THE MOSCOW PLAYBOOK

THE MOSCOW PLAYBOOK

HOW RUSSIA USED, ABUSED, AND TRANSFORMED SPORTS IN THE HUNT FOR POWER

BRUCE BERGLUND

Library of Congress Cataloging-in-Publication Data available upon request.

This book is available in quantity at special discounts for your group or organization. For further information, contact:

Triumph Books LLC
814 North Franklin Street
Chicago, Illinois 60610
(312) 337-0747
www.triumphbooks.com

Printed in U.S.A.
ISBN: 978-1-63727-748-5
Design by Nord Compo

To Vera, Nils, Marta, and Will

CONTENTS

INTRODUCTION

THE CROWD INSIDE the arena buzzed in anticipation. As skaters circled the ice to warm up, rock music thundered over the speakers—songs of Bon Jovi and AC/DC, staples of hockey arenas around the world. But this was a Russian arena—the $300 million Bolshoy Ice Dome, built for the 2014 Sochi Winter Olympics—and filling the arena was a Russian crowd.

Faces were painted with the colors of the Russian flag: white, blue, and red. Some fans wore jerseys of the national hockey team, emblazoned with the double-headed eagle of the imperial Romanov dynasty. One guy near the ice waved a Soviet naval flag—its red star and hammer-and-sickle insignia visible throughout the arena. In between Freddie Mercury singing "Another One Bites the Dust" and the opening riff of "Eye of the Tiger," fans chanted their country's name—"RO-SSI-YA! RO-SSI-YA!"—with all the intensity of Americans shouting "U-S-A!" at an international match.

Except this wasn't an international match. It was an exhibition game. Both teams warming up were Russian. On the ice were some of the greatest hockey players in the world—or more accurately, some of the greatest *retired* hockey players in the world. One team was made up of former members of the vaunted Soviet squads of the 1970s and '80s, winners of multiple Olympic gold medals and World Championships. They faced a collection of former

NHL players, some of the first Russians to play in the West in the 1990s, winners of the Stanley Cup and members of the Hall of Fame in Toronto.

But the star of the night was not a former Olympian or an NHL great. Before the game began, the loudest cheers went up for this last player to be introduced. A spotlight followed him as he stepped onto the ice. The announcer's deep baritone rumbled through the darkened arena, like the prelude to a heavyweight fight:

"President of the Russian Federation, Vladimirrrrrr Putin!"

From the starting face-off, all eyes were on Putin, both in the arena and on the nationwide TV broadcast. He moved down the ice with tentative strides, slower than the other players. Noise rose from the crowd in the opening minutes when he collected a teammate's pass. Viewers across Russia heard the commentator's voice lift in excitement: "Putin with the puck! The president skates to the goal!"

Defenders slowed to a stand-still, allowing him to stickhandle past. The goalie stiffened.

"Putin shoots! Goooooal!"

The camera zoomed on the president giving fist-bumps to his teammates. Inside the arena, the siren wailed, the music started, the spectators slapped their plastic thundersticks. Without expression, Putin skated to the bench and took his seat, as if it was the most natural thing in the world for him to score a goal against some of the best players to ever lace up skates.

Putin went on to score seven more goals this night. His team won 14–7. The president's hockey exploits have been repeated once or twice each year, usually with the same lineups, always with the same result: Putin scores a half-dozen or more goals in leading his team to a lopsided victory. The games usually mark a special occasion. On this night, the exhibition coincided with celebrations of the Soviet victory over Nazi Germany. In past years, there have been games on the anniversary of Yuri Gagarin's first space flight or the president's birthday.

Putin started skating in his fifties, and it shows. His strides are hesitant, his turns wobbly. He has taken his tumbles. On this night in Sochi, in May 2019, Putin famously face-planted while taking a victory lap after the game. As he waved to spectators, the president didn't notice a rug had been placed on the ice for the postgame ceremony. Down he went, to the horror of his teammates.

Admittedly, I felt a tinge of sympathy for Vladimir Vladimirovich in that moment. As I can attest from being a middle-aged amateur hockey player, it hurts to hit the ice. And at our age, it's hard to get up.

So why does he do it? Why does the Russian president risk embarrassment and injury to have former pros feed him the puck and let him score easy goals? Justin Trudeau is a seasoned skater, but he never got on the rink with NHLers during his years as Canadian prime minister. Barack Obama has played basketball his whole life, but he didn't make himself the star of nationally televised games against NBA old-timers. Why does Putin take the ice against some of the best players in hockey history, only to show he is clearly out of his league?

Putin himself says he took up hockey for exercise. His exhibition games are typically billed as charity events for the Night Hockey League, an amateur organization launched in 2011 to get more Russians involved in sports. To be sure, improving health and wellness is a worthy goal, especially in the country with the world's highest rate of heart disease. But sports in Russia are never simply about physical activity. The Night Hockey League is a good example. Unlike the community rec leagues or lunchtime pick-up games we play in, Russia's amateur hockey players compete in a nationwide, centralized association, linked to the government's

Ministry of Sport. And the whole idea for the league's founding is credited to one man: Vladimir Putin.

During Putin's two decades in power, the Kremlin has used sports to build his standing as president, a leader attentive to his people's welfare as well as a vigorous man of action. Putin's high-scoring hockey performances can be viewed alongside photos of him competing in judo or swimming in Siberian lakes or taking bare-chested rides on horseback over rugged mountains. Yet the aim is not simply the greatness of Putin. It's the greatness of Russia. The exhibition hockey game was more than an exercise in presidential image-building or a charity event for an amateur league. With the chants and flags, the faces painted in national colors, the legendary players who had won the Stanley Cup and Olympic gold, it was a celebration of Russia.

Putin's hockey games are not intended to be real competitions. They are a performance of victory.

Since the time of Stalin, Moscow's rulers have sent Russian athletes into the world with one command: you must win. Whether they wore the colors of the Russian Federation or the Soviet Union, Russian competitors at international events, especially the Summer and Winter Olympics, understood their victories had political meaning. Winning at sports showed the greatness of their nation, their motherland.

Of course, people of every nation want their athletes to win at world events, whether it's Argentinians watching soccer or Australians following cricket. I have watched the Olympics at home in the United States with friends and family gathered around the television, and I have sat in an Olympic ice arena surrounded by Koreans. I have watched international hockey with Swedes, international soccer with Germans, and international rugby with Italians. We all cheer for our own. We are lifted when our athletes win; we are disappointed when they lose.

In Russia, however, support for the country's athletes goes beyond *wanting* them to win. Russia's athletes *need* to win.

During the Cold War, the demand for victories had an ideological motivation. According to the Kremlin's propaganda, the Soviet Union was the most advanced, most equal, most just country in the world. Even more, the communist system enabled citizens of the USSR to reach new heights of production and creativity. It was difficult to prove, however, that the Soviet Union had the world's best scientists or coal miners. But you could prove that the USSR had the strongest weightlifters, fastest runners, and most skilled gymnasts. To confirm that Lenin was the world's greatest genius, Stalin was the world's greatest leader, and the Soviet Union was the world's greatest country, athletes from the USSR would compete against opponents from the bourgeois, capitalist West—and they would win!

At the same time, there were deeper roots to this drive for victory. The belief in Russia's unmatched role in the world goes back centuries before the 1917 Bolshevik Revolution, and it has lasted past the collapse of the Soviet Union in 1991. Yet while medieval Orthodox monks could only take it on faith that Moscow's czars had been chosen to rule in God's place, contemporary Russians can point to more objective signs of greatness. As one proud Russian told researcher Nina Kramareva, an expert on sports and politics, "You came in first—you are the best."

Of course, I can't fault anyone for thinking their country is the greatest on Earth. After all, my countrymen carved the heads of their favorite leaders into the side of a mountain. But Russian national pride has a twist that distinguishes it from the American variety: Russians are convinced of their country's greatness while at the same time being deeply self-conscious about its deficiencies. Historian Sergei Medvedev writes about these competing senses of superiority and inferiority as contributing to an "infantilism of the

Russian consciousness." Russia makes demands, throws tantrums, nurses grudges, and refuses to follow rules of the adult world. Stir in a tendency to black-and-white thinking, along with spirals of self-delusion and self-loathing, and you have a collective mentality resembling that of a teenager.

Medvedev sees this immature national consciousness as key to understanding Russian support for Vladimir Putin's authoritarian rule and his decision to invade Ukraine in February 2022. We can also point to these intermingling currents of pride and resentment, supremacy and failure, in Russia's drive for sports victories. Because Russia is great, wins were expected. Because Russia had to prove its greatness, wins were necessary.

It didn't matter how those victories were achieved. Take for example one of the most notorious episodes in Olympic history, at least from an American perspective: the gold-medal game in basketball at the 1972 Munich Olympics. In the game's final three seconds, with the US ahead by one point, referees gave the Soviet team three attempts to inbound the ball and take a final shot. On the third try, Ivan Edeshko made a full-court pass to Alexander Belov, who scored the game-winning layup.

For Americans, the Soviet win was fixed. "The powers that be determined that we would lose if it was close," said US team member Tom McMillen. For the Soviets, it was a hard-fought triumph, the culmination of years of work. "In those three seconds, our basketball players showed endurance and will," reported *Sovietsky Sport,* the USSR's daily sports newspaper. There was no mention of the last-second confusion. The game report simply stated that Belov scored the winning basket.

Today, Russian sportswriters acknowledge the botched officiating at the game's end. Nevertheless, a win is a win. The gold medal at Munich was a "great victory," whereas the Americans showed what poor losers they were by not showing up to receive their silver medals. Moreover, the Americans had no one to blame but themselves. "They just had to play defense for three seconds," said the Russian website Championat, "but they got nervous and did God knows what on the court."

The Soviets did not cheat in the 1972 Olympic basketball Finals. But they did cheat in other international contests. A lot. The USSR's decades-long dominance at the Olympic Games was based on a massive deception. At a time when the International Olympic Committee (IOC) enforced strict amateur regulations on athletes from the United States and other Western countries, the Soviets sent pros to the games. Moscow called them amateurs, and the IOC went along with the deceit. In truth, Soviet Olympians were paid to be full-time athletes.

Consider another Soviet team that grabbed headlines in fall 1972. At the same time as the Olympics were underway in Munich, the Soviet hockey team was playing a historic set of games. The Summit Series brought together, for the first time, top Canadian pros in the National Hockey League with the Soviet squad that dominated international tournaments for more than a decade. Earlier that year at the Winter Olympics in Japan, the Soviets had won their third consecutive gold medal, to go along with eleven titles in the annual Hockey World Championships.

To qualify for the Olympics, each Soviet hockey player—like Olympians in all other sports—had to sign a form verifying their amateur status. The form listed the athlete's occupation—most members of the Soviet team listed teacher, factory worker, or army officer. In fact, however, their job was hockey player. Players on the Soviet national team spent more time on the ice during the year than NHL pros. And they were paid just as much, relative to income levels in the USSR. Both Canadian NHLers and Soviet hockey players earned two to three times as much as the average salary in their respective countries.

In essence, the 1972 Summit Series was a showdown between two pro all-star teams. The eight-game series (four games in Canada, four games in Moscow) played out like a battle of titans. The Soviets won the first game in Montreal 7–3. For Canadian fans, the defeat crushed the belief that their hockey players were the best in the world. A week later, the crowd in Vancouver booed Canada's players off the ice after a 5–3 humiliation.

All that practice time Soviet players dedicated to their sport paid off. They had a style of play unlike anything seen in the NHL. They were fast and fit. They were disciplined and improvisational. Yes, they were pros disguised as amateurs. But there was no denying they were good.

We can imagine that a 19-year-old law student back in Leningrad was watching these Soviet victories in fall 1972. Vladimir Putin has not shared his specific memories of the hockey team's wins in Canada or the basketball team's triumph in Munich. We don't know if he watched Olga Korbut make her daring flip on the uneven parallel bars or Vasily Alekseyev set Olympic records in weightlifting. We do know, however, that sports were important to Putin from a young age, particularly martial arts. "If I hadn't been involved in sports, I'm not sure how my life would have turned out," he told an interviewer before his first presidential election.

Putin was also a fan who took pride in Soviet victories. After becoming president in 2000, he devoted a remarkable amount of attention to restoring the greatness of Russian sports. During a rough stretch for the national hockey team, for instance, he called the sport's top administrator in Russia to the Kremlin. "When will we start winning?" Putin asked.

The hockey boss skated around the question, assuring Putin that a new winning spirit was taking hold with the team. But the president had no patience for the dodging answer.

"I am asking," Putin interrupted, "when will we win?"

Putin was not putting the question to some no-name sports bureaucrat. The head of Russia's hockey federation was Vladislav Tretiak, star goalie for the Soviet team in the Summit Series, first Russian player inducted into the Hall of Fame in Toronto, and one of his country's most revered athletes. Yet here was Tretiak in the Kremlin, getting belittled by his president. As a comparison, picture Mike Trout being called to the White House after Team USA's second-place finish in the 2023 World Baseball Classic. Imagine Joe Biden grilling Trout about his game-ending strikeout in the championship. It's something we can't fathom. But that's what happens in Moscow.

For eight decades, this mixing of Russian sports and politics has followed the strategies in the Moscow playbook. As we'll see, the playbook has contributed to worthwhile changes in world sport. But its key chapters are dedicated to cheating at international competitions and manipulating world governing bodies. The tricks, lies, and maneuvers all have an official stamp of approval—as long as they bring wins.

Of course, there is no actual playbook sitting on a Kremlin shelf. But there is a Russian way of doing international sports. To chart Moscow's schemes and deceptions, I dug through documents in the Olympic archive in Switzerland, records of the government committees that ran sports in the USSR and East European satellites, and decades of Russian sportswriting, from old Soviet newspapers to current websites. This book reveals what I unearthed.

If the Moscow playbook did exist, it would have no better introduction than Putin's words to Russian Olympians setting off for the 2000 Summer Games in Sydney. The 435 athletes made a solemn visit to the Tomb of the Unknown Soldier and then received a blessing from Moscow's Orthodox archbishop. The ceremony's final send-off came from the new president, elected only five months earlier.

At competitions like the Olympics, Putin observed, the skill level among athletes was roughly the same. "It is the one with stronger character who wins," he said, "and the Russian land has always been strong in character." The Olympians would triumph not through individual talent or training or motivation, but through the moral strength they had as Russians. In return, their successes would strengthen Russia—in a way even the president could not.

"Victories in sports," Putin said, "can unite the nation more than a hundred political slogans."

CHAPTER 1

VICTORY MUST BE OURS!

"WAR MINUS THE SHOOTING."

George Orwell coined his famous jab at international sports just a few months after the shooting of World War II had stopped. The world did not yet know the words "Cold War" or "Iron Curtain," yet Orwell detected a growing tension between Stalin's USSR and the western allies. This "fresh animosity," as Orwell described it, was evident on the soccer pitch.

In November 1945, the champion of the Soviet league, Dynamo Moscow, played a series of matches against British clubs. This was the first time a Soviet team had visited the birthplace of football. It was also one of the first contests ever between top athletes from the USSR and the West. For the first match of the tour, at London's Stamford Bridge, curious spectators spilled onto the track and perched on the grandstand roof to watch the visitors take on Chelsea. When the whistle signaled the end of the 3–3 draw, fans surged onto the grass and lifted the Russian players on their shoulders.

While the amicable mood of the wartime alliance was still on display at the tour's start, growing suspicions between East and West came out at the end. A week after the Chelsea match, Dynamo took on Arsenal. The Soviet visitors had asked specifically to play the Gunners, winners of five league titles in the 1930s. Yet the North London club was still recovering from the war. Several players were stationed overseas, so Arsenal had to fill their depleted ranks with players borrowed from other clubs. Among the players wearing Arsenal red was Stanley Matthews of Stoke City, already regarded as one of England's best footballers ever.

The Soviets objected to these additions. Through his translator, Dynamo coach Mikhail Yakushin complained that his club was facing the English national team. Yet his own roster was bolstered with ringers. The most important addition was 22-year-old Vsevolod Bobrov, borrowed from CSKA Moscow, the club known as Red Army. Just a shade under 6′ tall, lean with broad shoulders, Bobrov resembled a young Babe Ruth with his round jaw, broad nose, and thick brows. The resemblance went beyond his boyish face: like the Babe, Bobrov was an extraordinarily gifted talent, an athlete for the ages. In his first season in the top Soviet league, he was the top scorer, with 24 goals in 21 games. Bobrov continued his run in Britain: he scored the late equalizer against Chelsea and then added a hat-trick in a 10–1 win over Cardiff City.

After the matches with Cardiff and Chelsea, anticipation swelled for Dynamo's contest with Arsenal. Spectators started queuing at midnight for the Wednesday afternoon match. There was talk in the morning of postponing due to heavy fog, but organizers did not want to risk losing ticket sales. The game went ahead. Or behind. No one could tell—not even the players.

According to tales passed down, the fog provided cover for all manner of rule-twisting. An Arsenal player was sent off, but he simply ducked into the mist, later claiming he didn't understand the Russian referee. Dynamo had twelve men on the field for a time: a substituted player didn't bother coming off. The Russian referee disallowed an Arsenal goal but also missed one by Bobrov. When the final whistle sounded, the Moscow players celebrated a 4–3 win. Out of the fog came accusations from both sides of rough play and cheating.

George Orwell wasn't in the stands that day, nor was he at the final match of the Dynamo tour: a 2–2 draw against Rangers in Glasgow. Still, he heard enough to comment on the hostility that emerged out of the matches. "I am always amazed when I hear people saying that sport creates good will between the nations," Orwell wrote in an essay for the *Tribune.* The Dynamo tour, like the Olympics or any international sporting event, showed that athletic contests only fanned tensions between countries.

"Serious sport has nothing to do with fair play," Orwell declared. "It is bound up with hatred, jealousy, boastfulness, disregard of all rules, and sadistic pleasure in watching violence: in other words, it is war minus the shooting."

Eight decades later, Orwell's remark still rings true, especially when it comes to Russia's sports contacts with the West. But because he wasn't at the matches in November 1945, Orwell missed something. The Russians were astonishing. Their style of play, tactics, speed, and physical stamina were unlike anything ever seen in England.

"Class football," judged Stanley Matthews.

"Dynamo was not an ordinary football team," reported a newsreel account of the Cardiff match. "They are a machine."

If the Dynamo tour set the template for eighty years of distrust, miscommunication, and mutual recriminations, it also showed why Russia would always be welcomed in world sport: the country's athletes were astounding.

Dynamo's 1945 tour of Britain was a turning point in the Soviet Union's engagement with the sports world. Prior to the war, sporting contacts between the USSR and the West were severed. Moscow kept its athletes away from events organized by "bourgeois" organizations like FIFA and the IOC. Governing bodies, in turn, followed the lead of western governments and cut ties with the revolutionary Bolsheviks.

As the globalized sports world took shape in the 1920s and '30s, a vibrant sporting culture developed within the USSR. Soviet propaganda encouraged men and women to join athletic clubs, with the aim of building fit bodies for labor and defense. Soccer clubs like CSKA, Dynamo, Spartak Moscow, and Zenit Leningrad drew tens of thousands of fans to stadiums. Crowds filled theaters and circus halls to watch boxing and wrestling. "The Soviet peoples were told that their lives had become better," wrote historian Robert Edelman. "Sports were to be part of that improved life."

As sports grew in popularity, coaches, officials, and journalists recognized that Soviet athletes needed to test themselves against competition from other countries. During the 1930s, when soccer clubs played friendlies against sides from France, Czechoslovakia, and Spain, Soviet managers saw their players had the ability to compete with the Europeans. What they were lacking was knowledge of European tactics and the competitive structure of a European-style league. As in economic development, the USSR had vast potential. And thanks to Stalin's leadership, the Soviet people were motivated to build an advanced country. All that was needed to pass the West was to better understand it.

This desire to beat the West is a constant theme in Russian history. Going back to Peter the Great in the early 1700s, Moscow's rulers believed that Russia's inexhaustible resources would bring the military and economic might needed to surpass its neighbors. But Russia had to first learn from them. As Peter remarked, "We need Europe for a few decades, and then we can turn our back on her."

Peter was impatient, however. So were his successors. Rather than waiting for processes of long-term development to bear fruit, Russia's leaders sought to make grand, immediate statements that would demonstrate the country's greatness—like St. Petersburg, Peter's European capital built on the Baltic Sea. Trailing European countries in railroads in the late 1800s, the Russian empire built the longest rail line in the world: the Trans-Siberian Railway. Behind in steel production, Stalin ordered construction of the largest plant in the world, at Magnitogorsk. Lagging in aviation technology, the Soviets unveiled the world's biggest airplane.

Of course, the longstanding Russian drive to surpass the West had an ideological element during the Stalin era. Founded upon a scientifically correct understanding of economics, history, politics, and social relations, as originally taught by Marx and Lenin, Soviet communism was leading the way to humanity's ultimate fulfillment. Freed from the bonds of capitalism, and guided by Stalin's wise leadership, the USSR was the most just, tolerant, and progressive society on Earth. Soviet citizens embodied humanity's future. Soviet workers achieved heroic feats of production. It was only natural that Soviet athletes do the same.

"Our best athletes must be better than those in capitalist countries," declared Politburo member Mikhail Kalinin in 1938. "Our football teams must be better than every bourgeois football team. We must develop strength, agility, skill, and organization to defeat bourgeois athletes on the football field, the running track, and in all other sports."

Kalinin's call for Soviet supremacy was reprinted often in newspapers after the war. With the Red Army occupying conquered Berlin, the Soviet Union was a world power. Moscow's need to demonstrate power in athletic competition was even more necessary. Like Russia's other bold statements of progress, the Kremlin's decision to enter international sports after World War II was a bid to show superiority over the West. A Communist Party resolution after the war called for nothing less than "world supremacy in major sports in the immediate future."

Dynamo's 1945 tour of Britain was the opening assault in this bid for world supremacy. Soviet newspapers hailed the soccer team as more than conquerors: they were representatives of the Soviet system.

"The success of Dynamo Moscow is not only an achievement of the eleven players," stated the daily newspaper *Sovietsky Sport*. "This is a victory of our football school, which is based on collectivism, organization, and an unwavering will to win—the distinctive qualities of the Soviet Man."

Just as victory over the Nazis on the battlefield proved the superiority of Soviet military and economic might, victories on the sporting field demonstrated the superiority of Soviet society. "The world has never known athletes like ours," declared *Sovietsky Sport* in 1949. Soviet athletes put their abilities at the service of the motherland. They took their strength from the people. At the same time, their success was fostered by the USSR's advanced science and technology. No victory was an individual achievement; it was a demonstration of collective commitment. Pursuit of sports victories required an organized, purposeful campaign by the communist state. The achievement of victories in sport confirmed the greatness of the state. As *Sovietsky Sport* made clear: "Every record is a triumph for the socialist system."

The man responsible for leading the campaign for sports victories was Nikolai Romanov, head of the government's sports bureau, the All-Union Committee for Physical Culture and Sports. Just 32 years old when he was appointed in 1945, Romanov had no sports experience at all. He trained apprentice workers at a Leningrad factory, then rose through the ranks of Komsomol, the Communist Party's youth organization. In many ways, he fit the mold of a Stalin-era functionary. His official portrait shows the bland face of a reliable apparatchik, with the pushed-back hairstyle of every Party hack in the Soviet Bloc.

Romanov was alert to commands from above. But he also had administrative talent—and ambition. When he was offered the job on the Sports Committee, he turned it down twice. In his view, heading the Sports Committee was a dead-end job in a minor branch of the massive Komsomol. Only at the direct urging of Stalin's deputy, Georgy Malenkov, did he take the role.

Part of Romanov's hesitation came from the demands of the job. His orders were to turn the USSR into the world's leading sports power in the "immediate future." As Romanov wrote in his memoirs, the push for sports supremacy was urgent after the Dynamo tour, especially as Cold War tensions grew. The problem was, Romanov recognized, supremacy was a long way off. In several sports, Soviet athletes were far behind competitors from the West.

Despite the gap, Romanov urged the Politburo to send a team from the USSR to the 1948 Olympics. To bring Soviet athletes up to speed, he recommended sending coaches to Europe and the United States to gain knowledge of western training methods. Romanov's Politburo bosses said no, both to sending Soviet coaches abroad and to sending Soviet athletes to the Olympics. There was no assurance of victory, and this is what the man in charge wanted.

"In order to gain permission to go to international competitions, I had to send a special note to Stalin guaranteeing victory," Romanov recalled. This was the only acceptable result for Soviet athletes. When the country's wrestling team placed second at the 1947 European Championships, Romanov received a stern reprimand from the "Great Leader" himself: "If you're not ready," Stalin said, "there is no reason to participate."

Romanov took Stalin's directive to heart—especially after losing his job. Following a lackluster performance by the Soviet men at the 1948 Speed Skating Championships, Romanov was sacked.

An ironclad rule was established in the Moscow playbook: losing has consequences.

His successor was Arkady Apollonov, a secret police colonel who ran the Moscow Dynamo athletic club. Like all Soviet sports clubs, Dynamo was more than a soccer team. It included teams in basketball, volleyball, gymnastics, hockey, and other sports. Apollonov brought a range of experience to his new post, but he didn't put that experience to use. His solution to the conundrum of guaranteeing victory was to not compete at all. During his time in charge of the Sports Committee, the USSR sent athletes to only a few international events. Party bosses did not approve of the stalling tactics—or to Apollonov's frequent vacations. After three years, Romanov was put back in charge of the Sports Committee, a position he held until 1959.

Romanov wasn't called back from Siberia; he was just down the hall, in the deputy chair's office. The fact that he was never removed completely from the Sports Committee showed he had backers in high places. He also had other skills useful for navigating Stalin's bureaucracy. Romanov was direct and cagey, persistent and adaptable. He knew how to cultivate his contacts in the Kremlin and use orders from above for his own ends. If we consider the sports program as one of the few things in the USSR that worked as intended, a Soviet initiative that ended up gaining world domination, then a good part of the credit must go to Nikolai Romanov, the person most responsible for setting its foundations.

The Soviet sports program was a product of the Stalin era, and it functioned like other Soviet institutions of that time. In the typical Western view, the Stalinist state was a totalitarian monolith. The Kremlin imposed orders from above. Down below, apparatchiks followed these orders out of fear of the Gulag. Western sportswriters expressed this view when Soviet athletes first competed at international events. "The Kremlin controls muscles just as it controls thoughts," jabbed Arthur Daley, sports columnist for the *New York Times*. In fact, the workings of the USSR in the Stalin years were far messier. This applied to sports as well.

The All-Union Committee for Physical Culture and Sports was like other ministries in the Soviet planned economy. For example, the Ministry of Light Industry had separate departments for production of steel pipes, leather goods, woolen cloth, and so forth. Top officials in the ministry received broad production targets from the State Planning Office, clarified those targets, and then passed them to the specific departments. Officials in the various departments then allocated resources, managed distribution, and set prices. This was Stalinist centralized planning in action. The plan was set in Moscow, but there was room for adaptation. Officials in the various ministry departments negotiated with factory managers across the USSR in determining how to meet the plan's goals.

Similarly, Nikolai Romanov ran a state agency designed to fulfill a plan. There were two broad aims to sports in the USSR: one, of course, was preparing elite athletes to set records and win international competitions. In Soviet lingo, this was called *masterstvo*—mastery. The second was to improve fitness within the population. This was called *massovost*—mass participation. As we will see, these two aims were not always in harmony. Over the decades, government resources were directed away from making sports programs widely available to preparing champions.

Romanov's committee was staffed by officials with broad responsibilities: sports and education, international relations, sports sciences. Then there were specific departments for soccer, hockey, gymnastics, track and field, weightlifting, and other sports. Based in Moscow, these various department heads were intermediaries between Romanov at the top, who reported to the Politburo, and coaches at sports clubs throughout the country.

Like the bottom rungs of the Ministry of Light Industry, here is where the plan was negotiated, debated, and put into practice.

Stir in some communist ideology, along with Stalin-era backstabbing and run-of-the-mill rivalry among clubs and coaches, and you had a potent brew of sports and politics. One example of how the gears turned was when Romanov quashed plans for the USSR to compete at the 1952 Winter Olympics in Oslo. The department heads in charge of skiing, speed skating, and hockey argued for Soviet participation. Their athletes were ready, they insisted. Romanov wasn't convinced, especially about the speed skaters, who cost him his job once before.

The department heads took the standard approach of Stalin-era bureaucratic wrangling: they went over Romanov's head, arguing to the Party's propaganda chief, Mikhail Suslov, that it would be "a grave political mistake" if Soviet athletes did not compete. Suslov asked for Romanov's opinion.

"The leadership of the Sports Committee has no confidence that Soviet athletes will be winners," Romanov replied.

Suslov underlined the sentence. Soviet athletes stayed home.

By taking the Winter Games off the calendar, Romanov and the Sports Committee could concentrate on the upcoming Summer Olympics in Helsinki. Athletes were released from school or work in January 1952, six months before the games, so they could devote themselves to preparing. They were lodged at training camps in Moscow, Leningrad, Kiev, Sochi, and Tallinn, along with coaches, physicians, nurses, cooks, and housekeepers. Political officers were there, too. Future Olympians were instructed in the tenets of Marxism-Leninism. According to a rosy report from Tallinn, "Athletes listened to the lecture 'Great Construction Projects of Communism' with particular interest."

Political lectures weren't the only characteristically Soviet feature of the training. Shortages and mishaps plagued preparations. The state budget office undercut Romanov's funding request for meals, limiting food for athletes. Training at every camp was stymied by substandard equipment, or no equipment: The equestrians needed better stables. The fencers needed better masks. The marksmen needed better targets. They also needed bullets.

Training also followed the Soviet model in its relentless quantification and analysis. According to the cardinal beliefs of Stalinism, economic development could be hastened with careful planning and rational analysis. As Romanov instructed his coaches, "It is our sacred duty to follow the instructions of Comrade Stalin, to resolutely develop self-criticism and organize effective verification of performance."

Yet despite the focus on intensive training and rigorous measurement of results, Romanov knew there were no certainties in sports. "Sometimes, when I signed a note to Stalin, I was not sure of victory," he wrote in his memoirs, "and some anxiety dwelled in my soul."

One group of athletes was subject to extra attention before the Helsinki Games: the Soviet soccer team. Romanov's plan for preparing the national team required the approval of no fewer than four Politburo members: Malenkov, the deputy premier; Suslov, the propaganda chief; Lavrenty Beria, head of state police; and Nikolai Bulganin, an Army marshal and former defense minister. Thirty-six candidates for the team were sent in January to the Black Sea village of Leselidze, in the northwest corner of Georgia. The team's coach was Red Army manager Boris Arkadyev, respected as one of the most innovative strategists in the Soviet league.

Arkadyev divided the candidates into two teams, who played each other in constant scrimmages. Romanov visited regularly and sent reports back to his Politburo masters. Players were cut, replacements called in. Backfield players were strong, forwards were not. The squad missed Vsevolod Bobrov, who was out with chronic injuries. Defenders in the Soviet league had learned the best way to keep him from scoring was to take out his knees.

With the constantly changing assembly of players, Romanov and Suslov decided it best to not reveal the national team's roster before the Olympics. For warm-up matches in May and June, the players were disguised as "Team Moscow." They fooled no one. After a few matches, Romanov tried a new trick. The candidates for the national team put on the shirts of Arkadyev's club, Red Army.

Even playing incognito, the Soviet team hit its stride in the warm-ups. In games against Poland, Czechoslovakia, Romania, and Finland, the Soviet side took only one loss. The most encouraging results came against Hungary, the top team in world football at the time. Led by the prolific scorer Ferenc Puskás, the "Mighty Magyars" had not been beaten in two years. In their two matches in Moscow, however, the Hungarians played to a draw and then took a 2–1 loss. Yet because the Soviets were playing as "Team Moscow," the match was not a sanctioned international friendly. The Hungarians left Moscow with their unbeaten streak intact and played two more years without an official loss.

Sanctioned or not, the victory over Hungary convinced Soviet officials their team had a chance for a medal in Helsinki, perhaps even gold. The final roster included players from seven different clubs. The captain's armband went to Bobrov, back from the injured list. Having never been much of a defensive player, the 29-year-old forward spent most of his time in the front half. Even on damaged knees, he provided the spark the Soviets needed, scoring six goals in the nine warmup matches.

The soccer team arrived in Helsinki ahead of the other Soviet Olympians. In total, the USSR sent 295 athletes to the 1952 Summer Games, more than any other country. The Soviet athletes were joined by a large retinue of doctors, trainers, typists, translators, reporters, and sports committee officials. The IOC conceded to Moscow's request that athletes from the fraternal socialist countries be housed separately from the Olympic village. Their fenced encampment was a slice of Soviet territory, complete with Russian cooks in the kitchen, Stalin's portrait above the door, and guards protecting the grounds. "They told us the capitalists would try to steal our women," one Olympian recalled.

The soccer tournament began four days before the opening ceremony. Bulgaria gave the Soviets a scare in the first match. The USSR needed Bobrov's goal in extra time to even the score. Four minutes later, teammate Vasily Trofimov put the Soviets ahead. They held the 2–1 lead through the rest of extra time. Next up was Yugoslavia.

A few sports contests during the Cold War stand out both for the intensity of athletic competition and the intensity of politics. The 1972 Summit Series is one example, the Miracle on Ice game another. But Cold War showdowns in sports were not only between East and West. Contests between the USSR and other communist states mixed fierce athletic rivalry and heightened political tension. One of the most notable was the soccer match between the Soviets and Yugoslavs at the 1952 Olympics.

Four years earlier, Yugoslavia's communist leader, Josip Broz Tito, had broken from Moscow over Stalin's interference in his country's affairs. Tito's insolence enraged Stalin, and the break led the Soviets to tighten their hold over the rest of Eastern Europe. Moscow ordered a blockade of Yugoslavia. Beria's NKVD made plans to assassinate Tito.

On the morning of July 20, the day of the match, hundreds of telegrams arrived from home to encourage the Yugoslav team. The only encouragement Soviet players received was from the officials on hand, who reminded them that victory over the Yugoslavs was politically necessary. The Soviet players also found little support among the 16,000 spectators. Memories of the Soviet invasion of 1939–40 were still strong in Finland. Over 20,000 Finns had died in the Winter War, and more than 400,000 people had fled territory seized by the Soviets. The crowd in Tampere loudly supported the blue-shirted Yugoslavs.

There was plenty to cheer in the first half. Yugoslavia scored three goals in a 15-minute flurry to end the first half, then scored a fourth immediately after the break. Bobrov finally put the Soviets on the board in the 53rd minute, but the Yugoslavs answered right away, giving them a 5–1 lead. Firmly in command, Yugoslavia started using time. The Soviets slowed as well. Only Dynamo Moscow striker Trofimov kept up the pace. With 15:00 remaining, he took the ball from the right side into the center, dribbled past two defenders, and fired a shot into the corner. The strike energized the Soviets. Just two minutes later, Bobrov scored his second goal, cutting the score to 5–3.

"They're tired!" Bobrov shouted to his teammates in red.

Six months of nonstop training bore fruit for the Soviets at the end of the match. "These are machines," remarked a Yugoslav sportswriter.

The battered Bobrov took the lead. His legs were so tightly wrapped, he couldn't bend his knees. "It wasn't blood in Bobrov's veins," the team doctor later said, "it was Novocain."

"Bobrov surpassed everything I have seen in my football life," recalled Croatian forward Stjepan Bobek years later. Coming from a player who shared the pitch with Pelé, with Puskás, with the great Alfredo di Stéfano of Real Madrid, this was high praise. Unable to stop or change direction, Bobrov charged forward with clenched teeth. In the 87th minute, he rushed forward to meet a corner kick. The Yugoslav keeper got a hand on the ball but couldn't make the save. Bobrov had a hat trick. Yugoslavia's lead was cut to a single goal.

By this time, the fans had shifted. Tampere was a stronghold of the Finnish Communist Party, and reds in the crowd cheered for the socialist motherland. In the closing minutes, the action was entirely in the Yugoslav box. Bobrov hit the crossbar, and a Yugoslav defender cleared the ball over the back line. Less than a minute remained as Konstantin Beskov jogged across the field to take the corner. He looked for Bobrov, but the captain was surrounded by three blue shirts. Instead, Beskov lifted the ball out of the box. Midfielder Alexander Petrov raced forward and drilled the ball along the ground. It skipped through the box, past the scrum of red and blue, and found the lower corner.

The whistle blew. Nikolai Romanov and the band of Soviet officials celebrated the comeback. But the match wasn't finished. With dusk approaching, English referee Arthur Ellis started extra time right away. The Soviets kept up their pressure. Bobrov and Petrov both hit the woodwork. The Yugoslavs were exhausted. Even the Yugoslav radio announcer lost his voice and had to hand off the microphone. But the Blues held on. The match finished in a 5–5 draw.

This was the age before penalty kicks, which meant a second match was scheduled two days later to decide which team would advance. Yugoslavia's coach gave his shell-shocked team the day off. The Soviets, meanwhile, put in a full workout in the July heat. Even more officials made the trip from Moscow to give extra encouragement. To add even more pressure, Romanov received a telegram from the Kremlin. In his view, the message was unnecessary. "It was already clear to the players what was expected of them," he wrote in his memoir. But a telegram from Stalin could not go unread.

Perhaps inspired by words from the Great Leader, the Soviets started the second match on the attack. In the sixth minute, Bobrov hit the top corner from 20 meters out. More chances followed, but the Soviets could not convert. Then they began to slow. The Yugoslavs evened the score midway through the half. Minutes later, a Soviet defender got an arm on the ball in the box. Yugoslavia took the lead on the penalty and then scored a third goal just after halftime. The previous day's practice session started to take its toll. Soviet players could not keep pace and started playing rough. Arthur Ellis had to give a stern warning late in the match. A few minutes later, he sounded the whistle. Yugoslavia 3, USSR 1.

"We beat Stalin's Russia!" shouted a blue-shirted player into the radio microphone. In Belgrade, Zagreb, and other cities, cheering crowds filled the streets. It would not be the last time citizens of a communist country celebrated a sports victory over the Soviets.

Coach Boris Arkadyev was instructed to take the first flight back to Moscow. The players boarded the train home the next day. The platform at Leningrad Station was empty when they arrived. Without smiles, they climbed aboard the connecting trains to rejoin their clubs.

Nikolai Romanov stayed in Helsinki. He still had important work: the Soviets might have lost in soccer, but they could still win the Olympics.

In 1952 the unofficial "winner" of the Olympics was determined not by medal count but by a points system that tallied the top six finishers in each event. American newspapers assigned 10 points for every gold medal, five for silver, four for bronze, down to one point for sixth place. Newspapers in the US reported each day on the back-and-forth struggle between the Soviets and Americans atop this points table.

Romanov likewise kept a points tally of the top six finishers. But his system made an adjustment. Aware that the Soviets could not best the Americans in winning gold medals, he assigned seven points to the winner of each event rather than 10. With the Soviets' large contingent of athletes and competitors in every event, Romanov expected that his team would have a surplus of top six finishers. The classic Russian strategy applied in the Olympics as it did on the battlefield: overwhelm your enemy with numbers.

Romanov's strategy worked brilliantly. At the end of the first week of competition, the Soviets were ahead of the United States by 106 points. On July 31, as the games neared their close, the Soviet lead had grown to 126 points. The editors of *Sovietsky Sport* were confident enough to dedicate a full page to the Soviet Union's Olympic heroes, under the banner FOR THE GLORY OF THE MOTHERLAND. The paper compared the feats of athletes in Helsinki to those of workers across the USSR—all accomplished under the leadership of Stalin: "Reflecting on the building projects of communism, reflecting on the magnificent victories of Soviet athletes competing for the first time at the Olympic Games, the Soviet people say thanks to the inspirer and organizer of our victories, the wise and great Stalin."

The celebration was premature, however. In the final three days at Helsinki, the Americans stormed back with multiple medals in swimming, diving, and boxing. The basketball team's 36–25 win over the Soviets in the gold-medal game sealed the comeback.

U.S. OVERTAKES RUSSIA TO WIN 1952 OLYMPICS, announced the *Los Angeles Times*.

Yet this so-called victory was according to the American formula for counting points. In the USSR, the math came out differently.

ATHLETES OF THE SOVIET UNION TAKE FIRST PLACE, declared *Pravda*.

Even with Romanov's finger on the scales, the calculations were close: 494 points for the USSR, as opposed to 490 for the Americans. The tight result put some anxiety in Romanov's soul. Immediately after the closing ceremony, he was summoned to appear before the Council of Ministers in Moscow. He presented his equations at the Kremlin, then went to the Sports Committee offices to await his fate.

"I waited for hours—almost an eternity," he recalled.

Finally, the call came from the Kremlin.

"Tell your comrades," said Malenkov: "The performance of athletes at the Olympic Games was generally recognized as successful. You have a lot of work to do. We need to figure out what to do next. Take it easy. Go home and rest."

Romanov spun a terrific story in his memoir, but he left out one important detail: he lied to his bosses. Fifty years after the USSR's first Olympics, sportswriter Axel Vartanyan pored through the results and added up the points. The correct tally, according to Romanov's own formula, was 495 for the Americans, 487 for the Soviets. "A common practice in those days," Vartanyan said. Like any Stalin-era minister, Romanov fulfilled the plan by reporting fake numbers.

Nikolai Romanov kept his job after the Olympics, but there were still punishments to be handed out. The track team was hit hard. Six weeks after the games, the daily newspaper *Komsomolskaya Pravda* denounced athletes by name. "Conceited.... Self-satisfied.... Amoral.... Lacking the necessary will to [attain] victory." The newspaper made clear that the poor showing by the men's track and field team was not due to inadequate performances but inadequate character. These were not Soviet men.

The harshest penalty, however, was reserved for the soccer team. The Council of Ministers asked Romanov who should be held responsible for the national team's loss to Yugoslavia. Malenkov followed up with a phone call to Romanov, asking if the Sports Committee should disband the Red Army team. After all, Red Army won its warm-up matches in Moscow, then put on Soviet shirts in Finland and failed. Romanov tried to explain that the national team included players from different clubs. But Malenkov was having none of it. Romanov did not understand the seriousness of the loss to Yugoslavia.

"If you refuse to resolve the issue yourself," said Malenkov, "then it will be resolved without you."

Romanov understood the threat: it was either his job or disband an entire football club. He wrote the directive and signed it:

> I ORDER
> 1. For the failure of the team at the Olympic Games, for serious damage to the prestige of Soviet sports, the Red Army team should be removed from the Soviet league and disbanded.
> 2. For unsatisfactory preparation of the team and for its failure at the Olympic Games, the senior coach of the Red Army team, Comrade Arkadyev, is to be removed from his position and deprived of the title Honored Master of Sports.

The loss in Helsinki was intolerable. *Sovietsky Sport* and other newspapers didn't even report the score. But there were other forces at play. It's possible that the dissolution of the Red Army soccer team had more to do with rivalries in the Politburo than international tensions.

For Lavrenty Beria, the success of his favored club, Moscow Dynamo, had always been an extension of his political clout. In 1942 he ordered the arrests of the four Starostin brothers, leaders of the popular club Spartak, to strengthen Dynamo's position in the Soviet league. In the early 1950s, Arkadyev's Red Army club blocked Dynamo's path to the championship. The solution was simple. As historian Robert Edelman writes, "Beria succeeded in eliminating his team's greatest rival with one mendacious stroke."

Once Red Army was removed from the table, individual punishments were not long lasting. Some players finished the season for another military team hastily assembled to take Red Army's place; others joined different clubs. Arkadyev's exile from the league lasted all of a month. He was put in charge of last-place Lokomotiv Moscow and led the team to four wins in the last five games, enabling the club to avoid relegation. Five years later, Lokomotiv won the USSR Cup.

Dynamo could not take advantage of the scheme their boss concocted. Even with Red Army gone, Dynamo finished third. Lavrenty Beria would not live to see his team win the league again. The following year, after Stalin's death, the dreaded chief of the NKVD was arrested and executed.

For all the political maneuvering, for all the backstabbing and threats and careerist denunciations, Soviet sports of the 1950s still featured athletes of remarkable talent. Among the Olympians at Helsinki were young men and women who had endured injury, starvation, and the loss of family during the war. Ukrainian gymnast Viktor Chukarin was captured by the Germans in 1941 and spent the next four years in 17 different prison camps. When he was freed by the British on the last day of the war, he weighed less than 90 pounds. At Helsinki, he won more medals than any other athlete.

If there is a face of Soviet sports in the 1950s, it is the boyish mug of Vsevolod Bobrov. After his performance in Finland, Bobrov went on to even greater international success in a different sport. When his battered knees forced him out of soccer, Bobrov dedicated himself to the game he loved all along—hockey. In 1956 at the Winter Games in Cortina d'Ampezzo, he captained the first Soviet hockey team to win Olympic gold. At age 33 he was also the tournament's top goal-scorer. He remains the only athlete ever to captain a team at the Summer Olympics and Winter Olympics. Before Bo Jackson, there was Bobrov.

Today, Vsevolod Bobrov is revered in Russia: a talent of historic proportions who excelled in both international football and international hockey. He is so respected that the Russian navy launched a support-and-rescue vessel in 2013 that bears his name. The United States Navy will likely never launch the USS *Babe Ruth*, nor will the Royal Navy ever commission the HMS *Stanley Matthews*. But that's not the case in Russia. Only there, in a country where sports are an extension of state power, would a military ship be named in honor of the nation's greatest athlete.

CHAPTER 2

A CHAMPION FOR THE MOTHERLAND

MICHAEL PHELPS LEANED over the edge of the pool, ready to put his name in the record books. Here at the 2012 Summer Games, Phelps was about to win his 19th Olympic medal, the most ever by an individual athlete. There was no question he would get the record: when he dove into the water, Phelps' teammates in the 4x200 freestyle relay had built a lead of more than two body lengths. More than 17,000 spectators packed the London Aquatic Centre to witness the historic swim. Their cheers rose as Phelps finished the final two laps, well ahead of the other swimmers. They erupted when he touched the wall.

High up in the stands, a 77-yeard-old woman in a Team Russia tracksuit joined the cheers. Larisa Latynina had won 18 Olympic medals in the 1950s and '60s as member of the Soviet gymnastics team. Nine of those medals were gold, a mark Phelps already surpassed at the 2008 Beijing Games. Latynina was gracious as her records fell. Reporters from different countries stopped her for interviews inside the Aquatics Center. A smiling *babushka* with sparkling eyes and red-dusted hair, Latynina insisted she had held the record long enough. "Phelps deserves the record," she said. "He is such a talented athlete."

Latynina reveled in the attention at the London Games. "I was never as popular as this during my career," she admitted. No gymnast was that popular in Latynina's day. When she competed, women's gymnastics were relatively new at the Olympics, certainly not the spotlight event of today. Black-and-white clips of Latynina's performances offer a look back to a distant age. While elements of her routines are familiar, there are none of the gravity-defying acrobatics we see today. Latynina's movements have the expressive grace of a dancer, particularly in her floor exercises. Standing 5′3″ tall, Latynina would tower over today's gymnasts. She didn't wear ribbons in her hair, or wave enthusiastically to the crowd. She smiled warmly; indeed, she loved to perform. But she was composed—a woman rather than a girl. When she competed at her last Olympics, the 1964 Tokyo Games, Latynina was nearly 30 years old, a member of the Kiev city council, and mother to a five-year-old.

Before Olga Korbut charmed the world at the Munich Olympics, Soviet champions like Latynina were little known in the West. When the USSR burst into international competition in the 1950s, western media dismissed the country's athletes as faceless Reds. Their success was due to promised rewards from Moscow, or threats of exile to Siberia. Victories in "minor events," like gymnastics, were discounted altogether.

In her own country, Latynina was a hero: hard-working, committed to her studies, willing to sacrifice for her training. Like most Soviet athletes of her generation, Latynina's childhood had been shaped by war. She grew up in the Ukrainian port of Kherson, a city occupied by the Germans for two and a half years. Profiles of the gymnast always noted her father had been killed at Stalingrad and credited her hard-working mother for raising little Larisa alone. "My mother dragged me through cellars and bomb shelters," she recalled.

Ballet had been Latynina's first love. After the war she was able to see the famous Bolshoi dancer Olga Lepeshinskaya perform in Kherson. "For the first time, I understood what real art is," she told an interviewer decades later. "You can enchant the entire audience without uttering a word." Only one dance studio was open in the war-ravaged city. Latynina's mother worked two jobs to pay the fees. "She was completely illiterate, but she was determined I would achieve something in life," Latynina recalled.

The 11-year-old's dreams of performing were soon dashed, however, when the studio closed. "It was a catastrophe!" Latynina said. She quickly discovered a substitute: an activity that looked much like ballet. Within three months of taking up gymnastics, Latynina won her first competition. Like many Soviet athletes, she paid tribute to her coach. Mikhail Sotnichenko was demanding yet wise. "He was like a father to me," she said. Sotnichenko recognized her talent immediately. Once victories came, he was firm in correcting her. "Stay here, Larisa!" he ordered one day as Latynina was hurrying to leave the studio. "Do you think that if you beat the other girls, they should carry your mats for you?"

"He taught me that I should never put myself above others," Latynina said of her coach. "There was no talk of any star mentality. In any event, there were no stars at all in our time."

By contrast, Latynina saw later gymnasts as hopelessly infected by a star mentality. This was one source of her feud with Korbut when Latynina coached the Soviet women's team at Munich. "She understood that she was Olga Korbut," Latynina said, "that a lot of what she did would be forgiven."

It was likewise the case with Russian gymnasts in the post-Soviet years. Speaking to a reporter in 2000, Latynina compared her generation to the stars competing in Sydney. "They say we had a 'Soviet' upbringing," she said. This was a time when young Russians disparaged anything—or anyone—they judged as Soviet.

"Perhaps that's so," Latynina continued. "But we competed and fought as a unified team. We lived with a fighting spirit. Each of us wanted to win. Each of us strove to win. And I tell you: We loved our motherland. Those aren't just words. We were united by a patriotic impulse."

Supremacy in world sport was the goal when the Soviet Union entered international competition after World War II. In 1956 Soviet athletes fulfilled the Communist Party's order. At the Summer Olympics in Melbourne, held in the two weeks bridging November and December, the red banner of the USSR was raised over the medalists' podium more than the flag of any other country. The Soviets topped the Americans in gold medals 37–32 and finished with 24 more total medals than the US. The Soviet Union was the new power in world sports.

Victory was especially needed in 1956. In February general secretary Nikita Khrushchev denounced the abuses committed under Stalin, who had died three years earlier. The revelations of his speech to the Communist Party congress sent a seismic wave through the country, stirring hope for change among some, disillusion among others. International events brought further turmoil. In November the Suez Crisis stoked rumors of war with the West. At the same time, Soviet troops were in Hungary, putting down an armed uprising against communist rule. The Spanish and Dutch boycotted the games over the Soviet military action. Fearing for his athletes' safety, Khrushchev wondered if the Soviet team should withdraw as well.

With tensions at their height, the Melbourne Games became notorious for the "Blood in the Water" match in the men's water polo tournament. The tense semifinal was marred by kicks and punches from both teams. Printed in newspapers around the world, the photo of Hungarian player Ervin Zádor with a bloody gash below his right eye was further proof of Soviet brutality.

Inside the Soviet camp in Melbourne, there was confusion about the storm encircling the games. Officials had little information from Moscow about what was happening in Hungary. They even provided money to the Hungarians, whose funding had been cut off by the fighting in Budapest. Soviet officials gave mealy answers to the press about the international situation. With their own athletes, they conjured conspiracies. When the women gymnasts arrived to a half-empty hall for the first day of competition, their coaches said an Australian millionaire had bought up blocks of tickets. He wanted to insult the Soviet team with empty seats.

There were plenty of empty seats at the West Melbourne Stadium, but it was not because of Cold War pettiness. Women's gymnastics was completely unknown in Australia. The three women selected to compete for the host country had answered a newspaper ad and then trained on makeshift equipment in the coach's backyard. Likewise in North America and Europe, women's gymnastics received little attention in the sports press. *Sports Illustrated*'s thick Olympic preview issue included no mention of women's gymnastics.

In 1956 the biggest event of the Summer Olympics was still men's track, and at Melbourne the biggest star in the biggest event was a Soviet runner: Vladimir Kuts. The 5′8″ veteran of the Soviet Navy did not look like a distance runner, with his barrel chest and muscular legs. Kuts had been a boxer after the war, before stepping on the track in 1949 as a last-minute substitution to the 5000m race at a military track meet. Five years later and 20 pounds lighter, he set a world record in the event at the European championships, beating the reigning Olympic champion, Czechoslovakia's Emil Zátopek.

After setting a new record in the 10000m as well, Kuts came to Melbourne as the runner to beat in both races. Before the games began, he went from being an expected medalist to a celebrity.

During press day at the athletes' village, he told a Melbourne reporter about his fondness for cars. The reporter offered the keys to his Chevrolet. Kuts happily jumped in for a test drive. But the right-side steering wheel was confusing, and then the door suddenly unlatched. Kuts took his eyes off the road and smashed into a telephone pole. US newspapers treated the episode as a comic fender-bender, with the runner's injuries limited to a cut on his chin. Describing Kuts as a stocky, smiling blond, the story was a rare instance in the 1950s when American media presented a Soviet athlete as human.

In fact the runner's injuries were more severe. Kuts banged his knees in the accident, then went out immediately afterward for his training run. "I looked at the Olympic Games as a combat mission," the former Navy gunner wrote in his memoir. "I had to complete this task successfully. My team and my homeland needed my victory."

Later that night as he was lying in bed, his swollen knees burning, Kuts heard an unexpected knock on his door. It was one of his teammates, with news from the Australian papers: they were saying the Soviets' top runner was out with a concussion. "The news had a negative effect on our guys," Kuts recalled. He knew what he needed to do.

Lifting himself out of bed, Kuts got dressed and went to the Olympic Club, the one place in the athletes' village where men and women were allowed to mingle. A roar went up when Kuts burst into the room. He made his way through the cheers to Australian hurdler Shirley Strickland and asked for a dance. As the two striking blonds took to the floor, Kuts' teammates came up to him, poking his shoulders to make sure he was there in the flesh. "Of course, I hid from the guys that I didn't feel well," Kuts later admitted, "and I wanted to dance about as much as I wanted a hole in the head. But I persevered."

Three days after his performance in the Olympic Village, Kuts seized the spotlight on the first afternoon of competition. For the first 21 laps of the 10000m race, Kuts ran just ahead of his rival Gordon Pirie of Great Britain. With four laps to go, the Soviet runner slowed to let Pirie catch up. Running side by side, Kuts could see that Pirie was struggling to keep pace. In his crimson top, the Soviet runner pulled away. Pirie was broken; he faded into the pack and finished eighth. Kuts won by 80 meters. He then took a victory lap around the Melbourne Cricket Ground, waving to the cheering crowd of more than 100,000 people.

"It wasn't the fact that he beat me," Pirie said afterward. "It was the way he did it. He murdered me."

Kuts took gold in the 5000m race later that week, breaking Zátopek's 1952 Olympic record by an astonishing 27 seconds. "His mind is as tough as his body," said Roger Bannister. The famed English miler was walking back remarks he had made in *Sports Illustrated* before the games, that Kuts was "no more than a relentless running machine." Now, Bannister acknowledged the brilliant tactics Kuts had shown in the 10000m. Yet this mental side to the Soviet's arsenal was just as "remorseless" as the physical. Bannister's judgement echoed that of other Western commentators of the time: Soviet athletes were robots—built according to scientific design, hardened in relentless training, and programmed only to win.

In the view of both Soviet athletes and their competitors, relentless training was the key factor in the country's early success. Kuts himself emphasized in his memoir the benefits of carefully planned, year-round training. "The foundation for achieving sporting success is, first of all, systematic, regular training," he wrote.

Soviet gymnasts likewise dedicated themselves to several hours of training each day. In 1961 when the men's and women's teams gave an exhibition at Madison Square Garden, coach Alexander

Mishakov described the daily regimen to reporters. "The standard training technique called for shorter exercises that were designed to develop either strength, suppleness, or grace," Mishakov said through an interpreter. "Now we stress longer combinations to improve all these abilities at the same time."

As Mishakov explained, the gymnasts' training program had been revised since the 1952 Helsinki Games. Even though Soviet men and women dominated that first Olympic competition, coaches still saw a need for improvement. This was a hallmark of the Soviet system, not only in gymnastics but other sports as well. At physical education institutes in Moscow, Leningrad, and other cities, researchers worked with coaches to refine training, fitness, and performance. Scientific analysis and rational planning were essential to success—as were intensive inputs of time and work.

In the case of Mishakov's top champion, Larisa Latynina, the demands of training precluded other interests. After winning national tournaments as a teenager and earning top grades in high school, Latynina had moved from her home city of Kherson to Kiev, where she enrolled in the technical university to study mathematics. She continued her gymnastics training and caught the attention of Mishakov, who taught at the physical education institute. Decades later, she remembered his ultimatum: "If you want to be an engineer, stay in technical school." There was a gym at the technical university, Mishakov told her. She could practice there if she wanted exercise. "But if you want to be a great athlete," he said, "then you need to transfer to the physical education institute."

Mishakov convinced Latynina to give up her chosen field of study, but she still nursed a love of performing. Seeing an announcement for a city choir, Latynina signed up for an audition. Mishakov beat her to the rehearsal hall. "He persuaded the director to say I had no voice or ear for music," she recalled. Even that desire was taken away from her. "It was very disappointing," she admitted.

Disappointments aside, Latynina remembered decades later how much she loved training. "I never regretted it," she told an interviewer in 2004, "even when I was tumbling on the mat for the thousandth time, while my girlfriends were walking around town without a care, stuffing themselves with ice cream. I just loved gymnastics." She enjoyed the camaraderie of the gym in Kiev. "We laughed and sang like crazy," she said of her teammates.

Latynina also came to see training as an outlet for her artistic side. Mishakov saw this as well, and tried to wring it out of her. "You keep trying to drag ballet into the gym," he grumbled. But Latynina held firm. She was creating something beautiful, she insisted. Her coach harrumphed and waved his hand.

Intensive training was essential to Soviet athletes' early success, but it wasn't the only path to victory. In planning the Soviet Union's entrance into world competition, Nikolai Romanov devised a strategy that played to the country's strengths. The best example of how that strategy worked was Larisa Latynina.

First, Latynina competed in a sport that was hardly practiced in the United States. Today women's gymnastics typically draws the highest television ratings for NBC's Olympic coverage. In 1950s America the sport was little known. Derived from the fitness movement founded in 19th-century Germany to train young people for service to the nation, gymnastics had deep roots in East Central Europe and Russia. In the United States, by contrast, gymnastics were practiced only at immigrant community halls, inheritors of this European tradition. When Romanov first proposed sending a team to the Olympics, he saw that gymnastics offered low-hanging medals. "Our chances are high," he wrote to the Politburo, "especially for women."

Romanov's prediction was right. Over three decades, Soviet gymnasts dominated the Olympics. In nine tournaments, Soviet men won gold in 39 events and claimed 94 total medals. And as

Romanov recognized, the women were even better. From 1952 to 1988, Soviet women won the team gold at every Olympics but one. The exception was 1984 when Moscow's boycott ceded the stage to the Romanians, winners of the team title, and the first American ever to win the individual all-around, Mary Lou Retton. But Los Angeles truly was the exception. From Helsinki to Seoul, Soviet female gymnasts won 33 Olympic gold medals. For all the success of Simone Biles and other Americans in recent years, the USSR still has two dozen more Olympic gold medals in women's gymnastics than the United States.

Another sport Romanov saw as a Soviet strength and American weakness was Greco-Roman wrestling. He knew wrestlers in the US did not compete in the classical form of wrestling. Wrestling at American high schools and colleges followed freestyle rules, which allows holds below the waist. In Russia, on the other hand, Greco-Roman wrestling was a popular spectator sport already in the 19th century. Early Soviet Olympians grew up idolizing the country's famous wrestlers. Heavyweight Anatoly Parfyonov read books about legendary wrestlers as a boy on a collective farm. He saw his first matches while visiting Moscow after the war, when he was a 26-year-old injured veteran. Five years later, the spade-jawed, iron-chested, hairy-shouldered village strongman led his teammates to five gold medals at Melbourne.

When it came to these two sports, Nikolai Romanov proved to be a sharp handicapper. From 1952 to 1988, the USSR won a total of 1,010 medals in the Summer Olympics, including 395 gold. Athletes in Greco-Roman wrestling and gymnastics alone accounted for a quarter of all these medals and 27 percent of Soviet gold.

Along with participating in a little-known event, Larisa Latynina competed at a time when women's sports were almost completely neglected in the West. Avery Brundage, the American who headed the IOC from 1952 to 1972, tried more than once to ban women sports from the games, or at least limit participation to events that were properly feminine. "I will probably be outvoted," he grumbled privately.

In fact, the IOC president reflected a common opinion in America: sports were strictly for men. *New York Times* sports columnist Arthur Daley complained how women "clutter up the joint" in his report from the 1960 Rome Olympics. "It doesn't seem right to watch a female leap clumsily over the bars, throw the weights awkwardly, or scamper over a track in unladylike fashion," Daley wrote. "They lose all their daintiness and appeal."

The view was different in Moscow. "If the Soviet has its way," Daley griped in his Rome dispatch, "this international show will wind up as a completely coed production." After joining the Olympic movement, Soviet delegates pressed constantly for expansion of women's events. Moscow framed this advocacy of women's sports as part of their larger campaign to make the Olympics more progressive. The IOC was led by "representatives of reactionary ruling imperialist circles," charged Romanov. From the start, Soviet officials pressed the Olympic barons for reform, not only more women's events but also expansion of the IOC to include countries newly independent from European empires.

Moscow deserved credit for these efforts to open the games. Of course, there was also a practical benefit. In evaluating the Soviets' chances at the Olympics, Nikolai Romanov recognized that women athletes gave his country the edge. Only 40 women were on the Soviet team at Helsinki in 1952, alongside 255 men. Yet this small female contingent accounted for a quarter of the Soviets' gold medals and a third of their total medals. Moscow recognized that more Olympic sports for women would bring more runs up the flagpole for the hammer and sickle.

Take, for example, the most American of women's team sports: volleyball. Invented in 1895 at the YMCA in Holyoke, Massachusetts, volleyball was widely played in community gyms and physical education classes across the US in the first half of the 20th century. But unlike basketball, the other sport invented at a Massachusetts YMCA, volleyball didn't take hold as a competitive spectator sport in America. By contrast, volleyball clubs in Europe and the USSR had large followings. At the 1952 Men's and Women's World Championships in Moscow, tens of thousands of fans filled Dynamo soccer stadium for outdoor matches. This was at the same time American volleyball clubs competed for the national title in places like Scranton and Duluth. The sport entered the Olympics thanks largely to the Soviets, who were driving members of the international volleyball federation. Moscow's appeals paid off on the podium. After the introduction of women's volleyball in 1964, the Soviet team won gold four times.

American sportswriters responded to the success of Soviet women with snorts of derision. Women's events at the Olympics were dismissed as "lesser sports." The Soviets' contingent of hardy females also provided an unfair advantage. "These 1952 games wouldn't even have been close between Russia and the United States save for the almost complete dominance of the Russian women in the heftier field events," wrote Shirley Povich of the *Washington Post*. Legitimate women's events were in "the non-bicep division," sports like swimming and diving, "where feminine form counts more than feminine muscle." In these competitions, Povich assured readers, "the American girls were all-conquering."

Povich's remarks about brawny Soviet women were repeated by sportswriters across the country. Female competitors from the USSR were described as husky and unattractive. Avery Brundage joined the chorus, complaining that Soviet women were hardened by hauling bricks and pushing plows. "What do these women look like?" the IOC president asked a reporter. "Get a picture for yourself." American writers especially targeted Irina and Tamara Press, winners of six medals in track and field in 1960 and 1964. While Soviet media hailed the sibling athletes, Americans charged the "Press brothers" weren't even women.

For all the slurs about burly peasant women from the Soviet steppes, American sports officials realized something had to be done. If the Soviets were going to win the Olympics with women athletes, then the United States needed some women athletes of their own. In 1958 the US Olympic Committee created a women's advisory board. College sports opportunities for women slowly increased in the early 1960s, leading to the 1966 creation of a governing body, the Commission on Intercollegiate Athletics for Women.

But old attitudes were hard to change. When *Sports Illustrated* profiled the US women's track team before the 1968 Summer Olympics, the athletes' appearance got as much attention as their running times. With team members described as "dainty," "lissome," and "tiny-waisted," the message was clear: American girls looked nothing like the Press sisters.

The American stereotype of Russian women athletes as muscle-bound Amazons was upended by the gymnasts. When the Soviet team made their two-week tour of the United States in 1961, crowds at college gyms were astonished by the male gymnasts' feats of strength. But the biggest response was for the women. Larisa Latynina played to the audience at a Pennsylvania stop on the tour, smiling and waving after landing her dismount from the vault. "There goes a doll," said an admirer.

Her teammate Polina Astakhova was less animated (the *New York Times* reporter called her "haughty"), yet the slender blonde drew the loudest cheers. "I didn't think Russian girls would look so feminine," remarked a male spectator at a New York gym.

At the tour's final performance, the exhibition at Madison Square Garden, men greeted the "bouncy belles" with catcalls. Latynina, Astakhova, and their teammates "were a far cry from the stereotype of the female athlete," noted the *Times* writer. "They were more like chorus girls."

By contrast, media in the USSR did not compare women athletes to showgirls or fashion models. There was talk of their femininity, but this was associated with traits like composure and cultivation rather than appearance. Latynina was praised for her charm, grace, and intelligence.

Latynina also represented the model Soviet athlete. Media celebrated her dedication, hard work, and willingness to sacrifice for her training. She wrote an essay for *Sovietsky Sport* in 1963 about the pride she felt for her country when she won in Melbourne: "The flag of my motherland was raised, and the melody of the Soviet anthem filled the hall. I stood there joyful and moved." The words were genuine. "I was so patriotic," said an older Latynina, looking back.

Something Soviet media did not emphasize about Latynina was that she was a wife and mother. In the late 1940s and early '50s, many of the first women to represent the USSR in international competition were celebrated as mothers. The Party's message changed, however, after Khrushchev came to power. Motherhood was downplayed. Instead Soviet women were told they could be engineers and physicians, even athletes and cosmonauts. They were building socialism, just like the men.

In the Cold War rivalry with the United States, Moscow touted the standing of women as further proof of the Soviet Union's superiority. Soviet women—including Soviet women athletes—were intelligent and engaged citizens, contributing their abilities to the strength of the country. A front-page story in *Sovietsky Sport* in 1959 remarked on Latynina's nomination to the Kiev city council. A large photo above the fold showed the gymnast at her apartment's kitchen table, studying for one of her courses at the physical education institute. "Latynina not only trains hard and gives her all in competitions, but she is also an excellent student," the newspaper remarked. There was no mention of the baby she had delivered a month earlier.

Meanwhile, American media typically commented on the appearance and marital status of any female subject. Coverage of the 1961 Soviet gymnastics tour noted that the "button-cute" Latynina was married to an engineer while the "trim" Astakhova was single. The *Sports Illustrated* piece on the 1968 track team closed with a commentary on the runners' prospects for finding mates. "If you get them running early, the girls can see that they're going to get a lot of attention," a coach told the magazine's reporter, "and they get to meet a lot of boys that way."

Only years later, after her competitive career was over, was Latynina's status as a mother incorporated into her story. Indeed, today's profiles of the gymnast describe the events surrounding her daughter's birth as her most impressive achievement as an athlete. As she tells the story, Latynina was training for the 1958 World Championships when she took ill. She visited the chair of the obstetrics department at the Kiev medical school, Dr. Alexander Lurie, a widely esteemed physician and researcher who twice won the Order of Lenin. Having treated Latynina earlier for an ectopic pregnancy, Lurie announced what he thought was happy news: she was pregnant. Latynina broke down in tears.

"Everything is fine," the doctor assured. "Everything is going well."

"But I have a World Championship," Latynina explained, "in three months."

"Listen, young lady," Lurie said. "I treat many ballerinas. They are still jumping up to the sixth month. If you are a brave person, you can compete in this championship. You have such strong muscles. I guarantee everything will be fine."

The doctor then added a word of advice: "Just don't tell anyone."

Watching black-and-white newsreels of the championships in Moscow, it's clear how someone without an expert knowledge of maternal health would have kept Latynina from competing if they had known she was pregnant. At the end of routine on the uneven bars, she launched into a dismount from a handstand on the top bar—almost 8′ above the mat. Latynina was certainly brave, and she followed Dr. Lurie's instruction: she kept the news from her coach, from the team doctor, even from her friends. At the 1958 World Championships, she won the individual all-around title, along with gold in vault, uneven bars, and balance beam.

"I just wanted to be finished," she recalled, "so I could tell everyone I was pregnant."

Even more satisfying for Latynina was her triumph in the individual all-around two years later at the 1960 Summer Olympics. After she gave birth to her daughter Tamara, many believed Latynina's career was over. "There was already talk behind my back," she remembered. When the Soviet team set off to Rome, the talented Astakhova had taken her place as the lead gymnast. Sports pages in the USSR predicted that Astakhova would lead the younger generation of gymnasts to follow the great champion Latynina. Commentators in the West, meanwhile, were more concerned with Astakhova's looks, dubbing the stately blonde "the Russian birch."

The Baths of Caracalla provided a fitting background to the dramatic showdown between the teammates. With the apparatuses, judging tables, and spectators' seats all set amidst Roman arches and ancient brick walls, the Finals of the women's individual all-around began with Astakhova in the lead after the compulsories. She was still ahead following the vault and uneven bars, followed closely by Latynina. Behind them were three teammates. Soviet gymnasts held the top five spots, all clustered within eight-tenths of a point. Next was the balance beam.

"I saw how tense she was, like a string pulled tight," Latynina said of Astakhova. "And she broke."

A fall from the beam cost Astakhova a full point. Television cameras showed her in tears as she sat down. There were no hugs or words of sympathy from her teammates. With one apparatus remaining, they were all in the hunt for medals.

The final event was Latynina's specialty: floor exercise. As always, she brought ballet into her routine, sweeping her arms in elegant arcs as she glided between tumbling passes. The judges raised their cards: 9.9—the highest score of the competition. For the second time, she was the all-around Olympic champion.

"No one counted on me winning, except for me and the coach," she said. "I proved to everyone that the time hadn't come to cross me off the list."

Although she kept her pregnancy secret while training and competing, Latynina and her doctor were not at odds with Soviet views on women's health. "I don't know gymnastics," Dr. Lurie told her, "but I do know medicine. The child will be healthy, the mother will be happy—and the doctor will be happy." This was at the same time physicians in the US were debating whether it was safe for girls to slide into base while playing softball.

Just as Moscow trumpeted the equality of women in the USSR, so did Soviet propaganda point to the training of athletes as a proof of the progressive Soviet system. "Scientific methods founded on achievements in Soviet physiology and education lie at the basis of sports instruction," declared an English-language pamphlet. At physical education institutes like the one in Kiev where Latynina trained, coaches worked with scientists and physicians to develop programs for elite athletes. Students took courses in anatomy, physiology, kinesiology, and psychology. Following their studies, they went on to serve as coaches at sports clubs and academies, where they trained the next generation of Soviet medal-winners.

Identifying and developing athletic ability in children was a particular concern in the Soviet system. The first sports academy for children opened in Tashkent in 1961. By the 1970s there were more than two dozen sports boarding schools across the USSR. Children were recruited at different ages depending on their sport—eight years for figure skating, 12 for track, 15 for weight-lifting. The review process was exact: Admissions were based not only on the child's abilities but also their parents' physical traits and athletic histories. All of this was measured against data compiled from past medalists.

Few were chosen for these elite institutions or the top sports clubs in major cities. Already by the late 1950s, mastery in athletics took precedence over mass participation. A 12-year-old girl wrote to *Sovietsky Sport* after being turned down for admission to a sports school. "Maybe I will not be like Larisa Latynina," she appealed, "but I really want to do gymnastics." She didn't know that the aim of Soviet youth programs was not "to do gymnastics"; it was to train future Latyninas.

For the young athletes who passed selection, training was demanding and intense. It was also innovative. Coaches searched for new techniques. Researchers at the physical education institutes filmed training sessions to break down athlete performance. During the late 1950s and early '60s, over 260 Ph.D. dissertations were completed at these institutes. From 1962 to 1969, the number of dissertations jumped to 495. The field of applied sports science, combining research in biochemistry, biomechanics, and psychology, had its origins in the work of these scholars. At first, this dissection of sports performance was widely rejected in the

West. Ultimately, however, the Soviets' scientific approach became the foundation for development, training, and competitive strategy in sports around the world.

For an example of how the partnership of Soviet researchers and coaches drove innovation, we can look to Larisa Latynina's sport. When she won her final Olympic medals at the 1964 Tokyo Games, Latynina was two months away from her 30th birthday. Once again, she beat out Polina Astakhova in the individual all-around competition. But for the first time Latynina fell short of gold, placing second behind Czechoslovakia's Věra Čáslavská. As they stood on the podium, Čáslavská, Latynina, and Astakhova represented the end of an era in women's gymnastics. A shift was underway, from mature women performing graceful routines to teenagers performing daring acrobatics. Not again until 60 years later, at the 2024 Paris Olympics, would all three medalists in the individual all-around be women in their 20s.

This change was spurred in the USSR. With gymnasts from other countries challenging Soviet dominance, a new turn was necessary. Male coaches, themselves former gymnasts, sought to introduce more elements from men's routines into women's performances. To do that, they needed the right kind of woman gymnast, with the build and mentality to take on riskier moves. What sport science researchers found was that these new gymnasts would not be women in their 20s with breasts and hips. Instead, they would be girls.

The trend was evident in Soviet gymnastics in the late 1960s. Teenagers Larisa Petrik and Natalia Kuchinskaya dominated the 1966 Soviet Championships and then led the national team to gold at the 1968 Olympics. The more influential figure was their younger teammate at Mexico City, Ludmilla Tourischeva. At the 1969 European Championships, Tourischeva performed a path-breaking floor exercise routine. Her tumbling moves matched those of male gymnasts. And with her white hair ribbons and a dramatic snap of her head at the start of her performance, Tourischeva set the template for Olga Korbut and other gymnasts for decades to come. The judges, however, didn't know what to make of her. They deemed Tourischeva's routines as too risky and lowered her scores, dropping the 17-year-old to third place.

The sport's transition was still underway at the 1972 Munich Olympics. Now more composed, Tourischeva won the judges' scores while Korbut won the crowd. Four years later, when Nadia Comăneci took the all-around title at Montreal, the transition was complete. Standing 5′0″ and weighing 85 pounds, the 14-year-old Comăneci was a clear contrast to gymnasts of the past, even Tourischeva, Petrik, and Kuchinskaya when they were teenagers. With her thin, immature body, her dynamic routines, and her seven scores of perfect 10.0, the Romanian gymnast confirmed the sport's new direction.

One of the strongest critics of this trend was the coach of the Soviet women's team at Montreal: Larisa Latynina. Insisting that the heart of gymnastics remained artistry and beauty, the former champion lamented Comăneci's acrobatics. The leaders of Soviet gymnastics, on the other hand, saw things differently. Even though the changes in the sport had started in the USSR, the wave had swept past the Soviets. Any obstacle to future success had to be removed. Latynina's former teammate Yuri Titov, now head of the Soviet gymnastics federation, asked for her resignation.

In interviews with Russian media in the 2000s, Latynina was still bitter. "Titov apparently forgot that gymnastic talents can appear in places other than the USSR," she grumbled. But the end of her coaching tenure was about more than "missing" a talent like Comăneci. Latynina opposed the style of gymnastics that Comăneci and Korbut represented—the style practiced by gymnasts today. When reporters ask about the current state of the sport, she repeats her criticism of acrobatic tricks performed by "puppet girls." The complexity of current routines is amazing, she admits. Yet the sport has lost its artistic center. "For me," she told an interviewer in 2004, "the main thing has always been that gymnastics does not become a bunch of unimaginable tricks."

In December 1956 Larisa Latynina and her teammates left Melbourne after having conquered the world. Sailing home aboard a passenger liner, the athletes carried 37 gold medals, 29 silver, and 32 bronze. The ship also carried 20,000 bottles of vodka. They were all drained in the three-week voyage.

On New Year's Eve the Olympians arrived at the snow-covered port of Vladivostok, accompanied by warships of the Pacific Fleet. Thousands gathered in temperatures of -22°F. "We realized how many people were waiting for victory," Latynina recalled. The athletes boarded the Trans-Siberian Railway for the eight-day trip to Moscow. Adorned with a banner declaring "For You, the Nation," the train was greeted by crowds at every town station and village platform. People brought cakes, Christmas trees, and buckets of vodka. At one stop, they met a bearded old man who walked 300 miles just to see Lev Yashin, the unbreakable goalkeeper for the gold medal–winning soccer team. The old man kissed Yashin and presented him with a dried whitefish from Lake Baikal.

"We felt something incomparably greater than curiosity," Latynina said of her teammates' trek across the length of the country. "We felt recognition, the recognition of a great country."

The triumphal procession ended at the Kremlin. Khrushchev began the tradition that Putin continues today, celebrating victorious athletes at the center of Russian power. "You have done well in showing your skill and ability," said the smiling general secretary in saluting the Olympians. "You have defended the sporting honor of the motherland."

Vladimir Kuts answered on behalf of his teammates: "We felt the care of all Soviet people while we were in Melbourne. All the telegrams and letters you sent strengthened our resolve to win for the Soviet motherland."

The highlight of the evening was a formal ball for the athletes. Movie cameras documented the celebration for a film on the Melbourne games. At a time when television sets were rare outside of Moscow, the film allowed people across the country to see the athletes they knew only from newspapers or radio. They saw Kuts running his victory lap and wrestler Anatoly Parfyonov with his arms raised after taking gold. They saw the football team defeat Yugoslavia in the soccer Finals, atoning for the loss four years earlier.

The film closed with scenes from the festive night at the Kremlin, the athletes dressed in their best. On cinema screens from Vilnius to Vladivostok, moviegoers saw the husband-and-wife gymnasts Valentin and Sofia Muratov dancing in the Kremlin's grand hall. And there was middleweight champion Gennady Shatkov, with the thick dark hair and brooding eyes of a movie star. The handsome boxer circled the floor with his partner, Larisa Latynina. Her long gown twirling, her smile buoyant, the young gymnast won the hearts of her audience.

Victory at the Melbourne Olympics strengthened the pride of the Soviet people at a pivotal time. The New Year's Day edition of *Sovietsky Sport* heralded good things to come after the trials of 1956. At the top of the front page, a cartoon showed a parade of Olympians—Kuts, Latynina, Parfyonov, Shatkov, and others. They hold aloft a platter, piled with medals. On top of the gleaming hoard stands the New Year's child, cheerfully announcing the arrival of 1957.

Indeed, the year 1957 proved to be a turning point for the USSR. In October the launch of Sputnik propelled the Soviets ahead of the United States in the space race. In years ahead the Soviet Union confirmed its technological superiority by sending the first man and woman into space: Yuri Gagarin in 1961 and Valentina Tereshkova in 1963. Young people who came of age during these years believed in their country's political and economic system. They believed in a communist future. The international success of Soviet athletes confirmed that the USSR was dynamic, progressive, and powerful—a model for the rest of the world.

The Soviet Union was indeed a model, when it came to sports. After their stunning entrance into international competition, the Soviets' program of intensive training became the norm around the world. Athlete development followed the advances in sports science first made in the USSR. Already a half century ago, the Soviets were preparing athletes the way we do today, from millionaire pros down to kids at the youth level.

Most significant was the Soviets' lead in opening the arena to women. Title IX is rightly viewed as the turning point for women's sports in the United States. Yet before the landmark 1972 law, rivalry with the USSR stirred the realization that female participation in sports might be valuable, if not for the women themselves then certainly for American prospects at the Olympics. Sports commentators no longer get away with the cringey sexism of the 1950s and '60s. Profiles of female athletes now laud their athleticism—as well as their smarts, civic engagement, and interests outside of sports—just as Soviet propaganda did decades ago.

Russian media still hails the country's greatest female Olympian as the model champion. Commentators perform front and back saltos to keep Latynina on the sports pedestal, even as her records are broken. When Michael Phelps was arrested for driving under the influence in 2014, Russian media leaped on his legal problems as proof that he was no Latynina. "Is Michael Phelps great?" asked the daily *Moskovsky Komsomolets.* Of course he is, in the pool. "But the greatness of an athlete is determined not only by the gold in his backpack."

When measured against another American athlete, however, the gold in Latynina's backpack makes all the difference. Russian media was gleeful when Simone Biles fell off the balance beam at the Paris Olympics, ensuring the American would not match Latynina's record of nine golds in gymnastics. "She is not worthy of comparison with Larisa," snorted one commentator.

And what did the champion herself think?

"It's very good my record could not be broken."

CHAPTER 3

BREAKING THE CODE

LARISA LATYNINA'S RECENT MEDIA appearances often read like complaints from your cranky Russian grandmother. During the 2016 Summer Games in Rio, a newspaper asked her about athletes biting their medals for photographers. "Why are they doing this?" Latynina groused. "In Soviet times, we didn't bite medals." Everyone knows gold medals are not made of pure gold, she went on. "This is wrong and terrible."

One of Latynina's few complaints about Soviet times was that she didn't get everything the government promised. Before the Melbourne games, the Sports Committee told athletes they would receive 20,000 rubles for each gold medal. On the voyage home after the Olympics, Latynina chattered with Viktor Chukarin about what they would do with their winnings. Chukarin had defended the all-around gold he won at Helsinki and added gold medals in the parallel bars and team competitions. He was due 60,000, while Latynina expected 80,000. "Crazy money," Latynina said of her expected windfall. "I was already planning what I would buy—a refrigerator, a car."

She was disappointed when she went to the accounts office back home. She signed a receipt for 50,000 rubles. After the state took its cut in taxes, she got 43,000. "In fact, money didn't play a role for us," she said. Easy for her to say. The bonus she took home was nearly five times the average annual salary of a Soviet comrade.

Latynina's grumbles reveal an essential ingredient to the success of Soviet sports. Yes, coaches in the USSR devised innovations in training and strategy. Yes, researchers transformed athletic development through advances in sports sciences. And yes, Soviet athletes surpassed their rivals in the time and energy they devoted to their sports. But at the root of it all was an inescapable fact about the entire sports system in the Soviet Union.

They were cheating.

When the USSR entered world sport after World War II, the amateur code still governed the Olympics. Under the leadership of Avery Brundage, the IOC held rigidly to the rules of amateurism and imposed these rules over the governing bodies of the various sports in the Summer and Winter Games. If a federation swayed from the IOC standard, Brundage warned, the sport would be cast from the Olympics. Athletes who violated the code likewise risked expulsion. To the end of his presidency, Brundage refused to restore the gold medals won by Jim Thorpe at the 1912 Stockholm Olympics. Thorpe had played semi-pro baseball before the Olympics. Brundage insisted the IOC was correct to strip his medals in pentathlon and decathlon.

The Soviet Union avoided this strict rule, as did other communist countries that adopted the Soviet model. Athletes in the USSR not only received prize money for victories, they were paid salaries to train and compete. The Soviet system of intensive training was possible only because the country's athletes were paid to devote themselves full-time to their sports. Larisa Latynina had other activities in her life—her studies, her service to the Kiev city council, her responsibilities as a mother. But her job was gymnastics. Even more, her status as an athlete brought enviable perks. "They gave us apartments," Latynina told a reporter, "and the opportunity to buy a car without being on the waiting list. We were not deprived of attention."

All along, the IOC and other governing bodies knew Soviet athletes were not amateurs—as did sports officials and journalists in other countries. Any challenge to the deception was swatted away. In covering up their system of "state professionalism," Soviet sports officials set down a fundamental strategy of the Moscow playbook: we will cheat, and the people in charge of world sport will accept our cheating, because they can't afford to lose us.

The professionalization of Soviet sports started before the USSR entered the Olympics. In the 1930s, with tens of thousands of fans attending soccer matches between top clubs, the sport's popularity spurred the need for paying players. Clubs wanted talented players on the pitch, both to win games and draw fans. Yet payments to players had to be on the sly. Marx and Lenin would not have endorsed pro sports, and zealous communists criticized club directors for being too much like "businessmen."

Club bosses devised a clever solution. Soccer teams in the USSR were extensions of factories, military units, and other entities of the Party-state. When a new player was recruited, he became an employee of the institution connected with that team. On paper, a Red Army player was a Red Army officer; a player for Lokomotiv or Traktor worked for the factory making locomotives or tractors. Several clubs were called Dynamo, located in Moscow, Kiev, Tbilisi, and other cities. These were all affiliated with the state police, and Dynamo players were all on the police payroll. Usually, their job title was "physical fitness instructor." In practice, however, all these so-called employees were paid to play soccer.

Athletes in the clubs' other sections—track and field, gymnastics, weightlifting, and so on—likewise received money for jobs on paper. For top competitors, the government offered bonuses. Even though Soviet athletes did not compete in international events before the war, Moscow officials wanted them to prove their superiority over bourgeois rivals by setting world records. To allow time for training and to add incentive, the government established a ranking system in 1934 called the Masters of Sport. The titles weren't just fancy words; they also carried a stipend, enough for the athlete to practice full time. Even athletes who were not Masters of Sports earned plenty. If their so-called job didn't pay much, they received food or clothes for winning races or matches. In the late 1930s it was better to get groceries than rubles.

Nikolai Romanov proposed an overhaul of this system when he became head of the Sports Committee in 1945. He suggested dividing the Masters of Sport—roughly 1,500 athletes at the time—into two groups: The larger group, about 1,000 people, were "athletes who have no serious achievement," as Romanov called them. These people could do actual work in an actual job while continuing their athletic activities. By contrast, the best athletes in the country would be under the complete care of the state. By providing full salaries for these athletes—record holders, Soviet champions, members of national teams—the Sports Committee would allow for "the necessary conditions for their intensive training and improvement." So an athlete like Vsevolod Bobrov would be fully employed by the state whereas a forward for a mid-table club like Moscow Lokomotiv would be expected to put in hours at the factory.

Romanov signed the order putting the Soviet Union's top 475 athletes on the state payroll. The directive was kept secret to avoid the attention of hard-core commies. The Sports Committee used all kinds of euphemisms to keep purists off the trail: Athletes weren't paid a salary, Romanov and other sports bureaucrats insisted. Instead, they received "necessary compensation" for salary they were not receiving from their regular jobs while training. Plus,

Romanov argued, athletes were doing "socially useful" work—above all, bringing glory to the motherland.

There was no getting around the fact that paying athletes was a violation of Soviet principles. After the Helsinki Games, the editor of *Sovietsky Sport*, Nikolai Lyubomirov, complained to Georgy Malenkov that the Soviet Union's 33 government-funded football clubs were entertainment rather than something "socially useful." The loss at the Olympics showed that players were only interested in getting paid. Soviet footballers had become "easy prey to harmful influences and moral degradation," Lyubomirov charged.

Romanov was not averse to limiting the Sports Committee's attention to soccer. Allocating more resources to developing athletes in other sports would serve the greater goal of sports supremacy. After the 1952 games the committee cut the top pay in soccer by a third. At the same time Romanov asked permission to expand the number of athletes in other sports receiving state money. In 1955 the Sports Committee added salary lines for over 1,300 athletes and coaches to prepare for the upcoming winter and summer Olympics.

Did Party officials buy Romanov's story that state pay was "necessary compensation" for athletes missing work? In their research on Soviet sport, Russian historians Elena Zubkova and Alexander Kupriyanov asked the question of who believed what. Party leaders could review Romanov's budget lines, but they didn't. They were concerned only with the larger goal: Soviet victories. "There was a 'tacit covenant' between sports functionaries and power," Zubkova and Kupriyanov wrote: Romanov and the Sports Committee "honestly" declared there were no professional sports in the country; the Party leaders "pretended to believe it."

The Sports Committee had to carry out a double deception to cover athlete pay. At the same time Romanov duped Party leaders into believing Soviet athletes were not professionals, he also had to convince world governing bodies that Soviet athletes were amateurs.

Sports officials in the West had no illusions about state support in the USSR. "Sport is a tool of the state," wrote Swedish administrator Tage Ericson in 1950 after a three-week visit to the Soviet Union. IOC president Sigfrid Edström circulated Ericson's report in anticipation of Moscow's application to join the games. Edström wanted the advice of other Olympic brass on how to proceed. "We must question ourselves if the Russian athlete can be considered an amateur," wrote Edström. "We must face the fact that many of them are professionals."

Edström's second-in-command agreed. "From all reports, the best Russian athletes are State protégés with all sorts of special concession and rewards," observed Avery Brundage, IOC vice president at the time. "They are certainly not amateurs."

Yet just a few months later, IOC members approved the USSR's application. The Soviet Olympic Committee declared it had "examined and accepted the rules of the IOC." Moscow admitted that athletes used to receive prizes, but the practice had ended.

Surely, Olympic leaders were not that gullible. What brought the change in opinion? Brundage's papers include his observations of the IOC's dilemma when the Soviets submitted their application. Most members knew athletes in the USSR were not amateurs, he wrote. Even more, there was no way to verify Soviet compliance with the Olympic Code. Other members, however, believed IOC membership would have an uplifting effect in the Soviet Union. Brundage summarized this view: "If Russian youth become acquainted with the Olympic Code of fair play and good sportsmanship, benefits might accrue, not only to the participants but also to the rest of the world."

Brundage saw two key factors in the IOC decision to admit the Soviets: First was the desire for the Olympics to be truly universal.

Whether out of ambition or noble belief in Olympic ideals, IOC members wanted the Games to be a global movement, which meant including the communist part of the globe. The other concern was the IOC's commitment to neutrality. The rich men who ran the Olympics understood that if they turned down Moscow's application, it would open them to charges of political bias. "There would be noisy communist outburst against the Committee," Brundage observed, "which would be charged with violating its own requirements against introducing politics in sport."

Caught between their principles of amateurism and political neutrality, IOC members chose the latter. In doing so, they undermined the former. State professionalism in the USSR and other communist states would be decisive in eroding amateurism in world sport. Even though Olympic athletes today are no longer required to be amateurs, the IOC and other governing bodies are in the same bind that Avery Brundage recognized in 1951. Leaders of world sport still hope Russian athletes, coaches, and officials will follow the rules. At the same time they recognize that nothing can be done when Moscow breaks the rules, since it opens federations to charges of political bias. The ideals governing world sport have changed, but the knots binding the leaders of world sport remain tight.

"It will be interesting to meet these Russian gentlemen," Sigfrid Edström confided to his assistant before the Soviets' first appearance at an IOC meeting, "but I'm afraid that our American friends will not like them as members."

By "American friends," Edström meant Brundage, the only member of the IOC from the United States. A businessman who made his wealth in that most American of ways—through government contracts—Brundage was rich and self-satisfied. Having risen from a hardscrabble background in Chicago, he had no time for left-wing politics. The Nazis' rebuilding of Germany was more to his taste. "We should follow the German model," he said in the 1930s. His rise in the IOC was due largely to his role in quashing American demands for a boycott of the 1936 Berlin Olympics.

The Soviets' disregard for amateurism also stung Brundage, at least at first. He lived the amateur code as a young man. As a student at a technical high school, Brundage fashioned rocks into shot puts. He competed in track and field while earning an engineering degree with honors at the University of Illinois. When he succeeded Edström in 1952, Brundage was the first IOC president to have participated in the games as an athlete. He was bumped up a place in the pentathlon at the 1912 Olympics when teammate Jim Thorpe lost his gold medal.

Given his politics and commitment to amateurism, Brundage's opposition to the Soviet Union was expected. But he made a notable about-face after becoming IOC president. In the summer of 1954 he took a three-week tour of the USSR. Brundage visited facilities and attended events in Moscow, Leningrad, Kiev, Odessa, and Tbilisi. His visit to Georgia even included a side trip to Stalin's hometown, the mountain city of Gori, where he watched the Finals of the district volleyball tournament. Everywhere he went, Brundage was impressed by the intensity of activity. From school children doing daily exercises to factory workers playing after-work soccer matches, Brundage saw people committed to the highest ideals of sport.

After his return from the USSR, Brundage wrote about his tour in the *Saturday Evening Post,* the most popular American magazine at the time. The article's title made clear Brundage's findings: "I Must Admit—Russian Athletes Are Great!" The IOC chief did not shy away from the authoritarian side of Soviet sports. "By American standards, it is harsh and severe," he wrote. Athletes took part in activities not as a pastime but out of obligation. Sport in the USSR, he said, "thrives on regimentation and fierce national pride."

Despite the authoritarian streak, Brundage argued that Soviet sports could provide helpful tips to the US. "We have become a race of grandstand and bleacher sitters," he charged. In the USSR, by contrast, Brundage saw people of all ages participating in sports. He didn't suggest a Soviet-style, state-run program. "That is not the American way," he wrote. "But we must, in this country, encourage amateur athletics in a broad, revitalized program, or we are doomed to a secondary position in the world of sports."

Brundage claimed to be a critical observer of Soviet sports. He was a noted opponent of communism, after all. Yet he repeated his hosts' inflated claims with little scrutiny: 4 million Soviet citizens took part in track and field; the USSR had 800,000 trained gymnasts; Ukraine had 60,000 soccer teams; 900 teams had competed in the district volleyball tournament in Georgia. Nine hundred volleyball teams in a rugged region of central Georgia? Seriously? Even the largest youth volleyball tournament in the US today only draws 750 teams.

Brundage was especially credulous in his meeting with Nikolai Romanov. The IOC president had come prepared with a file of articles questioning Soviet athletes' amateur status, all translated into Russian. Brundage asked Romanov point-blank if the country's athletes were paid. Romanov admitted they had been in the past, but now they were not. Soviet athletes were workers and students.

Brundage followed with a question about training. At the time, IOC rules allowed only two weeks of dedicated training before the games. "We never send a sportsman to a camp for more than 14 days," said the man who designed Soviet Olympians' six-month training regimen.

"We want to win," Romanov declared. "You don't criticize us for that, do you?"

"No," Brundage answered, "so long as you follow the rules."

Neither the *Saturday Evening Post* article nor Brundage's notes recorded what Romanov said in response to that point. Whatever it was, the IOC president left satisfied. When he returned to the US, Brundage repeated Moscow's lines word for word: "Very few of the Russians are full-time athletes," he told reporters. "The majority work or go to school." Yes, there were abuses, he acknowledged. But Brundage pivoted from any Soviet missteps to his bigger concern: college football. The real hypocrisy was at American universities, he charged. By contrast, athletes in the USSR did not have chances for generous scholarships or pro contracts.

Based on what Brundage saw, Soviet people were dedicated to sport for sport's sake, not for wealth or fame. They didn't have much fun, he admitted. But they abided by the amateur code. He had Romanov's word on that. "Now we have this on record," he told the *New York Times*, "and if we find any abuses, we can go to headquarters."

While Brundage waved Romanov's declaration as proof of Soviet amateurism, the Sports Committee chief was masterminding a fully professional system, funded and managed by the state. Along with paying salaries to top athletes and coaches, Romanov's office continued paying bonuses to athletes who set records in track and field, weightlifting, swimming, and other events. Romanov was a typical Soviet boss: he took care of his people. He lobbied Party leaders to provide benefits like disability pay when athletes were injured, stipends for players cut from the national team, and training for older athletes so they could transition to coaching.

In making his case to Soviet leaders for expanded pay, Romanov followed Brundage's argument: look at American universities with their athletic scholarships. "In addition, the US has hundreds of professional hockey and basketball teams," he argued. Just as he exploited Brundage's ignorance to spin tales of Soviet rectitude, he counted on his bosses' ignorance to create a picture of American deception. Of course, Romanov knew American pros did not compete in the Olympics. And there weren't hundreds of pro teams in basketball and hockey. The NBA had eight teams at the time; the NHL had six. But his exaggerations did the trick: Party leaders approved 12 government-funded teams in the Soviet hockey league to prepare players for the national team.

In 1959 the Council of Ministers brought some order to the system Romanov developed over the previous decade. The government stipulated a new pay scale for athletes. For winning the National Championship in team sports or an individual event like skiing, cycling, or gymnastics, athletes would receive 500 rubles (the equivalent of 5,000 rubles in the early 1950s, before the Soviet currency was reformed by chopping off a zero). A World Championship brought a bonus of 1,500 rubles, as did an Olympic gold medal or world record.

To make a comparison: IOC rules forbade an athlete in the West from receiving any prize over $50. At the time $50 equated to roughly 1% of the average salary in the United States. By contrast, bonuses for Soviet champions amounted to 5% percent of the average salary in the USSR.

Along with paying current champions, Romanov wanted to support future champions. The Council of Ministers initially rebuffed his requests to provide stipends to promising teenage athletes. Leaders of the Komsomol youth organization feared cash payments would corrupt young athletes. But by the end of the 1950s, Romanov's pressure won out—young athletes received stipends from the Sports Committee, provided they kept up their studies and political education.

Even though state professionalism contradicted Soviet ideology and violated the rules of international sport, the system was firmly in place by the 1960s. Soviet athletes trained year-round, for hours a day. Whether they received money from their clubs or directly from the Sports Committee, athletes' training and competition were treated as labor. For the most successful, rewards were impressive, thanks not only to their official salaries but also the special perks they received. For instance, members of the Soviet national hockey team earned the 1,500-ruble bonus every year during the 1960s for winning the World Championship or Olympics. A hockey player could also buy a Volga car for 6,000 rubles, without having to wait years for a car to be available, like ordinary Soviet citizens. He could then take the car to Tashkent or Tbilisi, where vehicles were especially rare, and sell it for 20,000. International tournaments brought the opportunity to buy foreign goods for even more black-market sales. "It was a good trip if you could make 3,000 rubles," recalled national team captain Boris Mayorov.

When it came to hiding payments to athletes, sports officials in the USSR were not as sneaky as they thought. Avery Brundage's personal files have plenty of reports on Soviet chicanery from American, Canadian, and European newspapers.

RUSSIAN ATHLETES DENY PAYOFFS, declared the *Los Angeles Herald Examiner.*

SOVIETS PAY AMATEURS CASH BONUSES, announced the West German paper *Der Mittag.*

Just a year after his visit to the USSR, Brundage forwarded the clippings to Moscow along with a request: "I wish you could give me some definite supporting evidence [that] might offset this growing indignation."

It took eight months for Moscow to work up a response. "In the Soviet Union, there is no professionalism," wrote Konstantin Andrianov, head of the Soviet Olympic Committee. "Our athletes train and participate in competitions in their free time from work or studies."

Brundage continued sending clippings in the 1960s, along with further requests for clarification. Soviet replies to questions about athlete pay set the template Moscow followed decades later in response to doping charges. These stock answers made up an essential chapter of the Moscow playbook: How to Respond When You're Caught Cheating.

Strategy No. 1: smear the source of information. When Brundage first confronted Romanov with questions about payments to Soviet athletes, his principal source of intelligence were athletes who had defected to the West. Romanov was blunt: you Americans wouldn't respond to a traitor's accusations, why should we? Stories from defectors were "not worth the ink with which they are written," Moscow officials maintained whenever Brundage forwarded charges from an athlete who fled the Soviet bloc.

Strategy No. 2: go on the offensive. Almost as soon as the IOC accepted the Soviet Union's application, sports officials in Moscow charged the organization with being undemocratic and backward. The Soviet Olympic Committee repeatedly proposed reforms: addition of more women's sports, admission of communist China, broadening of IOC decision-making. Certainly, some proposals were legitimate, but the strategy also served as an effective counterpunch. At a 1961 meeting in Moscow, Romanov fired a salvo at the IOC: "We won't refrain from exposing reactionaries in international sports." An English translation of the speech ended up at Olympic headquarters in Switzerland. It served as a warning: accuse us of violating the rules and we'll remind everyone you are bourgeois imperialist pigs.

Strategy No. 3: be a dedicated ally. Soviet sports officials understood that the way to Avery Brundage's heart was to join him in opposing commercialized pro sports. As the IOC president became even more zealous in his campaign against creeping professionalism and commercial sponsorships, Moscow joined in pointing fingers at the naughty Europeans and North Americans. "Professional sports and the Olympic movement have nothing in common," stated a 1968 editorial in *Sovietsky Sport*. Brundage couldn't have said it better himself.

Strategy No. 4: deny the evidence. In 1972 Canadian hockey officials appealed to Brundage with detailed evidence of Soviet state professionalism, uncovered by the *Montreal Gazette*. Brundage passed the complaint to Moscow. The reply was direct: "The 'facts' indicating the incomes of Soviet ice hockey players are not true and do not indicate the real situation." Other peoples' so-called facts were not facts. "Our athletes are amateurs," sports officials stated in reply. The quiet part wasn't included in their letter: "Because we say so."

Moscow stonewalled, and Brundage went along with it. In his view, the greater threat to the Olympics wasn't the Soviet state professional masquerading as an amateur, it was the Western amateur taking a college scholarship. Brundage also complained about the increasing quality of Olympic-level competition, which required athletes to devote more time to training. "Many participants have stated that to reach Olympic caliber, they do nothing else during most of the year," he groused. In his view, if an event was so difficult it required year-round commitment, then it should be eliminated from the Olympic program.

In his complaints about expanding training schedules, Brundage missed that trends in sport were driven by successful athletes and the most successful athletes came from the USSR. During the 1960s, athletes and coaches around the world intensified training programs to keep up with the Soviets. More training meant athletes needed material support. If Olympic hopefuls spent their waking hours practicing their sport, they couldn't hold jobs. Their needs had to be met somehow.

If we look at two sports the Soviets dominated in the '60s and '70s, we can see how their state-professional system, which allowed for year-round training, influenced their competitors. First, let's look at hockey. From 1963 to 1972, the Soviets swept every international tournament in the sport: seven World Championships and three Olympic gold medals. Most members of the national team played on the same club team, Red Army. The Red Army coach, Anatoly Tarasov, was also the co-coach of the national team. In essence members of the national team trained under a national-team coach and played alongside their national-team teammates for the entire season before going to the Olympics or World Championships. In addition, everyone on the national team went to a month-long training camp in the off-season. So much for the IOC rule limiting athletes to two weeks' preparation.

Canadian officials complained that the so-called amateurs from the USSR spent more time training than NHL pros. Plus, Soviet players were getting paid like pros. Nevertheless, Brundage refused to allow Canadian pros to enter international tournaments. Frustrated by this unfair system, Canada withdrew completely from international hockey. The country that invented hockey did not compete in the sport at the 1972 and 1976 Olympics.

The Swedes, meanwhile, also responded to the Soviet challenge in world hockey. In 1962 Sweden won the last World Championship before the USSR went on its dominant run. As bonuses, members of that championship team received trinkets from team sponsors. Players practiced three nights per week after finishing work. Off-season training was voluntary. Through the rest of the decade, however, as the Soviets won year after year, Swedish coaches and officials recognized their players needed more time on the ice. League administrators and club directors devised ways to pay players for their time. National team players earned money through endorsement contracts or jobs with sponsoring companies. By the end of the '60s, these jobs were just a way to cut a paycheck. In 1976 the Swedish league did away with pretending and became openly professional. Yet with the IOC still holding to amateur rules, officials had no choice but to follow the Canadians. Sweden also pulled their hockey team from the Olympics.

In gymnastics, competitors likewise had to adapt to the Soviets' intensive training. For example, the top American gymnast at the 1956 games, Sandra Ruddick, practiced her routines at the German community center in Indianapolis when she had time away from raising two children. She finished 51st in the individual all-around at Melbourne. By contrast when Cathy Rigby was preparing for the 1972 Olympics, she spent up to seven hours per day in the gym. She finished 10th—the best showing ever by an American. Rigby showed that more training brought better results. But how to provide for the athlete's needs while she's training?

In gymnastics, the solution was simple: get children to be the athletes. As former international gymnast Georgia Cervin explains in her history of the sport, from 1956 onward the American women's team was, on average, younger than the Soviet team. And they kept getting younger. Ruddick was 24 when she competed in Melbourne. At age 19, Rigby was the oldest member of the team that went to Munich. Four years later, the average age of the American team was just under 18. Without jobs to hold or families to raise, American teenagers could devote themselves to the full-time training required of Olympic gymnastics. A state-funded program was out of the question—this was the United States, after all. Instead, they trained at private gyms, and their parents picked up the tab.

"Soviet sports is a façade," wrote Yevgeny Rubin in the *New York Times* in 1979. Six months earlier, Rubin had been in Moscow, writing for *Sovietsky Sport*. He was in trouble repeatedly for reporting on payments to athletes. Now that he was in the United States as a Jewish refugee, he could write freely about what he knew: the salaries, the Moscow apartments, the cars, the trips abroad, and goods sold on the black market. The USSR had violated the rules of international sport for political propaganda, Rubin charged. "What prevents the athletes of the world from saying 'no' to the Moscow Olympics?" he asked. "Who can force amateur athletes… to go to the Olympics in a country that despises Olympic ideals?"

Rubin was right: Soviet sport wasn't guided by ideals; it was guided by wins. And with the 1980 Summer Games approaching, Soviet officials were determined to win. The USSR had to top the medal standings at its own Olympics.

To provide additional incentive, the government increased the amount athletes would receive for winning a medal. A gold medal would earn 10,000 rubles, 5,000 for silver, and 3,000 for bronze. However, when Jimmy Carter announced a boycott of the Moscow Olympics in protest over the Soviet invasion of Afghanistan, Soviet officials pumped the brakes on the bigger bonuses. If the Americans weren't going to be in Moscow, then why offer more money? Soviet athletes were going to dominate with the Americans away on their boycott, joined by the Japanese, West Germans, and others. Giving out big bonuses would only break the bank.

When it was clear their main rivals weren't going to compete, state accountants rolled back the bonuses. The 10,000-ruble bonus for gold was dropped to 4,000; silver paid out 2,000, and bronze brought 1,500. Quick-thinking bean counters saved the Moscow treasury a bundle. At the 1980 Summer Olympics, Soviet athletes set records for most gold medals (80) and most total medals (195). With the revised bonuses, the state cut its payouts by more than half.

Just like Larisa Latynina after the Melbourne games, Soviet athletes in 1980 discovered that what the state promised—even after revising the offered bonuses—wasn't what ended up in their pockets. A gold medalist would find their 4,000-ruble bonus reduced by 13% for income taxes. A male athlete without a family would have to pay an additional 6% tax for being childless. If you lived outside Moscow, the Sports Committee sent your bonus through the postal service, which charged a transfer fee. The further you were from the capital, the higher the fee. An athlete living in Uzbekistan, for instance, would pay 20% to get their money.

Even after the state took its cut, some Soviet athletes did quite well. "Just before the Olympics, I got an apartment in Moscow," recalled sabre fencer Viktor Krovopuskov, who won two gold medals. Gymnast Alexander Dityatin, winner of three golds, went on a spree: four-room apartment in Leningrad, furniture, car. Automobiles were a popular choice for medalists. Swimmer Vladimir Salnikov bought a Lada Riva, the new model built for export. Ukrainian swimmer Oleksandr Sydorenko gave the coupon allowing him to leapfrog the waiting list to his father. "He always dreamed of owning a Volga," Sydorenko recalled.

When the Olympics closed in Moscow, the pillars of amateurism were beginning to crack. Despite Avery Brundage's traditionalism, he guided the Olympics into becoming an international spectacle that brought in millions in television revenue. For all the money they were forking over, broadcasters wanted elite competition, not university students who turned rocks into shot puts. The athletes in turn recognized that everyone else was getting rich. "Amateur athletes sensed this hypocrisy," observed Matthew Llewellyn and John Gleaves in their history of Olympic amateurism. "They demanded a slice of the growing pie."

The Soviet Union's influence was decisive in turning the Olympics from amateurism. Following the Soviet model, coaches and athletes around the world adopted more intensive training methods, driven by applied research. Elite-level sport became a technologically advanced enterprise, with governments and corporations investing large sums. It was ridiculous to insist that the athletes, the objects of all this R & D, should remain part-time amateurs.

After Brundage retired in 1972, his successor, Lord Killanin, eased the IOC's hard stance on amateurism. The real turning point then came in 1980 at the IOC's Moscow meeting with the election of Juan Antonio Samaranch as president. Over the objections of the Soviets, who stood to lose most from the demise of the amateur code, Samaranch moved immediately to loosen rules against professionalism. In 1984 pro tennis players competed in a demonstration tournament at Los Angeles. The gates were then thrown open by the NBA stars who competed at the 1992 Barcelona Games. The Dream Team showed what was possible for the Olympics: a showcase for the best athletes in the world.

When Russian sportswriters today profile Soviet Olympians, a common question is how much the athlete was paid. What did they receive in salary and bonuses? What did they spend their money on? These stories are now part of the lore of Soviet sports. Yet there is no admission that these athletes were part of a state-run effort to game the whole structure of international sports. The great medal-winners of Soviet years are now national heroes in Russia. It would be unseemly to mention they were cheating.

CHAPTER 4

A NEW WAY TO CHEAT

AMATEURISM'S LAST HURRAH came at Lake Placid's Olympic Arena on February 22, 1980.

Sportswriters at the time equated the US hockey team's triumph over the Soviets to a high school football team beating the Pittsburgh Steelers, recent winners of their fourth Super Bowl. The Soviets were indeed like the Steelers of the 1970s—if the Steelers had poached players from the Cowboys, Raiders, and Rams, and then practiced eleven months a year. Just a year before, the Soviets embarrassed a squad of NHL all-stars at Madison Square Garden. The NHL team included 20 future Hall of Famers. The Soviets won 6–0. This was the team the Americans beat at Lake Placid, the best pro dynasty in hockey history.

But to equate the US Olympic team with high schoolers did them a disservice. This was a talented, well-prepared team. It was also an amateur team. Most players were fresh out of college; their average age was just under 22. The Soviet team included veterans who had spent more than a decade in the USSR's top pro league. Americans love underdog stories, and the hockey players at Lake Placid were true underdogs—real amateurs playing real pros. That's why the Miracle on Ice still resonates.

When interviewed by American media, former Soviet players cast blame for the loss in different directions. In the ESPN documentary *Of Miracles and Men*, players pointed to coach Viktor Tikhonov's strategic blunders. Slava Fetisov charged in a *Sports Illustrated* interview that Tikhonov deliberately blew the game so that he could dismantle the national team. When Fetisov later played in Detroit, he would needle Red Wings teammate Mike Ramsey, a member of the US team. "Fucking lucky," Slava chirped across the locker room.

Yet old Soviet players tell a different story to Russian reporters.

"They were doped up with something," said Viktor Zhluktov. "I don't doubt it at all. There was no one who could keep up with us for a whole game."

"Back then, there was no drug testing like at today's Olympics," said Vladimir Petrov. "We suspect the Americans could not have done it without drugs."

"You can look at the photos and see it in their eyes," said Alexander Maltsev.

To be sure, there were American athletes who took performance-enhancing drugs during the 1970s and '80s. Hurdler Edwin Moses, gold medalist in 1976 and 1984, said that over half of US track and field athletes took drugs to improve their performances. When surprise drug tests were announced at the 1983 Pan-America Games in Venezuela, a dozen athletes caught the first flight back to the US. Doping was an epidemic in international sport, and American athletes were guilty of shooting up.

In the Soviet Union, however, doping had a different dimension. Rather than an individual athlete seeking an edge over rivals, doping was an integral part of the state's strategy for winning. As the rest of the world started keeping pace with Soviet athletes, by adopting Soviet methods, Moscow needed to regain the lead. Doping became a new way to ensure victories.

Even for the invincible hockey team. The irony of the hockey players' doping charges against the Americans is that they had been getting doses from their own team doctors. The doctors said the pills were supplements, allowing the players some deniability. To this day, Fetisov insists the strongest drug his teammates used "was the name of our country on our uniforms."

Doping in sports is nothing new. Ever since the games of the ancient Greeks, athletes have sought elixirs to give them an advantage. Early cyclists relied on all kinds of drugs: ether to deaden pain, nitroglycerin to stimulate the heart, cocaine for endurance. During the Cold War, the time-honored practice of finding a chemical boost turned into a pharmacological arms race. Just as neither superpower could let the other build more missiles, so could neither country allow the other to gain an advantage in drugs.

From the start, the Soviets made pharmaceuticals part of their plan. At the training camps Nikolai Romanov set up before the 1952 Helsinki Games, physicians gave athletes various pills. Reports back to the Sports Committee referred to distribution of "vitamins" and "special concentrates for nutrition." One letter from the Kiev training camp asked Moscow officials to "resolve the issue of stimulants."

Maybe nutritional supplements were simply that. But the Soviets were also experimenting with more potent stuff. We have this inside information on good authority: one of the team doctors, who admitted what the Soviets were up to over drinks in a hotel bar.

As a chapter of the Cold War, it's fitting that the doping race began in Vienna—one of the main stages of East-West espionage. In 1954, when the city was still occupied by American and Soviet troops, Vienna hosted the World Weightlifting Championships. On the same stage of the famous Konzerthaus where the Vienna

Symphony Orchestra performed, the world's strongmen hefted iron. Among the American contingent was Dr. John Ziegler, the team physician. A weightlifter himself, Ziegler would have stood out even among the hulking competitors. Standing 6′4″, he was typically dressed in Western-style clothes. Back home in Maryland, friends called him "Montana Jack," even though he hailed from the Midwest.

As Ziegler later told the story, he ended up having drinks in Vienna with the Soviet team doctor. His counterpart pestered him with questions.

"What are you giving your boys?" the Russian asked at one point.

Ziegler dodged. More drinks were downed. The Slav broke before Montana Jack.

"We give our team testosterone," the Soviet doctor admitted.

Ziegler's ears perked up. Along with his medical practice and side job with the weightlifting team, Ziegler also did research for Swiss-based Ciba Pharmaceuticals. In particular, he did work on post-traumatic treatments, an interest of his after being injured in the war. Ziegler used testosterone to treat burn patients, but he hadn't thought to use it in the gym. On his return to Maryland, he gave doses to lifters he knew—and he tried some himself. No one reported improved results, except for one guy who got an instant erection whenever he saw a woman.

Undeterred, Ziegler began working with the Ciba chemists on something more effective than testosterone: anabolic steroids. Scientists in Ciba's Swiss labs had been researching steroids since the 1930s, and in 1958 the company began marketing Dianabol, the first widely used steroid, as a treatment for burn victims. Ziegler brought the little pink pills to the gym and handed them out as "diet supplements."

Eager for scientific data, Montana Jack found an ideal testing subject, a 34-year-old weightlifter and medical student named

Louis Riecke. Two weeks after starting on Dianabol, Riecke saw a 6% increase in his lifting bests. More tellingly, he didn't tire after a workout. "I feel like lifting all the time," he told Ziegler. Riecke had not qualified for the last Olympics, yet two months after starting on Dianabol, he was lifting weights that would have won the bronze medal. Four years later, he set the world record with a snatch of 325 pounds.

Dianabol quickly spread among weight gyms across the United States. At the same time, Ciba's pills and steroids from other labs circulated in Europe. By the mid-1960s, athletes were trading pills at international meets. One of the first American athletes to admit taking steroids, hammer thrower Hal Connolly, testified to Congress that he got his first dose in Finland. When he took the world record in 1964, it was no secret among rivals that he was doping. Four years later at the Mexico City Olympics, athletes from various countries were dosed with steroids, competing in weightlifting, track, and other events.

At first, Ziegler believed he had found a way for athletes to lift weights that were, in his words, "superhuman." Yet already by the late 1960s, he was concerned about lifters gobbling down drugs. "They figured if one pill was good, three or four would be better," he said in a 1969 interview. "They were eating them like candy." Decades later, he expressed regret at the widespread abuse. Yet he still tried to convince himself that his motives had been justified. "The Soviets were doing it first," he told himself. Like weapons in the arms race, it was necessary to cut off the enemy's advantage.

By the 1970s, when I was watching weightlifting on ABC's *Wide World of Sports*, the world's greatest lifter was unquestionably Vasily Alekseyev. Bursting from his red singlet, with enormous belly and hairy shoulders, Alekseyev looked nothing like a world-champion athlete. Yet in 1970 he started a decade-long run of dominance in the sport: two Olympic gold medals and 80 world records, including the first lift ever of 500 pounds in the clean and jerk. *Sports Illustrated* put Alekseyev on the cover in 1975, beneath the headline: WORLD'S STRONGEST MAN.

As a teenager in the coal-mining city of Shakhty, in southern Russia, Alekseyev had made his own barbells from scrap metal. He was a late bloomer in competitions: only in 1968, at age 26, did he start winning meets. By that time, Alekseyev had already broken from coaches, preferring to follow his own training program. In interviews, Alekseyev gave occasional glimpses into his secret regimen: lifting lighter weights for several reps, practicing cleans in a swimming pool. He also stopped trying to control his weight. As his belly grew, so did his strength.

Alekseyev's self-devised training program fit his personality. He was lifelong tinkerer. During his short tenure as coach of the Russian national team, he had lifters using equipment he created. When a reporter visited in 1999, the retired champion showed off a device he made for catching rats. The reporter asked why he didn't market his inventions. Alekseyev waved a hand and said President Yeltsin would take everything. The best way to make money was to become a criminal, he added. "But I can't," he laughed. "I'm too famous."

Alekseyev was always good for a quote. Garrulous, unfiltered, with a deep voice and booming laugh, the champion regularly welcomed reporters to his house in Shakhty before his death from heart failure in 2011. Typically, reporters sought him out for opinions on the current state of weightlifting. Like Latynina the old gymnast, the old lifter had plenty to grumble about. In particular, he complained about doping. Current lifters were all doping, he charged, just like all of his old rivals. Alekseyev proudly recalled how Soviet team doctors pressed him to take steroids before competing at the 1976 Montreal Olympics. "Take them yourself," he said. Then he went out and lifted a total of 970 pounds—an Olympic record.

The doctors told a different story. "Vasya loved steroids," recalled team physician Sergei Sarsania. Certainly, Alekseyev was innovative in his training, Sarsania acknowledged in an interview shortly before his death in 2021. And the champion was indeed a prodigious physical specimen. "He would break a grilled chicken in half and swallow it," the doctor said of Alekseyev's midday meals. "Four bottles of beer and two chickens—that was his lunch." As for the records, however, Sarsania was blunt: that was drugs.

Arkady Vorobyov admitted as much to the Sports Committee when Alekseyev was still competing. A two-time gold medalist himself, Vorobyov earned his doctorate in sports medicine while serving as coach of the Soviet weightlifting team in the late '60s. By the time Alekseyev joined the team, Vorobyov had left to become head of research at Moscow's physical education institute. In 1970 the strongman-turned-scientist got a call from Alexey Pavlov, head of the Sports Committee. Alekseyev had just set a new world record. "The chair called me and demanded an explanation of how he achieved it," Vorobyov recalled in an interview. "It's anabolics," he replied.

Pavlov gave a different report to the Sports Committee. "Some scientists say these are anabolics," he said, as Vorobyov looked on. "But in fact, these are advanced training methods."

Privately, Vasily Alekseyev professed his fondness for drugs. "The barbell jumps off the chest by itself," he told Sarsania. But there were side effects to contend with. At a competition in Cuba, he had to be restrained from throwing a teammate out a hotel window. Before a competition in Bulgaria, he went into a rage. Swinging a barbell like a club, the steroid-crazed Alekseyev destroyed an entire gym. The Bulgarians sent angry messages to

Moscow, but complaints were brushed aside. This was the strongest man in the world.

"When the goose lays golden eggs," Sarsania recalled, "all is forgiven."

Alekseyev was not the only Soviet weightlifter to pump himself with steroids. And Sarsania and Vorobyov were not innocent observers. According to Sarsania, he first learned of steroids from Vorobyov. At the training camp before the 1968 Mexico City games, when Vorobyov was the weightlifting coach, he gave Sarsania bottles of pills from Hungary and instructed him to administer the doses. "This was a gold mine of information," Sarsania admitted. "But no one knew the correct dosage or side effects."

The physician went to work. Leading a team of researchers at the Institute of Physical Culture, Sarsania conducted a four-year study into the benefits and drawbacks of anabolic steroids. Only 150 copies of his final report were printed, distributed to national team coaches and physical education institutes in the USSR. Although Sarsania's findings were kept under wraps, his report did not describe steroids as something illegitimate—except when foreign rivals used them to steal medals from Soviet athletes. Steroids were a scientific advance in sports training. "With a markedly increased competition between the leading sports powers," Sarsania wrote, "as a rule, the greatest successes are achieved by the country that best uses the latest achievements of science and technology."

In other words, the Soviet Union could use steroids to beat the Americans. Even better: the Soviets would beat the Americans with their own medicine. As Sarsania's report made clear, American athletes were the first to use anabolics, and researchers in the US and Western Europe had already conducted tests on steroid use. The USSR needed to catch up.

To discover the most effective use of steroids, Sarsania conducted trials with biathletes, weightlifters, track athletes, gymnasts, rowers, basketball players, and more. His team left no cell unturned: they measured heart rate, muscle mass, liver absorption, body size. The results were clear: "Anabolics cause a significant increase in energy, increased appetite, good mood, desire to train, and a more complete recovery after training."

Yet there were also side effects: ligament strain, headaches, irritability, liver damage, impotence, and sterility. These drawbacks were largely avoided when administering the proper dosages. The report did have one firm warning, though: "The use of anabolic steroids by athletes of both sexes under 18 years of age is strictly prohibited." Researchers found that steroid use delayed puberty, indicating that the study's subjects included children. For adults, on the other hand, Sarsania's report gave full approval. "Reasonable" steroid use brought improvements in strength, speed, and endurance. Moscow had another way to cheat.

Except steroids weren't cheating—at least not in the early 1970s. First of all, everyone was doing it. According to a survey conducted at the 1972 Munich Olympics, some two-thirds of athletes from the US, Europe, and the USSR had taken steroids.

Second, Soviet physicians and sports officials controlled how the drugs were distributed and used. At least on paper. Admittedly, there were abuses. Athletes and coaches in distant regions sought the recognition that steroid-boosted results would bring. Disregarding the warnings, they figured bigger doses would bring better results. Sarsania recalled a weightlifter from Volgograd who took 125 milligrams of Neurabol per day. The recommended dosage was 15 milligrams. "Naturally, things ended badly for that guy," he said. "He died from cirrhosis of the liver. Such were the times."

Third, taking steroids was not cheating because there were no rules against steroids. Attention to doping had arisen after the death of Danish cyclist Knud Enemark Jensen at the 1960 Rome Olympics. Jensen collapsed in the heat and fractured his skull. It was later learned he had been weakened by a dose of Roniacol, a blood-pressure drug administered by the team doctor to increase the cyclists' endurance. The IOC's concern about doping, however, was not so much the health of athletes but the purity of competition. Doping was a violation of the Olympics' amateur code, just like an athlete being paid or spending too much time training.

According to the Moscow playbook, sport was not a morally pure arena where fairness reigned. As Sarsania's report made clear, the leading sports powers competed *within* the arena of international political rivalry. Athletic success was politically necessary. Therefore, any advantage gained through science was to be used—especially if the rivals were already using that advantage. The Soviets held this view of steroids as a legitimate tool even after the IOC banned the drugs and instituted testing at the 1976 Montreal Olympics. Science had given athletes an advantage. Science would allow Soviet athletes to keep that advantage.

Already before British chemists devised a way to test for steroids, Soviet researchers were working on their own detection methods, so they could devise ways to confound the tests. Vasily Alekseyev boasted of being the only clean weightlifter at the 1976 Games. In fact, Soviet doctors figured out a way to wash out the drugs before his test. "Vasily Ivanovich was given a solution of citric acid," Sarsania reported. The strongest man in the world set his record, and no traces of steroids were found.

Sarsania's accounts of doping in the 1970s don't read like a centrally organized masterplan. Instead, the picture is much more Soviet: a bumbling circus of corrupt officials and coaches handing out drugs to athletes without any instruction. "Athletes were eating pills by the handful," he recalled, "without paying attention to the side effects." By contrast, other states in the Soviet bloc took greater control over steroids. Sarsania appealed to the Sports Committee to follow the practice of the Bulgarians, who distributed drugs through pharmacies. His bosses refused.

Sarsania recounted their stance to a Bulgarian colleague at a weightlifting meet. "Your first group of people will die from overdoses, and then you'll replace them," remarked the Bulgarian, an astute observer of the Russian mindset. "We're a small country. We can't squander our property."

In his appeals for central control, Sarasania pointed to another socialist state as an example of proper steroid use—the country now synonymous with drug-fueled athletic success: East Germany. In the 1970s relations between sports officials in Moscow and East Berlin were tense. Drugs were a big part of the problem. On paper the East German sports program shared the same goal as the Soviets and other members of the Warsaw Pact: show the superiority of the communist system. But East Germany had other goals as well. The aim of sport, declared Party boss Walter Ulbricht, was "to strengthen the German Democratic Republic." With a population of just 16 million, the GDR was dwarfed by West Germany, a country of more than 50 million people and one of the world's strongest economies. Sports were a way to prove the smaller, socialist Germany was the better Germany.

In building their athletic program, East German officials also looked east. In the 1950s the GDR dutifully adopted Soviet-style organization and training. But the East Germans were already devising techniques that broke from the Soviets, thanks to spying on West German training facilities. When the East Germans built their own advanced training center, they were more careful about keeping secrets safe. Even the Soviets were in the dark. Ulbricht himself gave the order: information on training methods "should not be handed out to the Soviet sports organizations out of 'friendship.'"

By the early 1970s Soviet sports scientists were openly complaining about the lack of cooperation from their so-called friends. At the time, East German sports was under tight control of the Ministry of State Security—the notorious Stasi. Security was especially tight in the "area of supportive means," doublespeak for doping. Dozens of Stasi informants were placed in steroid labs to make sure scientists weren't selling secrets to the West or the East. The Soviets "won't get a single thing from us," declared Manfred Hoeppner, head of the doping program.

The Soviets were worried about the East German doping program, especially when East German athletes started beating their own. At the Munich games, the GDR finished third in the medal table behind the Americans and first-place Soviets. Four years later at Montreal, the East Germans' 40 gold medals surpassed the Americans and nearly equaled the Soviet haul of 49.

The East Germans' centralized doping program not only produced results in competition, they also had good results with the urine vials. Bulgarian, Czechoslovak, and Polish athletes all failed drug tests at Montreal, but the East Germans came away clean. The Soviets did as well, although people like Sarsania knew more work was needed. By contrast, East German scientists were so confident in their ability to avoid detection they pushed for more stringent testing. At the 1972 and 1976 Olympics, the host countries managed testing. Before the Moscow games, East Germany called for international control of anti-doping tests. The Soviets were sweating. If they didn't run the testing, there was no way to ensure clean results. Moscow launched a warning shot to East Berlin: stop pursuing actions "that might be damaging to the Soviet Union."

The year before the Moscow Games, the Soviets took a practice run at managing doping tests when they hosted the World Hockey

Championships. Sarsania knew Soviet skaters were doping. He was administering the doses.

Prior to the tournament, coach Viktor Tikhonov summoned Sarsania for a consultation. Like his predecessor Anatoly Tarasov, Tikhonov coached both the national team and the Red Army club. Members of the Soviet team played for Red Army during the league season, then put on their CCCP jerseys for the World Championships or Olympics. Tikhonov's regimen was notorious: workouts on and off the ice during the season along with more training in the summer. This particular year, the national team also traveled to New York to play the NHL All-Stars. The Soviets paid a price for their 6–0 victory at Madison Square Garden. Two months later, players were exhausted.

"The team is dead," Sarsania told Tikhonov and the coach's boss, Viktor Koloskov, head of the Sports Committee's hockey department.

"What are we going to do?" Tikhonov asked. With the World Championships being played in Moscow, anything less than first place was unacceptable.

The players needed energy. Sarsania had the remedy.

"What about doping control?" asked Tikhonov.

"Don't worry," interjected Koloskov. The Sports Committee was responsible for testing at the World Championships, and Koloskov was in charge. "I'll take care of it."

In the late '70s, Soviet dominance in international hockey had been challenged by Sweden and Czechoslovakia. But at the 1979 championship, the Soviets served notice to their rivals. In the final round, the Soviets trounced Sweden 11–3 and beat Czechoslovakia twice, by a total score of 17–2. Tikhonov's squad took the world title. Everyone tested clean.

Yet Tikhonov didn't learn his lesson. The following year, he ramped up training in preparation for the 1980 Winter Olympics.

"The team was catastrophically overwhelmed by the workload," Sarsania told a Russian interviewer. Despite the doctor's successful prescription in 1979, Tikhonov didn't consult him before Lake Placid. "According to my calculations," Sarsania said, "it was the coach, not the players, who were to blame for the defeat."

With the Americans spending $1.5 million on doping control at Lake Placid, the Soviets would have been hard-pressed to sneak dirty samples through the lab. Things would be different in Moscow. Soviet officials fended off calls for international doping control. "There will be no control," Sarsania assured his Bulgarian colleague. "These are the Olympics of socialist countries. No one will allow us to lose face."

To ensure clean results, the Soviets borrowed a trick from the East Germans, putting their state police in charge of the anti-doping lab. KGB officers were responsible for collecting urine samples and then trading them out for clean samples. Soviet athletes were not the only ones to benefit from the scheme. Pole vaulter Konstantin Volkov, silver medalist at Moscow, recalled his visit to doping control. He handed his vial to a uniformed officer.

"We throw it all away," said the officer. "Here is your urine."

"I'm clean," Volkov protested. "I'm not afraid."

"We don't need accidents," the officer answered. "Go hand this one in."

"Is this the case for everyone?" Volkov asked. "My opponents as well?"

"Everyone. Without exception. Nobody will test for anything."

The Moscow playbook had a new chapter, one that would come in handy in 2014 at Sochi. Even though athletes were popping pills and jabbing needles, Soviet officials bragged that the 1980 Games were the cleanest Olympics ever. Not only did the country's athletes win the most medals in Olympic history, but Soviet officials also implemented the first drug-free games. They could proudly trumpet the words of the IOC's medical director: "In comparison with previous Olympics, the Moscow Olympics are the fairest."

The Washington-led boycott of the 1980 Olympics cast a cloud over Moscow's triumph, but not as dark as the Carter Administration believed. The Soviets' aim was to gain victories for political benefit, and their athletes gained the most victories ever. Soviet media pointed out that 18 world records were set in Moscow—proof that Americans weren't needed to have top-level competition.

The Soviet press didn't need to condemn the boycott. Americans did that for them. *Sovietsky Sport* quoted a *Washington Post* editorial criticizing the boycott. TASS featured the remarks of American athletes who slammed Carter for making political points. In responding to the boycott, Moscow shifted its line on sports and politics. Ever since the Soviet Union began competing internationally, officials stated repeatedly that sports were an expression of politics. "The view popular in the West that 'sport is outside of politics' finds no support in the USSR," declared an English-language booklet published for the Olympics.

With the boycott, Moscow reversed its message. "Faithful to the ideals of the Olympic movement, the USSR Olympic Committee condemns attempts to use sport as a means of political pressure," said Konstantin Andrianov, the committee chair. The playbook's old chapter on sports and politics was torn out and replaced with new instructions. International sports were about peace and understanding. They were about young athletes expressing their individual commitment and fulfilling their dreams. The Americans ruined this "holiday of sport" by turning the Olympics into a political instrument. Vladimir Putin would put this new chapter to good use.

Yet Putin would not be arriving in the Kremlin for a couple of decades. In the meantime, his Soviet predecessors were able to put their new line into practice. Four years after the Moscow Olympics,

Moscow announced that Soviet athletes would not attend the Los Angeles Games. Don't call it a boycott, the Kremlin declared. The Soviets reluctantly had to stay home because, once again, the Americans were politicizing sport. The Reagan Administration had created "a climate of hostility" in the United States, Andrianov told IOC president Juan Antonio Samaranch. "We cannot take the chance of seeing something happen, of having another Munich."

Moscow's stated reason for the Soviet withdrawal in 1984 was the American politicization of the Games. But what was the real reason? Contrary to what many believe, it was not a tit-for-tat response to the 1980 boycott. When the Politburo made the decision to keep Soviet athletes home, the government had already paid $2 million for television transmissions—a significant amount of money for the cash-strapped Soviets. At the IOC meeting in Sarajevo in February 1984, Soviet officials gave every indication their athletes would be in Los Angeles. And as the *New York Times* revealed in a 2016 report, Soviet sports doctors had their doping plan in place months before the game.

The doping plan was important. At the Winter Olympics in February, the master dopers of international sports, the East Germans, had pulled off a stunning upset. With nine gold medals, the GDR had topped the Soviets. The new head of the Sports Committee in Moscow, Marat Gramov, was worried. How would the USSR fare in the Summer Games, against the Americans on their home turf and the surging East Germans? Even with pharmaceutical assistance, victory could not be assured.

Moreover, it was doubtful that Soviet athletes could count on chemical help in LA. The person in charge of doping control, UCLA professor Don Catlin, announced that his high-tech lab was able to detect stanozolol—the Soviets' steroid of choice. Moscow's drug doctors believed stanozolol to be undetectable. Catlin threw down the gauntlet.

The Americans also scuttled the Soviets' scheme for a floating drug lab. Moscow planned to send a passenger ship to Los Angeles, insisting it was needed to care for their large team. Onboard the ship, Soviet athletes would have access to their own physicians, massage therapists, cooks, and so forth. What Moscow didn't say was that the ship also carried a lab to make sure Soviet athletes were testing clean. Once the floating lab confirmed drugs were not showing up, athletes would be sent ashore to submit their samples to Professor Catlin's lab. This way, there would be no embarrassing positive tests.

The Soviets got permission to dock at Long Beach. But Washington was suspicious of a Soviet ship parked in America's busiest harbor, miles from Southern California's defense-tech industries, at the height of the Cold War. The US government said communications off the ship would be blocked, and every person who came on and off would be searched. Moscow leaders claimed Soviet athletes would be in danger because of the lack of security in Los Angeles. It was more likely they feared too much security.

On May 5, 1984, the Politburo voted to keep Soviet athletes home from the Summer Olympics. Strong political winds were churning at the time: tensions with the United States were heightened. There had been a change in leadership only a few months earlier, and new Party boss Konstantin Chernenko was in poor health. But we can't dismiss the likelihood that Moscow feared, above all, a poor Soviet showing on American soil.

Soviet athletes faced a steep challenge in LA. It would have been even steeper without drugs. Of course, Moscow couldn't admit this. Instead the official line was that the Americans were injecting politics into the Games, endangering Soviet athletes and betraying the purpose of the Olympics. "The Olympic ideals are everlasting," Moscow stated, "and any attempts to flout them are doomed."

CHAPTER 5

THE RED MACHINE BREAKS DOWN

"GOODBYE, MOSCOW, GOODBYE," crooned the famous singer Lev Leshchenko at the closing ceremony of the 1980 Summer Games. "Farewell to the Olympic fairy tale."

As Leshchenko's velvety voice filled Luzhniki Stadium, a four-story balloon of Misha the bear, mascot of the Moscow Games, lifted from the field and floated into the August night.

The Olympics were indeed a fairy tale. Soviet television showed smiling spectators and smiling athletes. Over 5,200 men and women from 80 countries took part in the games. Did it matter the Americans were not there? Not at all. Washington's attempts to ruin Moscow's games had failed.

Four years later, it was the Americans' turn. From the start, the Los Angeles Games were a spectacle, with 84 pianists in teal tuxedos playing George Gershwin's "Rhapsody in Blue" at the opening ceremony in Memorial Coliseum. Over the next two weeks, American athletes won medal after medal, setting a new record for most gold at an Olympics (83). Did it matter that the Soviets weren't there? Not at all.

It certainly didn't matter to viewers across the country. ABC claimed that 90 percent of American households tuned into the network's broadcasts of the Games at one point or another. My friends and I were glued to the television, especially for the Finals of women's all-around gymnastics. Gathered around the TV at my friend Scott's house, we were transfixed by the dynamic girl with short brown hair and ebullient smile. To say we had crushes on Mary Lou Retton would be an understatement. But our love for Mary Lou ran deeper than surging hormones. We cheered her performances because she was one of us. In her leotard emblazoned with stars and stripes, her wins were American wins. The absence of Soviet athletes did not diminish our excitement in the least.

Mary Lou and Mitch Gaylord with their perfect scores in gymnastics. Carl Lewis and his four gold medals. Michael Jordan leading the basketball team to victory. The Los Angeles Games were the summit of 1980s America. The economy was surging, Ronald Reagan was in the White House, and *The Karate Kid* and *Purple Rain* were in theatres. But the pastel-hued, all-American Olympics had a tinge of Soviet red to them. In the eight years since the US had last competed in the summer games, training of Olympic athletes had been transformed—in large part due to the influence of the Soviet Union and other communist states. Aspiring athletes devoted more and more time to their sports. Training itself also borrowed from the Soviets, focusing on strength and endurance as well as skills of the sport.

A good example of this shift was America's sweetheart, Mary Lou. Two years before the games, when she was 14, Retton moved 1,300 miles from her family's home in West Virginia to train in Houston. Her coaches were Béla and Márta Károlyi, who had developed Nadia Comăneci before defecting to the US. The Károlyis came from Romania not the USSR, but they imported the Soviet-style institution they had created back home: an academy where talented young gymnasts from across the country would live, study, and train year-round.

The Károlyis' academy in Romania was so Soviet it upset the Romanians, which is saying something since Romania had the harshest regime in the communist bloc. The couple were a coaching team: Márta, a former gymnast, instructed the children in acrobatics and choreography; Béla, a one-time boxer and hammer thrower, led the physical training. He also led the school, with an iron fist. Romanian officials received regular complaints from parents. When doctors objected to the girls' nutrition and physical care, he had them removed. Károlyi had connections. He could do what he wanted—until the Romanian women's team lost to the Soviets in Moscow. When officials started interfering in the Károlyi kingdom, Béla and Márta bolted.

Béla later claimed he and Márta left Romania to escape government pressure. "They say you are living in this country, you have to make communist propaganda for everything," he told the *New York Times*. While he may have been a Stalinist in running his gym, Károlyi was a salesman when dealing with the press. Investors took notice, as did aspiring gymnasts and their parents. When the couple opened their Houston gym in 1982, they promised to train Olympic champions, just as they had done with Nadia. "We can develop a girl by 1984," Béla boasted.

The timing was perfect. The popularity of gymnastics was rising in the US, spurred first by Olga Korbut in 1972 and then Comăneci's performance in Montreal. Mary Lou was one of countless American girls to take up the sport after watching Nadia earn the first perfect score.

There was also a larger shift happening in American youth sports. Traditional community-based sports programs were being elbowed out by a new model: parents were signing up their kids for private clubs instead of school teams, enrolling them in off-season training camps, and even sending them away to newly opened academies, where they would practice their sports year-round.

At the same time US sports administrators and coaches adopted the Soviet model for developing Olympic candidates. In 1978 the US Olympic Committee opened a year-round training center in Colorado Springs. The same year, the USOC launched its own version of the Spartakiad, the annual Olympic-style competition bringing together athletes from across the USSR.

Founders of these new academies insisted that success in sports demanded full commitment and non-stop practice. The philosophy matched well with the mindset of Reagan's America: If you didn't succeed, you weren't working hard enough. Károlyi and other coaches knew their market—not the kids but the parents. The mother of gymnast Kim Zmeskal, who won the world all-around title after training at the Károlyi gym, admitted her concerns in a 1991 *Texas Monthly* article. It was unnerving that Kim spent more time at the gym than with her family. And she fumed whenever the temperamental Béla yelled at her daughter. "But," Clarice Zmeskal added, "I can't argue with his success."

At the same time American coaches and athletes were setting up Soviet-style programs, people involved with sports in the USSR were pushing back. In the early 1980s Soviet newspapers published complaints about exploitation of young athletes. Educators were especially vocal. In 1982 *Pravda* ran a letter from teachers at one of Moscow's sports academies calling out the practices of top-level soccer coaches. "The coach comes to a boy, promises him and his parents mountains of gold, and the boy abandons his school," the teachers wrote.

The academy teachers asked what will happen to their students. What will become of the boy who left school early if he does not have a career as a footballer? And what about those who never reach the top levels—what use will their sports training serve? "Our students train intensively," the teachers wrote. "Their interests are strictly focused. But how many will become a Master of Sport? Experience shows, not many. What about the rest? They will be left behind."

Criticism of the Soviet system even came from one of its most successful products. In the 1970s Irina Rodnina was among the Soviet Union's most famous athletes. With her short brown hair, round cheeks, and broad smile, she was famous across the country. Dominant in pairs figure skating for over a decade, Rodnina won 10 consecutive world titles and three Olympic gold medals. Her defining performance came at the 1973 World Championships in Bratislava, Czechoslovakia. During the final routine with partner Alexander Zaitsev, their music suddenly went dead. The couple did not hesitate, even when their coach called them to stop. Rodnina and Zaitsev skated to the end of their routine as the crowd clapped along in rhythm.

In 1980 as Rodnina prepared for her final Olympics, she gave a remarkably candid interview to the cultural journal *Literaturnaya Gazeta*. The beloved champion spoke about the thrill of performing to a crowd, the perils of competing in a judged sport, and the give-and-take of skating with a partner. Rodnina was grateful for all that sport had given her. But as she reached the end of her career, she lamented what little preparation she had for life off the ice.

The demands of being a Soviet athlete were especially hard, Rodnina admitted. "The most important thing is to win," she said. "Not only for yourself, but also for the spectators, for your family, your friends, and when it comes to the Olympic Games or World Championships, for the whole country. When I win, everybody wins."

This expectation carried a toll. Rodnina set aside the challenges of injuries or personal difficulties. She had to have the mindset of a "professional." No matter what struggle she faced, she had to perform. "We're always in the public eye," she said. "You can't hide. You can't explain why you didn't skate well."

For more than a decade, Rodnina stood on podiums around the world, with the Soviet flag raised above her. Now, at age 30, she faced the question of what she would do next. What could a Soviet athlete offer once their career was over? Former athletes did not become leaders outside of sports. They were unable to find other ways to contribute to Soviet life. The blame for that, Rodnina charged, was not with the athlete but with broader Soviet society.

"The athlete can't do it alone," she urged. "I think coaches, clubs, sports committees, and the community in general should be held accountable. They have a responsibility for the athlete's fate even after he's gone from the arena."

Seven years later, Rodnina had even greater reason to deplore the fate of the Soviet athlete. After two marriages, she was a single mother of two small children. She started coaching, but was disappointed at how her fellow coaches spent most of their time drinking. Meanwhile, the demands on young skaters had become even more intense. Still famous, still revered, Rodnina dropped a bomb on the system she had been part of her entire life.

"We have turned sport into monotonous, tedious work," she told an interviewer. "We push athletes who are still children into all kinds of competitions fraught with serious mental trauma and physical injury." Soviet athletes were little more than "obedient mechanical soldiers."

Rodnina unveiled the truth of Soviet sports: Young athletes were used not just by scouts or coaches. They were being used by society as a whole. She watched teenage skaters pushed to master increasingly complicated moves and then be cast aside after thousands of hours on the rink. "I am against 15-year-old champions who climb the podium only to disappear without a trace," she said.

Like any former athlete, Rodnina remembered her early years in the sport as a simpler time. In truth the Soviet system was always geared to create champions. With her own innovations

Rodnina advanced what was expected in figure skating. Soviet coaches, including the retired champion herself, built on those advances. Ever more demanding, ever more taxing, ceaselessly striving for higher accomplishments, the Soviet sports system pushed ahead despite the warnings.

It was not only Irina Rodnina's status as one of the USSR's greatest athletes that allowed her to speak so directly. By this time, Mikhail Gorbachev's policies of *perestroika* and *glasnost* had brought a new openness to the country. Introduced in 1986 the reforms were intended to revive a failing system. Gorbachev recognized the Soviet Union's deep structural flaws, particularly after the Chernobyl disaster in April 1986. More than anything, Gorbachev later stated, the nuclear-plant explosion "opened the possibility of much greater freedom of expression."

Soviet sports avoided its own Chernobyl moment. Finishing behind East Germany at Sarajevo turned on the warning lights. Rather than risk another failure in Los Angeles, Moscow took the system offline. Yet without the experience of the 1984 Summer Games, Soviet sports entered the doldrums. In 1987 the men's basketball team, 14-time winners of the biannual European Basketball Championship, lost the Final to Greece. Two years later, the Soviets stumbled to third. In women's basketball the Soviets were overtaken by the sport's emerging power: the United States. At the 1986 world cup in Moscow, the Americans defeated the defending champions by 20 points.

Skiers, weightlifters, and middle-distance runners all took losses in the 1980s. Even the vaunted hockey team, pride of the motherland, was beaten in the World Championships by Sweden and Czechoslovakia. At the 1985 tournament in Prague, one of the old ladies working in the arena cafeteria added insult to injury.

She served the Soviet players cups of tea steeped in the greasy water left over from cooking sausages.

With results lagging, sports journalists took up Gorbachev's call for openness. "The country is moving forward, but sport is standing still," declared veteran sportswriter Alexander Kiknadze in *Komsomolskaya Pravda*. Writers exposed drunk coaches and corrupt officials. An example of the new investigative approach was media coverage of scandals at the gymnastics training camp in 1985. One involved former world champion Dmitry Bilozerchev, who left camp without permission and crashed his car. The horrific accident injured two teammates, while Bilozerchev broke his leg in 41 places. Newspapers revealed that Bilozerchev had been drunk, something gymnastics officials tried to cover up. Meanwhile back at the training center, women gymnasts complained of food disappearing from their rooms. Once again, newspapers uncovered the truth: the missing food was being stolen by the team's coach and doctor.

The country's main sports daily, *Sovietsky Sport*, took the lead in *glasnost*-inspired investigations. "It's just impossible to compare the working conditions then and now," the newspaper's deputy editor, Vladimir Geskin, told the Associated Press. "Now I can say anything I'm thinking. Five years ago, it was just impossible."

One of the most shocking stories to appear in *Sovietsky Sport* was an exposé of the 1982 disaster at Luzhniki Stadium. Near the end of an early UEFA Cup match between Spartak and Haarlem, on a cold October night, hundreds of fans headed to the exit to catch the metro. When a roar went up after a late Spartak goal, fans near the gate reversed direction to get back inside. A young woman fell on the icy stairs; some people stopped to help her. They were the first to be trampled. As the crowd surged, more people fell over the bodies and were crushed underneath.

"People were falling over, knocking others to the ground like dominoes," recalled Andrey Chesnokov, a promising teenage tennis player. "I jumped over the railing to save myself and stepped over the bodies."

Newspapers at the time said nothing. "An accident took place," read a brief note in one paper. "There were casualties." The government investigated; the stadium director was sentenced to a labor camp. Everything was swept under the rug. The extent of the disaster became known only seven years later. LUZHNIKI'S DARK SECRET read the headline on *Sovietsky Sport*. The stunning story got immediate attention around the world, particularly its estimate of 340 victims, which would have made it the most deadly stadium disaster ever. Geskin had to backtrack when it became clear the casualty numbers were inflated. But it was the new era of openness. Journalists sought to expose failures. At the same time, they were selling papers. Geskin admitted this meant pushing sensational story lines.

"The problem in the Soviet Union is that every newspaper is seeing how far it can go, and we have to keep up with it," Geskin said. "Now we even have sensation and scandal, maybe more than necessary. Our newspaper now is very critical of everything, and the readers love it."

The new media was sensational. But it also had an effect on society. Driven to expose corruption, journalists stirred widespread skepticism in the pillars of Soviet life, including the vaunted sports program.

In spring 1989 the magazine *Smena* (Change) sent a shockwave through the Soviet sports world with an article on doping in the USSR. With a circulation of 2.8 million readers, the magazine of the Konsomol youth organization was one of the leading journals of *glasnost*. The article on doping was written by a well-known science-fiction writer named Zinovy Yuryev. Unlike other Soviet writers who took on doping, Yuryev did not push blame on the Americans. It didn't matter that the Americans were the first to use steroids, he declared. "What matters is that the monster is claiming more and more victims." In using the word "victims," Yuryev also shifted blame away from athletes. Other media articles claimed that doping was the fault of overly ambitious, un-Soviet athletes. Yuryev pointed out other culprits: Soviet sports authorities.

"More often than not, the doctor would just give us pills," an anonymous female athlete told Yuryev. "'These are vitamins,' he would vaguely say if you asked. Most chose not to ask. They knew what the vitamins were, and that if you refused, you'd be kicked off the national team."

Her competitive career over, the former athlete hoped to start a family, but the steroids had taken their toll. "Now I'm in constant pain, almost an invalid," she told Yuryev. "My hormones are ruined."

Yuryev pressed: "You didn't protest because you feared getting kicked off the team?"

"It's not that simple," she answered. "When you are programmed to win at any cost, the scale of values shifts."

Yuryev directed his attack above the level of team doctors and coaches, to the top rank of Soviet sports officials. Athletes were given pills, and then Soviet labs would test the athletes before competitions. If the athlete's sample was tainted, word would come from Moscow that they had to withdraw, to avoid embarrassing the Soviet motherland.

For those Soviet athletes who did get caught, authorities created an array of denials—similar to Russian officials in recent years. Yuryev saw through the deception of the Moscow playbook. "It was a lie purely for internal use, to fool us, you and me. No normal person abroad would take seriously all this nonsense, the kinds of excuses a first-grader gives."

Yuryev sounded a warning. He pointed to the number of positive doping tests at the annual Spartakiad. The results gave the appearance of control. In fact, lower-level athletes were busted, while athletes who competed internationally tested clean. Like an organized crime racket, the sports authorities had taken over enforcement and decided who was protected. "The criminals are entrusted with fighting crime," he wrote. Just like the Mafia, they had imposed a code of silence.

"Yes, medals are great," Yuryev concluded, "but let's think together, what is more valuable to us: Yet another medal, won unjustly and paid for with health of the athlete, or a fair competition? A human being's health, or the kind of cheating that violates the soul? The honor and dignity of our motherland, or the stigma of a country where the anabolic monster is rampant?"

The story in *Smena* hit a nerve. Officials in the Sports Committee were concerned enough to respond directly. *Sovietsky Sport* published the transcript of a special call-in meeting with the committee's deputy chairman, Vasily Gromyko. From across the country, coaches, parents, and ordinary fans called Moscow with questions they had after reading the *Smena* article. Gromyko held the line. Yes, he admitted, there was doping. But it was the fault of rogue athletes and coaches, who were drawn to dope "out of self-interest, bad judgement, or outright stupidity."

The Sports Committee was on the trail of these misguided cheaters, Gromyko insisted. "Believe me," he assured, "we are no less concerned than you about what is happening. The fight we are waging against doping is part of the larger fight for the purity of our sports."

The Sports Committee could talk the language of *glasnost*, with open conference calls and sympathies for ordinary people's concerns. Nevertheless, Gromyko was still lying. He lied directly when a caller asked about one of the most provocative revelations of the *Smena* article: that the USSR had sent a ship to the South Korean port of Incheon, not far from Seoul, with a $2.5 million lab aboard for testing Soviet athletes at the 1988 Summer Olympics. The floating doping-detection lab warned against any positive test results on the Soviet team. Gromyko admitted that the ship was there. But it was equipped with diagnostic and rehabilitation equipment, he explained. There were physicians and trainers aboard. "They did not deal with doping tests at all," Gromyko said.

In fact, the ship in Korea performed the same task planned for the Los Angeles Games—testing Soviet athletes for drugs before they submitted their urine samples to the official testing lab. The scientist in charge of the remote lab was Grigory Rodchenkov, who had to make sure no Soviet athlete would be caught. "We did do our job," Rodchenkov recalled in his memoirs. "And we had fun doing it."

The 1988 Seoul Olympics showed the Soviet sports machine had one last burst of fuel. The USSR finished far ahead of East Germany and the United States in the medal table: 55 gold medals, compared to 37 for the GDR and 36 for the Americans, and 132 total medals, compared to 102 for the East Germans and 94 for Team USA. The Sports Committee could still win the Olympics. Sports Committee apparatchiks could still deflect prying questions, now coming from Soviet journalists and ordinary citizens. But as 1989 unfolded, deeper problems in Soviet sports kept rising to the surface. The athletes themselves were ready to revolt.

The biggest shock came from within the most successful, most prominent, most heralded institution in Soviet sports: the national hockey team. In October 1988, eight months after the team had won its seventh gold medal at the Calgary Winter Olympics, first-line center Igor Larionov published an open letter to coach Viktor Tikhonov in the popular magazine *Ogonyok* (The Spark).

In the letter to his coach, Larionov pulled back the curtain on the entire performance of victory. During the season, when national team players wore the uniform of the Red Army club, no one watched their games. Because all of the country's best players were concentrated on one club, the league wasn't competitive. Red Army easily won most of its games. Nevertheless, Larionov and his teammates had to endure endless training and humiliating insults. Tikhonov was a dictator who had created "a reign of terror." Players weren't even able to see their families. "It's a wonder how our wives had children by us," Larionov wrote.

To put Larionov's letter in perspective, it would be like Steph Curry slamming Steve Kerr in *Time* magazine. Players do not take on their coaches publicly. They do not air grievances outside the locker room. Nowhere. Certainly not in the Soviet Union. But Larionov had enough—and so did other Soviet athletes. After Larionov's letter was published, the mutiny began.

The following year, 1989, Larionov was playing in the National Hockey League. Along with four other members of the national team, he was among the first Russians to sign with NHL teams. Soccer players likewise joined European clubs. World record-setting pole vaulter Sergei Bubka signed a sponsorship deal with Nike, while tennis players Andrey Chesnokov and Natalya Zvereva announced they would keep their tour winnings, rather than turn them over to the Sports Committee.

"Everybody is fighting with the Committee," said Chesnokov of athletes' campaign. "Everybody wants to change the situation."

Everybody included the Sports Committee. By 1989, as the Soviet economy was collapsing, the agency in charge of the country's sports program was running out of money. Desperate for cash, Soviet sports officials accepted that it was finally time to sell their most valuable assets—their athletes.

What brought down the Soviet empire—the bankruptcy of ideas, or the bankruptcy of treasuries? During the revolutionary year of 1989, communist leaders in Eastern Europe had to deal with crippling deficits in both departments, ideology and finance. They could find no solution, especially after Gorbachev let them know there would be no help from Moscow. By December, the bloc was finished.

The Soviet sports programs was hurt by both threats as well. Larionov's open letter revealed the failures of ideology: the vaunted Soviet hockey team was built on deception, tyranny, and ruthless disregard for the athletes. The revolt over earnings by tennis players and other athletes showed how difficult it was for communists to hold off the lure of the market. Top Soviet athletes knew they were among the best in the world; they expected to be paid like it.

Gorbachev's reforms opened up this new path for his country's athletes—competing not for the greatness of the Soviet motherland but for individual wealth. By the end of the 1980s, Soviet hockey and soccer players were joining pro leagues in the West while tennis and track stars were pocketing big paychecks at international events. Just as American sports culture adopted Soviet standards of year-round, intensive training, athletes in the USSR adopted the slogan that defined 1980s America: greed is good.

A new machine was being created: Soviet engineering would develop young athletes into champions, but they would be motivated by the highest prizes offered in the West, wealth and fame. This machine, with socialist design and capitalist fuel, still drives our global sports culture today.

CHAPTER 6

FREE AGENTS

THE SUMMER DAY in Moscow was overcast, but there were cheers on Red Square. At the site where victorious soldiers had once paraded, a new triumph was celebrated. Slava Fetisov and Igor Larionov were dressed in red-and-white jerseys, but these were not the colors of the Soviet national team. The USSR was no more. Fetisov and Larionov represented their new team, the Detroit Red Wings, and they had returned to Moscow with the Stanley Cup.

The celebration on Red Square was unplanned. A small crowd of enthusiastic Russians, surprised tourists, and stone-faced police surrounded the players as they lifted the silver trophy. They even took photos in front of Lenin's tomb. Surely, the embalmed corpse of Vladimir Ilych was spinning under its glass case. It was bad enough the state he founded had come to an ignominious end. Now there were Russians who had left the Red Army to make fortunes in America dancing on his grave with a silver bauble named for a Victorian nobleman.

Still today the 1997 Red Wings are beloved in Detroit. The Stanley Cup win was the team's first in 42 years, restoring pride to a once-proud franchise. A vital part of that team was its contingent of Russian players. Fetisov and Larionov arrived in Detroit in their late

30s, their careers seemingly on a downturn. But they found new life as respected leaders. Their younger teammates—Sergei Fedorov, Vladimir Konstantinov, and Vyacheslav Kozlov—represented a new generation of talented Russians who joined the NHL in the 1990s.

Red Wings coach Scotty Bowman sometimes put all five Russians on the ice together—Larionov, Fedorov, and Kozlov as forwards, and Fetisov and Konstantinov on defense. Bowman recognized that sending the Russians over the boards as a unit at key moments could change the tempo of a game. If the Red Wings needed a boost, the Russians' fast-paced, fluid style of play would provide it. "They were game-changers as a unit," Bowman said.

Whether on the ice together or with other Red Wings teammates, whether scoring goals or stopping opponents with crunching hits, Detroit's Russians were essential to the Stanley Cup run. Their time together was storied, but also tragically short. Just a week after the team won the cup, Konstantinov suffered debilitating injuries in a car crash. Yet in their brief stint with the Red Wings, the Russian Five secured a place in NHL history—and the history of Russian sports.

That same summer, another star athlete from Russia emerged on the world stage—someone a generation younger than Fetisov and Larionov, who would likewise have a lasting influence on her sport. In June 1997 unseeded Anna Kournikova surprised the tennis world by reaching the Wimbledon semifinals. Having just turned 16 before the Championships began, Kournikova was a highly touted juniors player making her debut at the All-England Tennis Club. She seized the stage, playing before packed grandstands at Centre Court. Former president George H.W. Bush was in the crowd for Kournikova's quarterfinal win. But her fan base steered more toward much younger males. Although talented and athletic, Kournikova's draw was less her game than her looks. The most prestigious tournament in tennis was her launch pad. In summer 1997 Anna Kournikova became an international celebrity far bigger than her sport.

Anna and Slava: the Slavic beauty and the man of character. In the decade after the Soviet Union's collapse, Anna Kournikova and Vyacheslav Fetisov came to embody the Russian athlete in the new, post-communist age. It goes without saying, their accomplishments and reputations would be vastly different. Yet each of them represented a stereotype commonly held in the West during the decade: the young woman whose looks brought the world to her feet and the seasoned veteran who stood against the Soviet system.

At the same time, Anna and Slava embodied different types of the post-Soviet Russian athlete for Russians themselves. Each gained success in the West, something that earned approval back home. Yet the ways they earned international fame, and what they did with that fame, were viewed quite differently. The stories of Fetisov and Kournikova reveal the tangled opinions that Russians had of the West—and themselves—in the turbulent 1990s. At a time when Russia was searching for its place in the world, the country's two most famous athletes pointed in opposite directions.

It is testament to Slava Fetisov's charisma that he became the symbol of Russian athletes' opposition to their Soviet masters. After all, it was Igor Larionov who fired the first shot in October 1988, with his article in *Ogonyok.* Fetisov, the national team captain, made his public statement against coach Viktor Tikhonov the following January, in an interview with a Moscow newspaper. Yet in most accounts of Soviet hockey's disintegration, Fetisov is hailed as the defiant hero. A 1995 profile by *ESPN: The Magazine* compared Fetisov to Muhammad Ali and Jackie Robinson. The most popular account of the Soviet hockey team, the 2014 documentary *Red Army,* is entirely Fetisov's show. Larionov's role in the fight against Tikhonov isn't even mentioned.

Fetisov "was always the real leader," Larionov acknowledged in his memoir. Larionov was an intellectual, known as "the Professor." Fetisov was a politician, in the best and worst senses of the word. He earned the respect of teammates and opponents. He knew how to work a locker room and an interview. Unlike Larionov the bespectacled intellectual, Fetisov was always good for a sound bite. At the same time, he was a master at building his reputation, deftly inflating his role in events. Media types bought it. After all, good stories need one hero. The Professor and the Captain gets muddled. Best to put the spotlight on the Captain.

To be sure, Fetisov took a brave stance in the winter of 1989. "I'm tired of Tikhonov's dictatorship—it's causing an unhealthy situation in the team," he said in his interview with *Moscow Komsomolets*. "I don't want to play anymore for a coach I don't trust." Tikhonov responded by cutting Fetisov from Red Army and thus the national team. One of the best players in hockey history spent the season playing for a low-level team sponsored by a pencil factory. Meanwhile, Fetisov spent days going from office to office at the Defense Ministry, dressed in his army uniform, seeking a discharge. Like most players for the Red Army club, Fetisov was an officer. His major's rank brought salary and benefits, but it also carried a 25-year service obligation. Fetisov hoped to be released so he could join the NHL's New Jersey Devils, who had drafted him in 1983. But Tikhonov had the upper hand: he would never let Fetisov play again, and the Soviet army would never let Fetisov go.

Thanks to Larionov, Fetisov returned from the factory league to the national team. One night, Larionov slipped away from the team's training camp and drove to the studios of Soviet Central Television, along with teammates Sergei Makarov and Vladimir Krutov. In front of the cameras, they made the case for their captain on one of the country's most popular news programs. If Fetisov was not restored to the team, they warned, then they would not play at the upcoming World Championships. A few weeks later, when Tikhonov's squad arrived in Stockholm, Fetisov was back on the ice. The Soviets won the tournament, and Fetisov was named best defenseman.

The Soviet national hockey team brought its 21st World Championship trophy back to Moscow in May 1989. But the flight home to Moscow was missing something important: one of the squad's most talented young players, Alexander Mogilny, was not on the plane. After the final match in Sweden, Mogilny slipped away from the team hotel. Two days later, he was in Buffalo, a newly signed member of the Sabres.

With Mogilny's departure, Moscow sports authorities recognized they couldn't keep their hockey players locked up. It was better to get something in return, rather than having them sneak away. The Sports Committee offered a deal to Fetisov, Larionov, and a few other veterans: the players would get 10 percent of their NHL contracts, while the Committee got the rest. Of course, the players balked. Larionov negotiated a 50-50 split of his contract with the Vancouver Canucks. Fetisov cut a different deal: he would control his full salary and donate part to the Sport Committee's children's fund. The officials agreed. In June 1989 Fetisov signed with the Devils.

"Maybe when I go back in three years, there will be no more Sports Committee," Fetisov mused to a reporter after his arrival in the US. "Someday it will be a normal country."

Half of Fetisov's prediction came true two years later. Between August and December 1991, the USSR broke into 15 independent republics. The Sports Committee was shut down in the process. Something like normalcy, however, was a long time coming. Sports officials in the newly independent republics faced the grim reality of post-Soviet life: dilapidated facilities, outdated equipment, and empty accounts.

At a meeting in Moscow in early January, just one week after Gorbachev handed over the keys to the Kremlin, leaders of the new countries' Olympic committees deliberated what to do in 1992, an Olympic year. Financial need required that they band together. Thanks to a last-minute gift of $800,000 from Adidas, athletes from the former USSR were able to participate at the Albertville Winter Games as the Unified Team. The German shoe company fronted even more cash for 475 athletes to compete later that year in the Barcelona Summer Olympics. When the Unified Team's 4x400 women's relay team took the podium after winning gold, they thanked their patrons by wearing Adidas T-shirts.

The runners could be forgiven for confusing where their loyalties lay. Already in the fading days of the USSR, sports officials increasingly relied on handouts from western companies. In early 1991 the Soviet Olympic Committee bartered away marketing rights to Xerox in exchange for two photocopiers. Later that year, when Moscow sent a delegation to an IOC conference in Switzerland, the hosts were stunned the Russians had no money for expenses.

In the '90s the need for cash was even more urgent. Western companies were willing to help, in hopes of gaining a foothold in Russia's opening market. Leading up to the 2000 Summer Games in Sydney, Reebok paid $15 million to be the official supplier to the Russian team. The infusion was welcome, but there was a big problem. The Russian national soccer team had signed its own deal with Nike. What would happen if the soccer players showed up in Sydney wearing Nike gear, while the rest of the Russian team was outfitted in Reebok? Russian sports authorities found themselves caught between two corporate giants—and their lawyers. Fortunately, the Slovaks knocked Russia out of the soccer qualifiers. Problem solved.

Perhaps the greatest testimony to the Soviet Union's sports program is that the country's athletes continued to win in the years after the USSR ceased to exist, even without any money. In 1992, the Unified Team topped the medal table at Barcelona and placed second at Albertville. Four years later, Russian athletes won the most gold medals at the Atlanta games. Overall, athletes from former Soviet states won 123 total medals at the 1996 Olympics, more than the host Americans or any other nation.

Yet there were signs of decline in Atlanta. The Russian women gymnasts finished second to the Americans, led by coach Béla Károlyi. The loss marked a shift in the sport's balance of power, away from Russia to the United States. The decades-long dominance of Soviet women's volleyball also came to an end at Atlanta: the Russians finished fourth.

The '90s were also a tough decade for the country's most popular team sports. The men's soccer team didn't advance from the group stage at the 1994 World Cup. Earlier that year at the Winter Olympics in Lillehammer, the hockey team finished fourth. It was the first time since 1956 that an Olympic medal in hockey was not draped over a Russian neck. At the annual World Championships, the Russian hockey team finished off the podium through the rest of the decade. The low point came in the 2000 tournament, hosted at St. Petersburg's new $60 million arena. Shut out by the Americans in the group stage and then eliminated by the Swiss, the Russians finished 11th on their home ice.

Both on and off the rink, the '90s were a time of troubles for Russian hockey. The problem was not necessarily money. Plenty of cash was coming into hockey coffers thanks to a special government rule allowing the federation to import alcohol and cigarettes without paying taxes. But in Russia of the 1990s, wherever there was money, there was corruption. Little money went toward building the sport. When Igor Larionov bought new equipment for the youth team at his old club in Voskresensk, he drove there himself, his car packed with pads and sticks, to make sure the kids received the gifts.

Money also attracted Russia's mafia. In 1996 the equipment manager and photographer for Red Army's hockey team were gunned down in separate executions. A year later, the soccer team's financial director, Larisa Nechayeva, was murdered at her *dacha* outside Moscow. "Anything can happen in Russia," Valentin Sych told an American journalist. As president of the hockey federation, Sych controlled the flows of money from imports and transfer fees. Just a few months after the interview, he met his fate as well. One morning in April 1997, as he was on his way to the office, gunmen ambushed Sych's car with AK-47s.

With their home country's sports establishment broken and busted, Russian hockey players fled to the West. In 1989–90, Fetisov and Larionov were joined in the NHL by only seven other Russians. When they won the Stanley Cup in 1997, there were 55 Russians on NHL rosters. At their peak in the 2000–01 season, Russians accounted for just over 8 percent of all NHL players.

For players who had grown up in the USSR, the NHL promised unimaginable riches. In 1997 Mogilny earned $3.5 million. Pavel Bure, the Canucks' high-scoring forward, took home $5 million that season. After the Red Wings' Stanley Cup win, Sergei Fedorov signed a new contract to stay in Detroit, with a $28 million bonus. Yet for all the money, the US and Canada were strange worlds for hockey players coming from Russia. The everyday stuff of North American sports—media interviews, contract negotiations, locker room pranks—were new and confusing. When these young men needed advice, no matter which team they played for, they turned to one person: Fetisov. Bure and Fedorov were the biggest Russian stars in the NHL during the 1990s, but Fetisov remained the Captain.

It wasn't only Russians who acknowledged Fetisov's role. "Statesman of the game," declared the *New York Times*. In his fight to leave the USSR, Fetisov "became a symbol for the country's hockey players and Russians in general." He sounded like any American athlete in interviews, saying he was "blessed" and speaking of "giving back." He described his fight with the Soviet brass as a struggle for human rights. He mused of owning a pro team someday, or launching a new global league, or even going into politics.

"I'd like to see sports superstars get involved in politics," he said, "because they are idols for the people."

Back home, Fetisov was indeed an idol. The hockey great was one of those rare athletes known by one name, like Michael or Serena. He was simply Slava. The name was fitting—in Russian, "*slava*" means "praise." Slava received plenty of *slava* in his homeland.

As Fetisov's playing days wound down, the Russian press gushed with anticipation over his next move. Rather than returning home, he stayed in America, taking a coaching job with the Devils after his retirement in 1998. The new position added to Slava's prestige. Russian sports writers avoided mentioning he was an assistant on the Devils staff. Instead, he was hailed as the mastermind behind the team's Stanley Cup win in 2000.

Moscow sports media touted Slava as Russian hockey's savior in waiting. "He is the one Russian who understands the NHL game," urged a Moscow sportswriter. The North American league was the pinnacle of pro hockey, and Fetisov had won the Stanley Cup as both player and coach. Success in America confirmed his greatness. An eager nation awaited his return.

Slava agreed: he was the only one able to bring Russian hockey back to the summit. "With the right approach you can build a team that will win," he said. "Our victorious tradition in hockey will be restored." But he played hard-to-get. He had so many offers in the NHL, and he had a comfortable life in America. Certainly, he could move back to Moscow, the city where he grew up. "But for what?" he asked a reporter. "Am I needed?"

Similar questions swirled around other Russian athletes who went abroad in the 1990s. Would they stay in America or Europe after gaining international success, or would they come back home? Life in the West offered riches and security. But Russia was their motherland.

In the late '90s, the Russian press focused on one athlete with particularly tangled connections to her homeland: Anna Kournikova. The young tennis player's parents had been on the lower rungs of Soviet sport: her mother Alla was a sprinter; her father Sergei, a wrestler. They started their daughter in lessons at the Spartak athletic club when she seven. From her first tournaments, Kournikova showed remarkable talent. In 1992, when she was 10, Anna and her mother set off to Nick Bollettieri's tennis academy in Florida. "This little girl comes and jumps in my ball basket and says, 'I'm here for the lesson!'" Bollettieri recalled in a 2015 interview. "I thought, 'Who the hell is this?'"

Bollettieri discovered this little girl was a good player. In her early teens, Kournikova dominated the junior circuit. As a 14-year-old she won tournaments in Europe and the US and was named ITF World Junior Champion. The following year she competed for Russia in the Fed Cup, helping Russia advance to the European Finals with wins in singles and doubles. That same year, she represented Russia at the Atlanta Olympics but bowed out with a first-round loss. A few weeks later, she advanced to the fourth round of her first major tournament, the US Open. By the end of 1996 Kournikova was ranked 57th in the world. Her future was bright. Even though she trained in Florida, Moscow sports pages claimed her as unquestionably Russian. She was "our star," or simply "our Anya."

The 1997 Wimbledon tournament was Kournikova's break-out party. In her third-round match at Centre Court, she came back from a set down to defeat seventh-seed Anke Huber. In the quarterfinal, she faced fourth-seed Iva Majoli, winner of the French Open earlier that spring. Kournikova had the speed to run from corner to corner, even making returns from beyond the lines. She also showed composure, easily taking the tiebreaker to win the first set. Up 5–4 in the second set, Kournikova broke Majoli's serve to win the match. Not since Chris Evert in 1972 had a woman reached the semifinals in her Wimbledon debut.

Next up was Martina Hingis, winner of that year's Australian Open and runner-up to Majoli in Paris. Hingis' match with Kournikova was billed as the Battle of Sweet Sixteens. It was not much of a fight. Hingis won 6–3, 6–2, and went on to take the title. In her post-match interview, the Swiss teenager was dismissive. Kournikova "made a lot of errors," Hingis said. "I was sometimes waiting for the mistakes." The press-conference performance confirmed the opinion among the media. "The self-possessed Kournikova is 16 going on 25," observed the *Washington Post*'s correspondent, "and Hingis is 16 going on, well, 17."

Russian media were especially tough on Hingis, branding her press-conference remarks as arrogant and rude. Papers back home also had plenty of excuses for Kournikova's loss. Because Hingis was 10 months older, ITF rules allowed her to play more tournaments, thus gaining more experience. And Kournikova was worn out after a doubles match right before the semifinal. Despite her loss, Anya had a promising future. "Don't despair," said a St. Petersburg sportswriter. "Kournikova has everything ahead of her."

At Wimbledon, Kournikova showed the world she was not only a rising tennis talent. She was also a certified sex symbol. Earlier in the year, *Australian Tennis Magazine* put her on the cover in a sports bra and exercise shorts. "Anna—Hot Pics Inside," the cover promised. At each tour stop, photographers hovered at her training sessions, snapping pics of her in skimpy exercise clothes. When they did catch her in a tennis dress, she was usually bending over. British tabloids had no shame in printing up-skirt photos of a 16-year-old. Kournikova didn't object either. "They ran all those pictures of my butt," she said of the tabloids. "But, hey, it wasn't fat. My pictures were great."

Kournikova's image as the "Lolita of tennis" was part of a deliberate marketing campaign. Anna Inc. was run by a shrewd, ambitious, and hard-nosed manager: the tennis star's mother, Alla. American reporters described Alla as the quintessential sports mom. "You can't fight Mama," said Bollettieri, a former paratrooper. For Russians, she was something else, something not entirely positive. "A tough, businesslike, capitalist person," judged *Izvestia*.

Alla Kournikova had dreams for her daughter—fashion model, cover girl, celebrity. Part of the plan was to surround Anna with admirers. Her rumored boyfriend in summer 1997 was the Red Wings' Sergei Fedorov, who sat in Anna's private box at Centre Court, alongside Alla. Fedorov was succeeded the next year by Pavel Bure, who reportedly proposed to Anna. She dismissed them both. "Every country I visit, I have a different boyfriend," she told an American reporter. "And I kiss them all." But only if the boyfriends could pay. When a gaggle of teenage boys called to her at Wimbledon, she tossed her blonde braid and waved them off. "You can't afford me, boys."

There were suitors who could afford her, with names like Omega and Adidas. Her ad campaign for the Australian underwear company Berlei brought worldwide attention: she was pictured in a sport bra, beneath the slogan, "Only the balls should bounce." By 2001 she was earning $10 million per year in endorsement deals—far more than her tennis winnings. One of her most lucrative deals was with a little-known publishing company in Modesto, California. Starting in 2001, John F. Turner and Co. released the Anna Kournikova wall calendar, offering sixteen months of Kournikova in swimsuits, miniskirts, and even tennis clothes. The calendar became an annual event, selling 200,000 copies per year. ESPN even filmed the photo shoots.

As one PR consultant observed, Kournikova was a "marketing monster." Yet this monster opened a path for other women tennis players to follow. After Anna, marketing execs and media producers saw women tennis players as a gold mine. Players took advantage, signing endorsement deals and modeling contracts. Immediately after Kournikova came Maria Sharapova, another Russian blonde who trained in America. Sharapova had more success, on and off the court. She won Grand Slam titles and held the number one ranking. She jumped from swimsuit calendars to capital investments and corporate boards. Still, she followed the direction marked by Kournikova. "Anna was unique in her own way," said Hingis, her former rival-turned-doubles partner. "She was one of a kind."

As Kournikova's popularity grew in the rest of the world, opinion of her dimmed back home. Soon after Wimbledon in 1997, she ceased to be "our Anya." The problem was not that she lost—defeats could be explained away. Rather, it was that she turned her back on Russia. Already before her Wimbledon breakout, there were concerns she was "too well liked in the West."

Speculation about Kournikova's ties to the West spiked soon after Wimbledon, with reports she was applying for permanent residence in the United States. Kournikova insisted the move was only for convenience in traveling from her training base in Florida. "I have never considered myself an American," she said. But the protests did not soothe fears. "Let's hope that she will keep her ties with Russia," mused one commentator. "There is no reason for pessimism."

In fact, pessimism was justified. Kournikova represented her home country only one more time in international play, losing three matches in the 2000 Fed Cup. If she had won more often, the Russian press might have been forgiving. But Kournikova never reached the singles Finals of a Grand Slam tournament. She could have been a champion, observers claimed. But she spent too much time on photo shoots, not enough on tennis shots.

With each tournament loss, Russian media heaped more criticism. "Anna became a victim of her own popularity. She turned out to be too successful," said a Moscow sportswriter. The undertone of these criticisms was clear: Kournikova had betrayed her homeland. She found riches in the West, but lost her soul. She was no longer "our Anya," an emerging tennis star who would bring victories to Russia. "Now Kournikova is just a model," jabbed the Russian press.

In a country that takes pride in its beautiful women, the sharpest cut was that Kournikova was basic. Wherever you went in the tennis world—Melbourne, Paris, London, New York—crowds filled the stands to see this blonde Russian girl. A Moscow reporter at Roland-Garros found it funny. "No matter how you try to explain it to them," he wrote, "these Western Chukchi do not believe she looks ordinary. For them, she is a beauty."

The word Chukchi was especially slicing—a turning of the tables in the 1990s, when Russia was struggling and the West had boundless wealth. The Chukchi were a small Indigenous tribe herding reindeer in Siberia. To call the crowds in Paris "Chukchi" was to brand them the most backward of bumpkins, people who wouldn't recognize a truly beautiful woman because they had never left the tundra. Kournikova was average at best, in the tennis department and the looks department. Still, the Chukchi flocked to her. Kournikova showed how easily the West could be duped.

Ultimately, Russian coverage of Anna Kournikova was about far more than tennis. It was about Russia and the West. The West was backward and unsophisticated: a land of uncultured fools who thought an ordinary Russian girl was a goddess. At the same time, the West was decadent and immoral. This Russian girl might have been ordinary, but she was once sweet and talented. Sadly, this girl, "our Anya," was lured away by riches and fame.

Coverage of Slava Fetisov likewise revealed facets of Russia's love-hate relationship with the West. Like Kournikova, Fetisov proved that Russians could succeed in the West—in his case, by virtue of talent, intelligence, and character. Already revered in the hockey world after his Soviet career, Slava's time in the NHL elevated his standing. Winning the Stanley Cup burnished his already impressive credentials, while his coaching role proved his qualities as a leader.

Slava himself projected the image that he was a success in America—respected, wealthy, with any opportunity available to him. However, he chose to return home. He sacrificed riches and fame to serve the motherland. "You know, choosing to be national team coach gave me nothing but huge obligations," he told a Moscow reporter from his New York home. "I already had an interesting job here. And there is no need to talk about the financial side. But I couldn't bear to see what Russian hockey was turning into, how its international prestige was falling."

When Slava was named national team coach in 2001, he had the support of Russian hockey's most important fan. That autumn, when he was still living in the US, Fetisov traveled from New York to meet with Vladimir Putin. The president was visiting Washington, and he invited Slava for dinner. "We talked for two hours—about hockey, about life," Fetisov said. Putin was a knowledgeable fan who cared deeply about the national team.

"He had one request for me," Slava said, "that the team should have a winning attitude and represent their country with dignity. I gave him my word that they would."

CHAPTER 7

SPORTS WARS START AGAIN

IT'S ODD THAT THE PRESIDENT of Russia would cut out of a trip to Washington, DC, to spend two hours talking about hockey. After all, a few other things were going on.

Putin's state visit took place in November 2001, when relations between the United States and Russia were the closest they had been in years. Immediately after the 9/11 attacks, Putin had called George W. Bush to pledge cooperation in the war against terrorism. During their November trip, Putin and his then-wife Lyudmila stayed at the Bush family's ranch in Crawford, Texas. At a student assembly in the town's high school, Bush introduced his guest as a "new style of leader." Putin was, Bush said, "a man who is going to make a huge difference in making the world more peaceful."

Bush's introduction could have been scripted by the Kremlin's PR department. At the time Putin was still something of an unknown quantity. The former KGB officer had worked in the St. Petersburg mayor's office in the early 1990s before moving to Moscow, where he was appointed to various posts by President Boris Yeltsin. After being named prime minister in August 1999, then taking over as acting president when Yeltsin retired on December 31, and then winning election on his own the following

March, Putin sought to project the image of an effective, cooperative leader. Fetisov could see Russia's improved standing in the US. "I can proudly say that the authority of Russia and our president is growing before my eyes," he told a Moscow reporter.

Putin led a country showing signs of dramatic turnaround. Russia's economy grew 10% during his first year in office. Right away, the new president went on a whirlwind global tour. In his first two years, Putin made 53 international visits, more than Yeltsin made in two terms.

With the country's renewed economic strength and international visibility, Putin wanted Russian sports to reclaim its prominence. The president himself chaired the committee overseeing preparations for the 2000 Sydney Olympics. At a meeting in the Kremlin a few months before the games, Putin heard reports and issued commands. The Finance Ministry was concerned about paying bonuses to medal winners. Just do it, the president directed. The head of the Russian Olympic Committee, Vitaly Smirnov, said there were insufficient training facilities for some sports. Fix the problem, Putin declared.

"There was never a meeting like this under the Soviet regime," said Smirnov, who was around in the days of Leonid Brezhnev.

Russia placed second in the medal table at the Sydney games. Reading the Moscow sports pages, you'd think they came in first. *Sovietsky Sport* bragged that Russia won medals in 23 different sports, more than any other country. And if you counted the medals won by athletes from all former Soviet states—48 gold, 48 silver, and 67 bronze—the USSR remained the world's sport superpower.

Expectations were high for the 2002 Winter Olympics in Salt Lake City. Russians looked to Fetisov to return the hockey team to the summit. "It's an opportunity to take revenge," said Slava's old teammate Vladislav Tretiak, who still felt the sting of Lake Placid.

The stage was set for the grudge match against the Americans in the semifinals. Russian hockey's old nemesis was even there. Herb Brooks, mastermind of the Miracle on Ice, was behind the Team USA bench. Now age 64, near the end of a coaching career that never matched the heights of Lake Placid, Brooks led a team made up of Stanley Cup winners and future Hall of Famers. Fetisov's Russian squad likewise featured a cast of NHL stars, including Sergei Fedorov and Pavel Bure as well as young phenoms Pavel Datsyuk and Ilya Kovalchuk.

The game started as a mismatch. The Americans led 3–0 after two periods. Russia showed life only in the third, but Team USA shut down the late attack. "We did not play well in the first two periods," admitted the Russian captain, 41-year-old Igor Larionov. "It was embarrassing."

Exposed as not quite the savior he claimed to be, Fetisov was quick to deflect blame. Referees wanted a USA-Canada Final, he complained. Russia at least took a medal after beating Belarus. But four years after taking silver, bronze was a step backward.

The disappointing finish in hockey set the tone for Russia's overall performance. Russian athletes won five gold medals and 13 overall, putting them far behind the nations at the top of the medal count: Norway with 13 gold and 25 total medals; Germany, 12 gold and 36 overall; and the United States, 10 gold and 34 total.

Like Fetisov whining about referees, sportswriters and officials diverted attention from the poor showing by pointing out the unfair treatment Russians received. There was a catalogue of offenses, from the speed skaters' poor accommodations to dismissive treatment of delegation members. Worst of all were the attempts to strip Russian athletes of their deserved victories. The Salt Lake City Olympics showed how determined the world was to tarnish the newly revived Russia. The warm vibes Putin experienced just a few months earlier went cold in the Utah winter. "We have entered the era of sports wars," declared a Russian newspaper.

The first provocation against Russia came in front of more than 14,000 people inside the Delta Center, home of the Utah Jazz. On this Monday night, three days after the Olympic torch had been lit, the medals in pairs figure skating would be decided. At the top of the standings after the short program were the Russian duo of Elena Berezhnaya and Anton Sikharulidze, two-time world champions and silver medalists at the 1998 Nagano Games. Just behind them were Jamie Salé and David Pelletier of Canada, most recent world champions.

In their final skate, the Russians were elegant, fast, and light as air. As always, their execution was superb, except for one small mistake: as the two skaters finished side-by-side double axels, Sikharulidze put down a second skate. The rest of the performance was flawless, punctuated by Sikharulidze throwing Berezhnaya high in the air. "It was like a work of art," declared Irina Rodnina to television viewers across Russia.

The eight judges gave the skaters a mix of 5.8 and 5.7 scores on technical merit, with the deductions coming for Sikharulidze's step on the axel. But in performance, seven of the judges gave the Russian pair scores of 5.9. Berezhnaya and Sikharulidze stayed in first place.

Salé and Pelletier took the ice next. The two skaters, who were a couple at the time, gave an emotional performance to music from the film *Love Story*. The crowd was on their side, sending up roars at each move. The Canadians' routine was not as demanding as the Russian pair's, yet they finished without a mistake. Chants of "Six! Six!" filled the arena.

"The pressure of the audience on the judges will be high," Rodnina warned.

The technical merit scores were better than the Russians, a mix of 5.9 and 5.8. The Canadians needed five performance scores of 5.9. They received four—from the Canadian, American, German, and Japanese judges. The Russian, Chinese, Polish, Ukrainian, and French judges gave scores of 5.8. Sitting in the kiss-and-cry, the rink-side bench where skaters await their scores, Pelletier dropped his head in his hands. With stunned eyes, Salé asked their coach if it was true. Had they lost? Yes, they had.

The arena erupted with boos and howls. Even before the judges reached their hotel, rumors swirled that something was amiss. In the hotel lobby, French judge Marie-Reine Le Gougne was confronted by British official Sally-Anne Stapleford, head of the International Skating Union's technical committee. The competition's referee, American Ronald Pfenning, wrote a letter that night reprimanding the judges who put the Russians in first. In a meeting the next day, Le Gougne broke down and admitted to her colleagues she had been pressured to favor the Russian pair. The push had come from her own boss, Didier Gailhaguet, head of the French skating federation.

Over the next days, with the games continuing in the background, the judging scandal took unprecedented twists. The International Skating Union and the IOC deliberated what to do with Le Gougne's admission. Le Gougne later retracted her words, insisting she had been pressured by Stapleford and Pfenning. But the damage was done: the ISU suspended her and Gailhaguet for three years. Four days after the skating Final, the governing bodies applied a Band-Aid: Salé and Pelletier would be awarded a gold medal, along with the Russians. The medal ceremony was repeated, with all four skaters standing atop the podium, the Russian tricolor and the Canadian maple leaf raised above them.

Salé and Pelletier left for appearances on TV talk shows and a photo shoot with *People* magazine. Berezhnaya and Sikharulidze left for home. Three years earlier they had moved to New Jersey for training. They practiced their English to make themselves more appealing to international judges. Now America revealed its true colors.

Americans and Canadians saw the judging scandal as another instance of Soviet-style cheating, a repeat of Commies and ex-Commies voting together as a bloc. Meanwhile, Russians saw the scandal as an example of American and Canadian privilege. Pouting when they couldn't get their way, the North Americans pressed the skating federation and IOC to give them what they wanted. The whole story about French collusion had been their invention, pushed on the poor Le Gougne until she broke. "All this happened under strong pressure from the North American press, spectators, and public," said the head of the Russian skating federation. "It has always been difficult for us to perform there."

The new chair of the Russian Olympic Committee, Leonid Tyagachev, was conciliatory to international media. Russia would respect the IOC's decision, he said. To the Russian press, however, Tyagachev was more direct: "Now anyone can just demand a medal."

Tyagachev pledged to make "an objective defense of our country." But in the weeks and months after the Winter Games, the figure skating scandal became even more tangled. An unexpected twist came courtesy of Italy's Guardia di Finanza. The police had tapped the phones of Alimzhan Tokhtakhounov, a Russian citizen living in a seaside villa in Tuscany. Originally from Uzbekistan, Tokhtakhounov was widely known as Taiwanchik, or "Little Taiwan." He was also widely known for connections to the Russian mob, allegedly involved in everything from gun running to moving stolen vehicles. One of his most notorious schemes was fixing Moscow beauty pageants.

In 2002 Taiwanchik was being investigated for money laundering. Yet while the tapped calls didn't reveal how he cleaned money, they did expose his conversations with Russian mob contacts about figure skating. The plan was that the French would help the Russians win gold in pairs skating, while the Russians would help the French ice dancing duo. What made the deal all the better was that the female member of the French ice dancing pair, Marina Anissina, was a Russian, with connections to Taiwanchik's confederates.

According to the phone taps, Taiwanchik was thrilled by the pairs Final. "Our French have amazed me in a good way," he said in a call back to Russia. "Our Sikharulidze fell, the Canadians were 10 times better, and in spite of that, the French gave us first place with their vote."

Taiwanchik was so pleased, he called Anissina's mother in Russia. Two or three judges were in on the fix, he told her. They were going to make her daughter an Olympic champion. "Even if she falls, we will make sure she is number one," he reported. Mom was grateful.

Anissina herself was not as appreciative when she called Taiwanchik a few weeks later. FBI agents had talked to Gailhaguet, head of the French federation. Anissina was nervous.

"Whatever craziness happened," Taiwanchik reassured her, "the French are responsible for themselves. They were doing a favor for the Russians."

Taiwanchik didn't explain the link between himself and the French judge in Salt Lake City. For her part, Le Gougne insisted she had judged the competition honestly, believing the Russians gave the better performance. Yet after news broke of the tapped phone calls, she dropped her appeal to the ISU and accepted the suspension. Gailhaguet did not appeal either. Instead, he blamed the "Anglo-Saxon lobby" for pressuring the French judge. "I'll wait for the truth to come out," he said cryptically to the French Olympic Committee.

The truth was kept under wraps. The FBI put out a warrant for Tokhtakhounov, based on the wiretap transcripts. Italian police made the arrest, but the courts did not extradite him to the United States. Taiwanchik returned to Russia, where he has been since 2003. "I would like the American audience to know the truth about me," he told a visiting ESPN journalist. "That all that's being written about me is completely untrue."

In Russia, the wire taps were evidence not of cheating but of American attempts to slur Russian athletes. The newspaper *Evening Moscow* printed transcripts of the conversations, then asked rhetorically: "What does this prove?" It was all a scheme by the FBI, Russian media charged. The Americans likely concocted the story because they could not find any evidence of Taiwanchik committing other crimes.

For Moscow newspaper writers, the entire scandal showed how the US had become gripped by madness since 9/11. America no longer cared for human rights, only for revenge. "The people of the United States are demanding blood, demanding revenge for their September 'aerophobia.' This is what the scandal with Alimzhan Tokhtakhunov was invented for." Americans were masters of creating a scandal out of nothing, declared *Sovietsky Sport.* They used Hollywood techniques to turn someone like the benevolent Taiwanchik into the ultimate villain: pimp, racketeer, arms dealer.

"If we simply list all the crimes that Tokhtakhounov is charged with, we would have to shoot him without trial," the sports daily argued. "That would be the end of it. But then, who would scare the children? After all, isn't this the most affectionate thing we can say of the Americans: that they are overgrown, spoiled children?"

The figure skating controversy sucked up a lot of oxygen at the Salt Lake City Games. Yet it was not the only scandal involving Russian athletes. Three days before the closing ceremony, at the

Soldier Hollow cross-country track in the Wasatch Mountains, four women on the Russian team prepared for the 4x5km relay. Two skiers, Olga Danilova and Larisa Lazutina, won gold in the race four years earlier at Nagano. Both skiers also won gold and silver in previous races at Soldier Hollow. Lazutina now had a total of nine medals in four Winter Olympics. Russian skiers had won this particular event four straight times. They were such a sure bet to win that the race was being broadcast live back home. Viewers would spend their evening watching the Russian women claim an assured gold.

Before the race began, Danilova and Lazutina were summoned to the drug-testing facility. For the first time ever, testing at the Olympics was being handled by the World Anti-Doping Agency (WADA), the organization established by the IOC in 1999 to monitor doping in sport. Like all athletes at the games, Danilova and Lazutina had already submitted urine samples. Today, they were randomly selected for blood tests. Samples were drawn and immediately tested for increased levels of hemoglobin and reticulocytes. If levels for either were above standard thresholds, it would indicate that the athlete had boosted the blood's capacity for carrying oxygen through the body. More oxygen in the blood meant more fuel for the muscles, which brought greater strength and endurance.

Less than an hour before the start of the race, Lazutina's results showed her hemoglobin levels were high. For verification, a second sample was drawn and tested. The result was the same. Lazutina was disqualified. There was no time for a substitute. Danilova, the team's lead, was already at the starting line when the Russians were forced to withdraw. Lazutina was crushed. Back home, viewers sitting down to watch the race were informed that the Russian women were not participating. "A stolen medal," announced *Sovietsky Sport*.

Lazutina's high hemoglobin count that day did not prevent her from skiing in later events. She returned to the track two days later for the 30km race. Having already announced her retirement from international competition, Lazutina would be skiing her final Olympic event. And after her forced scratch in the relay, she was on a mission. She took the lead from the start and had the fastest time at every split. At the finish, she was two minutes ahead of the next skier.

"I really needed this victory," she said through tears. "Without meaning to, I let down our team three days ago."

Her words of contrition were not an admission of guilt. She won the medal to seize back what had been "unfairly taken" from her and her teammates. "These are not our Olympics," she told a Russian reporter. "Good thing they haven't introduced points into skiing. Fortunately, you can't buy seconds in a race."

Lazutina's redemption was short-lived. Two hours after she received the seventh gold medal of her Olympic career, the IOC announced that both she and Danilova had tested positive for doping. Their urine samples contained traces of darbepoetin, a drug used to treat people with anemia and cancer patients by increasing red blood cells. The drug's manufacturer, Amgen, had released it to the market only five months before the games, so it was not on WADA's list of banned pharmaceuticals. It was, however, an analogue to the banned drug erythropoietin (EPO), the only difference being that darbepoetin was longer lasting and was not produced by the human body. If anyone had darbepoetin in their urine, it had to have been injected. The drug was also potentially dangerous. Because it generated production of red blood cells, darbepoetin caused the blood to thicken. An athlete using it was at risk of heart attack or stroke.

Whenever a new drug with performance-boosting potential is introduced, athletes take a calculated risk. They have a narrow window to use the drug before anti-doping scientists figure out a way to detect it. Lazutina used darbepoetin at races in December 2001, and she likely presumed the drug would still be undetectable at Salt Lake City. Just before the games, WADA informed federations and national Olympic committees that a testing protocol was in place for darbepoetin. Not everyone got the memo. Along with Lazutina and Danilova, Spanish skier Johann Mühlegg also tested positive. He was ultimately stripped of the three gold medals he won at Salt Lake City. The IOC stripped Danilova of her two medals, and Lazutina lost three.

Russian officials in Salt Lake City were furious—not at Lazutina and Danilova for doping but at the WADA scientists, the IOC, and the international skiing federation. The night before the punishments were announced, the IOC Medical Commission broke news of the tests to the head of the Russian delegation, Viktor Mamatov, and Dr. Nikolay Durmanov, the team's chief anti-doping officer. Right away, the Russians went on the offensive.

Darbepoetin was not a banned drug, they argued.

It was analogous to EPO, the IOC doctors answered.

There was no testing protocol, the Russians countered.

IOC doctors showed the testing announcement sent out before the games.

Throughout the sparring, the head of the IOC Medical Commission kept asking the same question: How did Lazutina and Danilova have darbepoetin introduced into their bodies?

That didn't matter, Mamatov declared. There was no legal basis for the proceeding because the testing was flawed.

Besides that, Durmanov added, there was no way for Lazutina and Danilova to get darbepoetin. It was only available in Western Europe. It was too expensive for Russians.

After arguing with IOC officials, Mamatov and Durmanov took on the WADA scientists: Jordi Segura, who ran the anti-doping lab in Barcelona, and Moscow's doping nemesis from the 1980s, Don Catlin of UCLA. The Russians grilled Segura and Catlin for an hour. Repeated explanations that darbepoetin was essentially similar to EPO and that the drug was easily detectable with long-established tests were pushed aside. Durmanov stood on his 20 years of experience: he was right; Segura and Catlin were wrong.

At the end, Mamatov eased off. "Sometimes our language is strong," he admitted, "but that is because we are defending our athletes."

The meeting came to an end at 1:30 AM.

Danilova and Lazutina immediately appealed the decision to the Court of Arbitration for Sport, the Lausanne-based body responsible for adjudicating disputes in world sports. Their lack of preparation was laughable. Danilova's American lawyer opened by calling for the three judges to recuse themselves. The judges were confused, especially the judge recommended by Danilova's own lawyers.

The judges asked if Danilova thought they would make biased decisions not based on evidence?

No, that wasn't the reason, her lawyer answered. When the judges pressed, he had no reason at all for requesting the recusals. The judges rejected the motion and moved ahead.

The lawyer interrupted again. Danilova was protesting, he said.

Protesting what? the judges asked. They hadn't decided anything yet.

Lazutina's team likewise phoned it in. Their written complaint to the court was five pages, simply a restatement of the arguments Mamatov and Durmanov had first made: the testing procedure was not verified, darbepoetin was not banned, and darbepoetin and EPO were different drugs. WADA scientists refuted the claims one by one, with reams of supporting documents. Durmanov spoke in Lazutina's defense, but he did not offer any counterevidence to the WADA scientists. Instead, he complained that Russian athletes were being treated unfairly.

"This was not the most helpful way for an expert to give evidence," the judges observed. They upheld the IOC decision.

Despite their failure, the skiers' appeals served as practice runs for Russia's later fights with the World Anti-Doping Agency. Moscow challenged the science and the process, trying to stir doubts about the analyses at the root of anti-doping work. When WADA chemists responded that this was science, the Russians responded: No, it's *your* science, and it's being used unfairly against *our* athletes.

Russian media trumpeted this refrain: international sports organizations were biased against Russian athletes. After doing its own research into the doping charges, *Izvestia* claimed to find procedural irregularities, lack of documentation, incompetence, unprofessionalism, and gross negligence. International sports officials conspired to cover up all of this, the newspaper charged. "There is an 'anti-doping mafia' operating in world sport, and we have become its victims."

Meanwhile, IOC officials were puzzled by the backlash over Danilova and Lazutina. Documents in the Olympic archive show that IOC staffers bent over backward to accommodate Russian appeals, despite their lack of merit. Officials discussed how to defend themselves in the Russian press. "If we had some friends in Moscow who could pull weight with one newspaper to lay out the facts," one staff member suggested. The staffer then conceded: "Russian press is not my area of expertise."

The Russian press was not the expertise of anyone in Lausanne. If it had been, IOC officials would have known that laying out facts would accomplish nothing. In Moscow's view, results from blood and urine tests didn't prove a thing. "For Russia, these athletes are still Olympic champions," declared *Sport-Express*, "not dopers."

Support in Russia for Danilova and Lazutina was unshakeable. Famous Moscow lawyer Anatoly Kucherena, whose clients included American whistleblower Edward Snowden, offered to represent the skiers free of charge. A Duma member called for the skiers to receive their full stipends as gold medalists. Even the zookeepers at the Moscow Zoo leant their support. A new polar bear cub was given the name Larisa. "From now on, the bear will be a symbol of the fact our athletes do not need any doping, and no one can defeat them."

The scandal made heroes of the disqualified skiers. Danilova returned to the Winter Olympics in 2006 and 2010 as an honorary guest of the Russian delegation. In the small city of Alexandrov, where she served as director of physical education, the local sports center was named in her honor. Lazutina also moved from sports to public service. In 2003 she was elected to the Moscow regional council as a representative of United Russia, Putin's political party. In no way did the doping results detract from their previous achievements. Rather, their status was bolstered: Danilova and Lazutina represented Russia not only as champions but also victims. It was unclear, however, who exactly the culprits were. Decades after the Salt Lake City games, Russian media still asks: "Who set up our skiers?"

"Twenty days of constant scandal," judged *Sovietsky Sport*.

According to the Russian press, the Salt Lake City games were a travesty. Conspiring with the Americans, the IOC and other governing bodies had stolen victories that rightfully belonged to Russians. They ripped away the skiing medals; they humiliated the figure skaters; they robbed the hockey team. American media then created stories of Russian cheating. The IOC, WADA, and other governing bodies needed villains. This was the only way to justify their existence. Russian athletes provided convenient scapegoats.

At the root of all evil was American greed. "The Americans bought everything in advance," declared *Evening Moscow*. American dollars could buy medals and bribe scientists and pay off hockey referees. Everything was for sale—except for Russia. When he met IOC president Jacques Rogge after Lazutina's ban,

Leonid Tyagachev warned that Russia would leave the Olympics if the insults continued. "We will unite those people who would compete in a 'clean' arena, with good refereeing," he told Rogge.

Alone in the world, Russia stood for pure sport, for competitions that were free of politics. For that reason, Russians could be proud. Despite all the cheating by the Americans, in league with the governing bodies, Russia was victorious. The Moscow playbook had a new defensive play: if a Russian athlete loses, it is still a victory—the triumph of moral superiority in the face of a global conspiracy.

"Who beat us?" asked *Evening Moscow.* "It turned out that the Americans, with all their billions, could not defeat Russia."

For this reason, Russian athletes and coaches held their heads high when Vladimir Putin welcomed them home from Salt Lake City. "The results of the Olympics will benefit Russian sport," the president said. "We have seen how much the country loves its athletes. But work needs to be done in areas where Russia was not successful, namely in legal and administrative matters." If success in international sport was going to be decided in the courtroom, then Russia had to be prepared.

Changes were necessary, and Putin had someone in mind to take the helm. Despite the hockey team's disappointing finish in Salt Lake City, the coach got a promotion. In April the president named Slava Fetisov chair of the State Committee for Sport and Physical Culture. Putin then doubled his budget.

Achievements in sports were hallmarks of a nation's strength, Putin declared. Salt Lake City was a setback, but the 2002 Winter Games provided useful lessons. The goal was clear. Russia would attain athletic success befitting its rising economic and political power.

"It is the worst thing to mope and cry," the president said. "We need to win."

[illegible] the [illegible]

[illegible]

CHAPTER 8

THE OLIGARCH'S EMPIRE

IT'S MORE ACCURATE TO SAY: Putin needed to win.

In the years since Vladimir Putin came to power, there have been many attempts to get a glimpse behind his steely eyes and expressionless face, to understand what drives the man. One thing Russia experts keep coming back to is that Putin has to win. Even the brief moment of cooperation after 9/11 was less a genuine partnership than a strategic move to secure Russia's international standing and Putin's power. As Sergei Medvedev pointed out, Putin applied the philosophy of judo: "Do not counter an overwhelming opponent, but use his force to your own advantage."

Putin always stated his appreciation for judo. He credited the sport's discipline with saving him from the rough streets of his youth. But it was more than a physical activity for him. "I think it's also a philosophy in a way," he said in an NPR interview during his 2001 visit to the US. "I think it's a philosophy that teaches one to treat one's partner with respect."

Talk of respecting others played well with the NPR crowd. Yet there was another side to Putin's love of judo: it helped him beat people up. As *New Yorker* writer Julia Ioffe showed in her podcast biography of the Russian president, Putin's personality was shaped by his early years in the *dvor,* the courtyard inside a socialist apartment bloc. The *dvor* was the common scene of a Soviet childhood, a place of pickup soccer and hockey games as well as fist fights and gang brawls. For boys of Putin's age, the *dvor* was the state of nature. Toughness, violence, confrontation were part of the code. The lesson of the courtyard was that "everything is a zero-sum game," Ioffe stated. "If I'm winning, that means you're losing, and if you're winning, that means I'm losing, so I better change that."

For a small, slight boy like Putin, the courtyard was a menacing place. Judo gave him the skills he needed to carry himself in this rough world. Through martial arts, he learned to defend himself against larger rivals. And he gained the confidence to make a quick, unexpected show of force—something he did on a few occasions as a teenager. Yes, judo enshrined values of respect. But, as Putin noted, "It's not for weaklings."

In Putin's view, Russia had been ruined by weaklings. Mikhail Gorbachev had naively, foolishly, criminally, steered the Soviet Union to collapse—the "greatest geopolitical tragedy of the 20th century," Putin said. Boris Yeltsin had kept the Russian Federation intact, but only at the cost of ceding Moscow's power to regional officials. Yeltsin also looked weak: an overweight, white-haired grandpa with a bad heart and a weakness for vodka. Immediately after becoming president, Putin showed that he was a different kind of leader. He was photographed in flight gear, arriving aboard a jet fighter at the war zone in the breakaway republic of Chechnya. In his first year as president, photos showed Putin skiing and sparring in judo. He started taking off his shirt a few years later.

Putin didn't just present the image of a strong leader, he also took action. Right after his election, Putin moved to consolidate presidential authority in Russia's federal system. A slate of reforms gave him power to appoint governors, dismiss regional legislatures, control expenditures, and oversee local police and courts. Putin insisted the reforms were necessary: "They used to say in Russia, 'Our land is rich, but there is no order in it.' Nobody will say such things about us in the future."

Wins for Putin were wins for Russia. In taking authority over the federation's 55 regions, 22 ethnic republics, 5 autonomous regions, and 2 federal cities, the new president aimed to bolster the unified Russian state. From the beginning of his time as Russia's ruler, Putin has seen the state's sovereignty and the sovereign's authority as one and the same. Still today, defending Russia's sovereignty is essential to Putin's politics; indeed, this was one of his rationales for the invasion of Ukraine.

Along with asserting power over the kaleidoscope of regional jurisdictions, Putin had to bring his fist down on another challenge to the Kremlin's authority: he needed to show he had the oligarchs under control. Russia's oligarchs amassed vast fortunes during the turbulent Yeltsin years, when industries formerly owned by the Soviet state were transferred to private ownership. Privatization was to be the first step in transforming the broken-down planned economy into a flourishing market economy. But there wasn't much flourishing at first. Much of the wealth in Russia ended up in the accounts of former Soviet bureaucrats, thanks to insider schemes and cozy deals with the Kremlin. By the end of the 1990s, oligarchs owned billions worth of oil and gas, mining, transportation, and communications companies, while Russia had one of the highest inequality rates in the world.

Reining in the oligarchs was good politics for the new president. As a group, they were hugely unpopular, widely seen as having unjustly fleeced Russia for their own greed. Putin pledged to cut them down to size. "These people who fuse power and capital," he declared, "there will be no oligarchs of this kind as a class."

Putin also needed to put a check on the oligarchs in his own quest for power. Russia's oligarchs had kept Yeltsin in office, they had given the nod to his choice of successor, and they helped Putin win election on his own. ORT, the broadcast company owned by Boris Berezovsky, was especially important. Thanks to the network's admiring coverage, the unknown Putin became the most-respected politician in Russia and won the March 2000 election. He would never rely on the oligarchs again.

Soon after dropping the title "acting president," Putin summoned the oligarchs for a show of fealty. On July 28, 2000, he hosted 21 of Russia's richest men at the Kremlin. The guests were likely nervous when they arrived. A member of their club, Vladimir Gusinsky, had been arrested a month earlier on tax and corruption charges. After Gusinsky spent a few weeks in jail, the charges were dropped, and he set off for Spain. It was not known at the time that the government had forced him to sell his assets and go into exile.

For those who didn't get the message of Gusinsky's arrest, Putin made things clear at the Kremlin: the government would allow the oligarchs to keep whatever they gained in the 1990s as long as they stayed out of politics and paid their fair share of taxes. The oligarchs were quick to heel. In a statement released after the meeting, they pledged to uphold Russia's interests: "The most important task for business is to preserve and increase the national wealth," they declared. It was time to start working for the motherland.

One well-known oligarch was not present for Putin's scolding. Roman Abramovich was the youngest of Russia's billionaires, just 33 at the time. He was also the only one with something like a rags-to-riches story. Orphaned at age three, he was raised by his uncle in the far northern region of Komi. Trained as a welder and mechanic, he got his start in black-market trading during his obligatory military service. The future tycoon convinced drivers in his unit to siphon some gasoline from their vehicles, which they gave to Abramovich in exchange for sweets for their girlfriends. Abramovich then sold the contraband fuel at below-market prices to officers, who used it for their personal cars. In setting up the scheme, Abramovich showed the skills that would characterize his management style in decades to come: a friendly demeanor, a soft-spoken persuasiveness, and an ability to invent profitable schemes. "He could make money out of thin air," recalled an army buddy.

In the perestroika years, Abramovich expanded into other products: dolls, timber, sugar, pigs. His specialty remained fuel—getting it from the people who had it to the people who wanted it. By 1994, at age 28, Abramovich controlled companies based in Russia, Switzerland, and Germany that were shipping over 3.5 million tons of oil products. For all his success, however, he was still a small fish in the oligarch sea.

Yet Abramovich was a small fish with a big idea. The oil products he shipped came mainly from a refinery in western Siberia still owned by the state. Abramovich recognized there was a bundle to be made by combining the refinery with the state-owned production facilities in Siberia, which would then link to his trading operations. To make the plan work, he needed the help of someone connected to Yeltsin's circle. Enter Boris Berezovsky, the media tycoon. Berezovsky agreed to make the pitch, in exchange for $30 million a year.

In 1995 Berezovsky struck a deal with the Kremlin on Abramovich's behalf: His network would help President Yeltsin before the 1996 presidential election. In return, the government would consolidate Siberian oil operations into a single company, privatize the company, and give Abramovich the inside track on ownership. It all played out according to plan. Abramovich paid a discount price of $100 million for the new company, called Sibneft. Berezovsky put ORT to work for the Yeltsin campaign, with Abramovich picking up the network's costs and paying Berezovsky's retainer. And Yeltsin stayed in power. After polling in the single digits at the start of 1996, the president made a stunning turnaround by the June election, thanks to ORT's fawning coverage. He won a second term with 54% of the vote.

Abramovich earned his own place in the Yeltsin circle with his next deal. With money from his oil operations, he bankrolled the creation of an aluminum conglomerate that became a key source of revenue for the president's family. Now trusted in the Kremlin, Abramovich was rumored to have a hand in the selection of Putin as Yeltsin's successor. Then he was rumored to be close to the former prime minister, turned president.

With Abramovich, most of what was known was just rumors. The oligarch was notoriously tight-lipped. Granted, the lips were usually curled in a disarming smile. Abramovich had a talent for putting people at ease—Berezovsky admitted this even after suing his former partner for billions in supposedly unpaid Sibneft assets. Berezovsky lost the 2012 case in British court, with the London judge finding him unreliable and dishonest. Abramovich, on the other hand, earned the court's approval for being thoughtful, careful, and responsible.

So why wasn't Abramovich at Putin's summit with the oligarchs? Russian media ran through the theories: Was he on the outs with Putin? Was he next to face legal charges, after Gusinsky? After all, in the Kremlin meeting Putin noted that Sibneft was delinquent on taxes.

Not at all, answered the Kremlin. Abramovich could not attend the meeting because he was busy with the Chukchis. Not the so-called "western Chukchis" in Paris, but actual Chukchis, herding reindeer on the edge of the tundra.

Chukotka is Russia's easternmost province, on the shores of the Bering Strait. Five times the size of Montana but with a population of just 50,000 people, Chukotka is a beautiful, barren, brutally cold land of snow-covered mountains and lichen-covered tundra. At the end of the 1990s, it was also woefully poor. The reindeer herds dropped from half a million to fewer than 100,000. The desperate Chukchis had to eat them.

Russians were baffled when Roman Abramovich decided to run for governor of the province in 2000. A few Moscow reporters took the 10-hour flight to Anadyr, the region's capital, to find out what the oligarch was doing. Was he planning to tap Chukotka's mineral and oil reserves?

"It wasn't profitable," Abramovich answered.

Was he seeking to win Putin's approval, perhaps ensure immunity from some future prosecution?

"An excellent theory," Abramovich said. "I'll go with that."

The oligarch then added, "Why doesn't anyone believe that I actually find this interesting? I think I can change things here."

Change things he did. In Abramovich's two terms as governor, new schools and hospitals were built. Rates of crime, alcoholism, and infant mortality all dropped; wages and life expectancy increased. Even the reindeer made a comeback. Much of the funding for these improvements came from Abramovich himself. Registered as a resident of Chukotka, his huge tax payments went to the region. He also made direct donations amounting to tens of millions of dollars. Abramovich stuck around to see how his money was being spent. "Charity is not like feeding pigeons in the square," he told a British reporter who made the trip. "It is a process that requires professional management."

What does Abramovich's arctic adventure have to do with Russian sports—other than the ice arena, fitness centers, and football pitches he built there? Chukotka reveals something of the impenetrable brew of motivations that drove Russia's most prominent, most perplexing oligarch: an instinct for profit, a desire to do something that matters, a restless impulse to take on wild schemes. Mix in as well, in some unknown measure, an interest in staying on Putin's good side while keeping the president at a distance.

We have to keep all this in mind as background to Abramovich's purchase of Chelsea FC in July 2003. Today big-money foreign owners are commonplace in British football, whether Gulf-state sheikhs or Hollywood stars. But when Abramovich bought Chelsea, it was something wholly new, something unexpected—like a billionaire setting off to Siberia.

Reportedly, the deal was outlined in 15 minutes: £60 million for ownership and another £80 million to cover Chelsea's debts. When the surprise purchase was announced, the Russian press was stunned. Was Abramovich buying an expensive bauble, a step up from cars, yachts, and mansions? Was he moving money into safer Western markets? "He invests his money in the reputation business," said a Moscow journalist.

Or maybe it was because he liked soccer. "He told me it was a boyhood dream," said a prominent radio journalist. "I remember when we talked about football, his eyes lit up. He said that when he was a kid, he realized he couldn't play but he still wanted to be involved. It's a dream come true."

That's how Abramovich himself explained the move. "It's really about having fun," he told the British press, "and that means success and trophies."

Some Russians were not only stunned; they were angry. Despite his work in Chukotka, Abramovich never escaped the stigma of being a devious oligarch, pilfering wealth from Russia for his own gain. Even worse, now he was pilfering for the gain of English football fans. "It's a shame that Russian football doesn't interest him," said one newspaper writer.

Sergei Stepashin, head of the government's accounting office, threatened to investigate: "Money from our oil companies should not go to buying football teams, but to drilling new wells and developing the Russian economy."

There was also speculation that Putin was behind the move. In the early 2000s, Russian media were still able to raise pointed questions about the president. One paper hinted that the Chelsea purchase was a PR move by an oligarch with close ties to the Kremlin. Yet if Abramovich was making an investment to boost his prestige, or Putin's, it didn't work out right away. Everyone suspected Abramovich was up to something no good, whether he was building hospitals in Chukotka or buying a football club in London.

With Russians pelting Abramovich, the Chelsea faithful didn't exactly roll out the red carpet. "We need to look at the source of his money, what his track record has been in Russia, to establish whether he is a fit and proper person to take over a football club in this country," declared Tony Banks, a Chelsea supporter, member of Parliament, and former sports minister. One of the club's all-time greats, Jimmy Greaves, was more direct: "Nobody knows anything about the bloke."

One of the biggest concerns among English football watchers was that Abramovich would fleece Chelsea for its assets. "Most people expected that he wanted the land around Stamford Bridge for property development," explained sports economist Stefan Szymanski. Right from the start, however, Abramovich surprised everyone by investing in the club. "Abramovich got very good press," Szymanski told me. "Clearly, he wasn't taking money out. He was putting money in."

Abramovich was putting in a lot of money. Soon after taking over the club, the new owner went on a spending spree the likes of which English football had never seen. During the summer transfer window, Chelsea added eleven players at a total cost of £111 million. Prior to that, the most any English club had paid in total transfer fees had been £58.6 million, by Manchester United in 2001–02. Abramovich proved right away he was going to open his wallet in the hunt for trophies. And his wallet was fat.

One of the few British reporters to get an interview with Abramovich was freelancer Chris Stephen, who made the trip to Chukotka a few weeks after the sale. Like all journalists who reached Abramovich's inner sanctum, Stephen described a soft-spoken, unassuming man, dressed casually in jeans. This was no hard-driving entrepreneur, like his former associate Berezovsky. He was also no rah-rah owner. Chelsea was not going to win anything this season, Abramovich admitted to Stephen, a supporter of the club. "Time is needed to make a team, then you hope for a result," he said.

When the 2003–04 season began, it looked as though the owner's prediction of a slow building process would be proved wrong. After opening with a 2–1 win at Liverpool, Chelsea played the next seven matches without a loss. But this was the season of Arsenal's Invincibles, the first English team to finish a season undefeated since 1889. Chelsea fans had reason to be hopeful: their club finished second to a once-in-a-century team and reached the semifinals of the Champions League before losing to Monaco. Abramovich, however, was not as patient as he let on. Two weeks after the season's end, he sacked manager Claudio Ranieri. Abramovich hired the young manager of Porto, the team that beat Monaco in the Champions League Finals. "I'm European champion," said José Mourinho at his introduction, "and I think I'm a special one."

With his new manager in place, Abramovich went shopping again for players. That summer, Chelsea spent £20 million for the mainstay of Porto's defense, center-back Ricardo Carvalho, £12 million for Dutch winger Arjen Robben, and £24 million for Ivorian striker Didier Drogba. The best value came from the £7 million spent for Petr Čech, who would become one of the best goalkeepers in soccer history. Together with English players Joe Cole, Frank Lampard, and John Terry, the new additions drove Chelsea's success for years to come.

In the first season under Mourinho, the club won the league title for the first time in 50 years; they repeated the following season. In 2006–07 Chelsea took the FA Cup and League Cup. With the new owner fulfilling his pledge to bring trophies to the club, Chelsea supporters became Abramovich stans. Before each match at Stamford Bridge, fans clapped along as the Russian folk song "Kalinka" played over the speakers. After Chelsea won European soccer's biggest prize in 2012, the Champions League, fans fixed a banner to the stands in tribute to their owner. Set against the blue, white, and red of the Russian flag, an image of the smiling Abramovich looked over the West London grounds. "The Roman Empire," declared the banner.

Abramovich's success in England got attention back home. Some Russian newspapers continued to grumble, reporting on his feuds with managers (Mourinho left after three seasons), rumors that he was selling, and even that his 11-year-old son sat uninvited in a player's locker-room chair. By contrast, sportswriters devoted regular attention to the club. Just as Fetisov reported proudly on Putin's reception in Washington, DC, a *Sovietsky Sport* correspondent at the 2012 Champions League Final in Munich reported on Abramovich's esteem among European fans. "Believe me, Abramovich is the main star of London's Chelsea," the writer announced.

Thanks to Chelsea's victories, the oligarch finally got some credit in Russia. A few weeks after the club won the Champions

League, Abramovich made a rare public appearance in Moscow, at a benefit concert for a children's orchestra. Wealthy patrons were there, alongside theatre directors and gallery owners. After settling into their seats, before the concert began, the affluent and cultured of Moscow broke into chants of "Chel-si! Chel-si!"

Abramovich's feats caught the notice of oligarchs as well. He made a risky investment in a foreign country, in a field even more uncertain than the commodities market, and it paid unexpected dividends. Abramovich was not only rich, he was also popular—something no other oligarch could claim. Members of the fraternity decided to try the strategy for themselves.

It's still unclear how much nudging the Kremlin gave to oligarchs who invested in foreign sports teams. The first Russian billionaire to follow Abramovich into the sports-ownership biz was reputedly close to Putin. After buying a minority stake in Arsenal in 2007, Alisher Usmanov told the *Guardian* of his admiration for Putin. Usmanov said he was "proud to have such a leader for his country."

Russian media were far more generous with Usmanov than they were with Abramovich. "He is kind and friendly in the Asian way," said one profile of the Uzbek-born magnate, whose riches were in metals and mobile phones. The Jewish Abramovich never received such a glowing introduction. Usmanov's reputation also got a boost from his purchase of a collection of Russian art long held by émigrés in the West, including prints of beloved Soviet-era cartoons. He could not be accused of failing to use his wealth for Russia's benefit.

Mikhail Prokhorov likewise earned good press when he bought the NBA's New Jersey Nets in 2009. PROKHOROV SAVED AMERICAN BASKETBALL FROM DESTRUCTION, blared an exaggerated headline. It would have been enough to say that Prokhorov was the first foreign owner of any American sports franchise. Unlike the mercurial

Abramovich, the Nets owner made himself available to Russian and American media. When a *Sovietsky Sport* reporter visited the US, he asked if Prokhorov's move into basketball was a "call of the soul" or a "bequest of the state." The oligarch answered diplomatically: he hoped his NBA experience would raise the level of basketball in Russia. And he still funded youth teams at Moscow's Red Army club, Prokhorov pointed out. Another oligarch doing good things for the motherland.

For the oligarchs abroad, questions about Putin were an occupational hazard. After *Forbes* charged that Usmanov's holdings were a front for Putin's own money, the oligarch sued. Suspicions arose again when the Panama Papers were released in 2016. The leaked financial records showed Usmanov moved hundreds of millions of dollars among his various offshore bank accounts. There was speculation the money belonged to the president, but none of it could be tied directly to Putin.

Prokhorov's ties to the Kremlin were likewise mysterious. In 2012 he ran for president of Russia—*against Putin!* The last oligarch to challenge Putin publicly had been Mikhail Khodorkovsky, Russia's wealthiest man at the time. In a televised meeting at the Kremlin in February 2003, Khodorkovsky argued with the president about government corruption. Eight months later, he was arrested for fraud and had his assets frozen. A presidential pardon allowed Khodorkovsky to finally go into exile in 2013, after ten years in prison. By contrast, Prokhorov's challenge to Putin did not bring arrest or exile, perhaps because it wasn't intended to be a challenge at all. In her profile of the oligarch, Julia Ioffe speculated that the campaign was concocted on the Kremlin's suggestion—a bid for office by a well-known oligarch to prove Russia was a functioning democracy. Prokhorov earned 8% of the vote. He stayed out of jail and kept his loot.

As for the original oligarch in the sports world, the connection to Putin was always murky. In her book *Putin's People,* British journalist Catherine Belton wrote that the president planned for a Russian to buy Chelsea a year before Abramovich purchased the club. According to one of Belton's sources, Putin himself asked Abramovich to buy Chelsea. Abramovich took Belton to court over the charge. The author and her publisher, HarperCollins, stood by her sources, but fighting a billionaire's band of lawyers was daunting. After agreeing to a settlement, Belton changed the wording of the paragraphs about the Chelsea purchase for the book's paperback edition, clarifying that Abramovich insisted the idea was his alone.

To be sure, whoever came up with the idea was a visionary. In 2003 the idea of a Russian oligarch buying an English football club was on nobody's radar. And success was by no means assured, as the experiences of other oligarchs proved. Arsenal's board blocked Usmanov from buying more shares in the club, while Prokhorov sold his stake in the Nets and their Brooklyn arena after nine years. It's not surprising Putin wanted to take credit for Abramovich's success. He had a habit of claiming other people's good ideas as his own. After all, he had to win.

Rafa Benítez gave all the credit to Abramovich. "He started a revolution," said the Liverpool manager in 2006, as Chelsea was on its way to a second consecutive league title.

Roman Abramovich did bring a revolution—a transformation of global pro sports rivaling what the Soviets did in the Olympics decades earlier. The Russian oligarch was the original tycoon-messiah of the global age, someone who swooped in from abroad and then transformed a club with massive infusions of cash. He was never able to entirely wash away the odor of ill-begotten riches. During 19 years as Chelsea owner, he was always hounded by questions about shady privatization deals and connections with

Putin. But he also gained a measure of public esteem rare for multi-billionaires, even those who devote time and treasure to reviving remote corners of Siberia. Abramovich showed other billionaires that spending their way to sports victories was a good way to win friends.

Abramovich's years at Chelsea also transformed the economics of pro sports, especially European soccer. During his run as owner, the club spent a total of £2 billion in salaries and transfer fees. In 19 years, the club won 21 trophies, including five Premier League titles and two Champions League trophies. With more wins came more fans. Before 2003 Chelsea had been consistently in the middle of the table, its support largely limited to West London. The year after Abramovich's purchase, Chelsea leaped past Juventus and Barcelona on the list of the world's highest-grossing clubs. Chelsea's blue shirts are among the top ten bestsellers in the world, and the club has over 130 million followers on social media. Investors from around the world followed Abramovich's lead. Current owners of English clubs hail from India, Thailand, China, the UAE, Saudi Arabia, Switzerland, and the United States. Thanks to a Russian oligarch, English football clubs have become the most-prized assets of the world's super-rich.

For peons like us, Abramovich's revolution also brought a transformation. Fans around the world, in every sport, hope for someone like Roman Abramovich to swoop in, buy their team, and invest millions, billions, whatever it takes to win a championship.

Indeed, Abramovich started a revolution. Yet just like the Soviets who revolutionized world sport decades earlier, he cheated. As other clubs responded to Abramovich's challenge by finding their own billionaires willing to drop loads of cash, leaders of English and European football realized they needed to set restraints. Introduced in 2009, Financial Fair Play rules were intended to set limits on super-rich owners. Abramovich, however, found a way to get around the rules—creating a loophole that came right out of the Moscow playbook.

Thanks to another set of leaked documents, these coming from Cyprus, British journalists discovered that the account books of Abramovich's various companies included Chelsea-related expenses. By using offshore accounts, Chelsea made payments hidden from the Financial Fair Play watchdogs. Even more troubling is where the secret payments went. Eden Hazard's agent received millions of euros before the Belgian star's transfer to Chelsea. The owner of a Russian club received money before sending Chelsea his star players, Willian and Samuel Eto'o. Romelu Lukaku's agent received £10 million from an Abramovich company in the Virgin Islands. Abramovich's club not only skirted limits on how much they could spend, they also spent money under the table to tilt the transfer market in their favor.

For months after Abramovich sold Chelsea in 2022, supporters still chanted his name. Meanwhile English and European football authorities investigated the financial cheating. UEFA, the governing body of European soccer, imposed a $10.8 million fine. Major sponsors stepped away from the club, and balance sheets went deep in the red. For a time, there were rumors of exclusion from the Premier League. The banner at Stamford Bridge finally came down, yet Chelsea still had to clean up the ruins of the Roman Empire.

CHAPTER 9

NATIONAL CHAMPIONS

THE BRAZILIAN STRIKER sprinted into the box, his dreadlocked hair draped over the shoulders of his red-and-blue jersey. The keeper leaped forward to intercept the crossing pass, but the ball skipped just out of reach. Alone at the goal, the striker powered a shot into the net. Lisbon's Estádio José Alvalade went quiet. More than 47,000 supporters of Sporting CP had watched their club lose its halftime lead. The visitors were ahead 3–1, with only 15 minutes left to play.

When the final whistle sounded, the Brazilian striker celebrated with his teammates. His name was Vágner Love. He had joined the team only months earlier, after being sold by his home club in Rio, Palmeiras, the club he belonged to since he was a boy. Just 19 years old, he traveled more than 7,000 miles to a strange land, to the club long known in the West as Red Army, CSKA Moscow. He endured a Russian winter. Now, on this May night, he was lifting a European trophy, the UEFA Cup.

In 2005 CSKA Moscow looked like any other top-level soccer team in Europe, with its mix of international and home-grown talent. Half of the players were Russian. A few others were from nearby countries like Latvia, Lithuania, and Serbia. Vágner Love was one of three Brazilians on the team. He and Daniel Carvalho had been the club's top scorers during the season. They were joined in the starting eleven by Nigerian midfielder Chidi Odiah.

With this international roster, the Red and Blues reclaimed their Soviet-era glory. The ownership group, fronted by businessman Yevgeny Giner, led the turnaround after buying CSKA—Central Sports Klub of the Army—from the Ministry of Defense. The win over Sporting was important not only for the team but for all of Russian soccer. This was the first win ever by a Russian club in a European competition. Yet Giner didn't get credit in the football press. Instead, tributes went to his friend, Roman Abramovich. The money to buy players like Odiah, Carvalho, and Love had come from one of the best sponsorship deals in world soccer. In 2004 Abramovich's company, Sibneft, bought a place on CSKA's red-and-blue shirts. The club's annual take was equal to the $18 million Manchester United received each season from its shirt sponsor, Vodafone.

CSKA's deal with Sibneft drew the attention of UEFA, the governing body of European soccer. It was a no-no for someone to have an ownership stake in two major clubs. Abramovich insisted he was just a sponsor. UEFA gave him a pass, but the Kremlin took interest. Abramovich was using Russian oil money to buy trophies for an English club. The CSKA win showed Russian oil money could also bring trophies to Russian clubs.

CSKA's victory in 2005 established a new model for pro leagues in Russia. The country's riches would buy big-name foreign athletes and pay for new stadiums and arenas. Russian leagues would boast of having the world's best players, in sports from men's soccer and hockey to women's volleyball and basketball. Meanwhile Russian athletes would compete against this top-level talent, preparing them for international events. Russia's sports culture would finally shake off the dust of the 1990s. Its pro leagues would match those in Europe and America, and Russian athletes would again win world titles.

The key to the whole strategy were the large resource-producing conglomerates Putin called Russia's "national champions." The Kremlin had an ownership stake in these companies and played a direct role in helping them expand operations. In return their executives funded Putin's plans for Russian sports victories—and even served as the president's lieutenants in putting his plans into action. This was a role they eagerly accepted. Like Putin, leaders of Russia's economic revival wanted to revive the sports success of their youth, when they watched Soviet athletes conquer the world for the socialist motherland. The profits their companies generated would make that happen again, for the capitalist motherland.

Putin's fight against the oligarchs was not only about neutralizing political threats. There was also an economic dimension. In the 1990s oligarchs like Abramovich, Boris Berezovsky, and Khodorkovsky enriched themselves by gaining ownership of formerly state-controlled assets. In the 2000s this process was reversed.

The legal threats against Berezovsky and Khodorkovsky were part of a campaign to gain state control of Russia's wealth. When Khodorkovsky was arrested in 2003, his company, Yukos Oil, was broken up and transferred to state-owned companies. By contrast, Berezovsky had been smart enough to escape Russia in 2000, before his own arrest. Once safely in Britain, the oligarch then sold his assets to Roman Abramovich, his junior partner. Abramovich paid $150 million for Berezovsky's stake in the ORT media company and gave the exiled oligarch another $1.3 billion as a final payout for his role in the Sibneft deal. Abramovich then handed control of both companies to the Kremlin. In the case of ORT, he kept his shares but did not claim any seats on the board of directors, essentially leaving the broadcaster under state authority. Sibneft was another matter. Ten years after buying the company from the state in a rigged deal, he sold it back to the state for $13 billion—a nice return on his original investment of $100 million.

Sibneft no longer appeared on the shirts of CSKA or any other club. The company was wholly absorbed into Gazprom, the main producer and exporter of Russian natural gas. Formed in the late Soviet period, Gazprom was the poster child for Yeltsin-era corruption. Company chairman Viktor Chernomyrdin, who also served as Russia's prime minister, stripped Gazprom assets for the benefit of himself and other executives. In the late '90s the company lost holdings equal to Exxon-Mobil's total worldwide reserves. The assets were sold off to shell companies owned by Chernomyrdin and his cronies for six cents on the dollar.

Putin cleaned house at Gazprom after becoming president. Chernomyrdin was removed and given the face-saving job of ambassador to Ukraine. Putin then installed two of his most trusted friends from St. Petersburg at the top of the company: Alexey Miller as CEO and Dmitry Medvedev as chairman of the board, a job he held while also serving as Putin's deputy chief of staff. With ties forged between the Gazprom boardroom, Kremlin halls, and Putin's circle of friends, the company became the super-heavyweight of the president's national champions. Indeed, Putin coined the term to describe companies like Gazprom: resource-producing conglomerates partly owned by the state. The government provided support for the companies to build global market share; the companies, in turn, used their profits to benefit Russia as a whole, rather than individual Russian oligarchs.

Certainly, individual Russians did get rich. In the case of Gazprom, there was a lot of wealth to spread around—to the executives who ran the company, and to the foreign investors who owned stock. During the early 2000s the Kremlin helped Gazprom regain most of its stripped assets and become the principal gas supplier to Europe. When Medvedev stepped down as chairman in 2008 to succeed Putin as president, Gazprom's market capitalization was over $300 billion, up from $7.8 billion in 2000. The company heated homes from the UK to Ukraine. Soon the Gazprom brand would be likewise inescapable, seen on television screens and soccer pitches across the continent.

"As long as I can remember, I have been a football fan," said Alexey Miller in an interview. "Mom still worries about Zenit and doesn't miss a game on TV."

Zenit was the club of Leningrad kids like Miller and Putin. For Miller more so than Putin, his former boss in the St. Petersburg mayor's office, soccer was a passion. He lived and died with Zenit's up and downs. At the end of the 2005 season, Miller was dying. Zenit dropped three straight matches in the final weeks, including a 1–0 loss to Amkar, a Siberian club at the bottom of the league. The loss plunged Zenit to sixth in the standings. Miller got on the phone to his friend, Sergei Fursenko.

"Sixth place!" fumed Miller, interrupting Fursenko's dinner at a high-end restaurant.

"You can't drive a car without taking the wheel," Fursenko answered.

Miller made the decision right away. Previously a Zenit sponsor, Gazprom paid $36 million to take full ownership. Fursenko was put in charge as the club's director. Below Miller in the Gazprom org chart, Fursenko was director of the subsidiary responsible for shipping gas throughout northwestern Russia and the Baltics. He was also a longtime friend of Putin. In fact, Fursenko was partner in one of Putin's few above-board business ventures: a development of *dachas* on lakefront property outside St. Petersburg.

Fursenko and Miller were friends of one of the most powerful men in the world, and they ran one of the largest companies in the world. Yet they were also sports fans who wanted their club to win. "They were simple Leningrad boys with the same headache as other Zenit fans," recalled a longtime club official.

So what happens when simple Leningrad boys who are also Gazprom executives buy their favorite club? They spend a ton of cash. Before Miller and Fursenko took over, Zenit's annual budget was about $10 million, compared to the $50 million Yevgeny Giner spent each year at CSKA Moscow. Fursenko increased the budget to $60 million in the first season of Gazprom's ownership. Three years later, the club was spending $100 million per season.

The investment paid off. In 2008 Zenit matched the European success of their Moscow rivals, with a win over Glasgow Rangers for the UEFA Cup. The St. Petersburg club then did CSKA one better. Three months after the UEFA Cup win, Zenit met Manchester United in Monaco for the UEFA Super Cup, the single-match showdown between the winners of the Champions League and the UEFA Cup. CSKA had lost their 2005 Super Cup match to Liverpool. Zenit came better prepared. Five days before the match, the club paid $44 million for Portuguese striker Danny. Starting as Zenit's attacking midfielder, Danny scored in the 59th minute to put his new team ahead 2–0. Danny's goal proved decisive. After Man U scored later in the half, Zenit held off a last-minute attack to win a second European trophy.

Fans lined the streets when the club arrived in St. Petersburg late the next night. An exuberant group made their way to the Portuguese consulate, to give thanks for their team's newest star. "We are the strongest team in Europe," one fan yelled to a reporter. "Now everyone—Real Madrid, Juventus—is not so scary."

Zenit didn't pose much challenge to the likes of Real Madrid or Juventus, and the club never repeated the European success of 2008. But it became the dominant club in Russia, winning the league 10 times in the Gazprom years, including a run of six straight titles. Being Russia's richest club certainly helped. Gazprom money paid for a string of high-profile European managers. And in 2012 the club paid the highest transfer fees ever in Russian soccer for two stars of Portugal's Primeira Liga: $50 million to Benfica for Belgian midfielder Axel Witsel and $76 million to Porto for Brazilian forward Hulk.

The Portuguese sports press grumbled about the loss of two of their league's best players. But Gazprom money was a welcome boost for the clubs. Both Porto and Benfica had recently moved into new stadiums, and the huge transfer fees allowed them to pay off construction debts. As club directors across Europe would learn, Russian money had its benefits.

Massive transfer fees were good for the teams that did business with Zenit, but they didn't do much for Gazprom. There was no plaque at Porto's Estádio do Dragão thanking the Russian company for the money it spent on Hulk. A better use of the company's cash were sponsorship agreements. Thanks to these deals with clubs and associations, Gazprom became one of the most recognizable brands in Europe.

Of course, Gazprom was not like other corporate sponsors. The company was an extension of the Russian state. Its purpose was to not only enrich investors but also advance Moscow's interests.

There was no better example of this mix of business, politics, and sports than Gazprom's sponsorship of the German club Schalke 04. When the deal was announced in October 2006 at a press conference in Dresden, Sergei Fursenko was there in his Gazprom-exec role. Also on hand was Vladimir Putin, back in the city where he worked in the '80s as a KGB agent.

The president was there to sign the contract with Schalke club president Clemens Tönnies. That's right—the president of Russia was signing a shirt-sponsorship deal with a soccer club. Clearly, this wasn't any ordinary sponsorship. In total Germany spent one half of one percent of its entire gross domestic product on natural gas imports from Russia, much of that supplied by Gazprom. The shirt sponsorship was a way for the company, an asset of the Kremlin, to build PR in this essential market. Schalke had one of the largest fan bases in Germany. Thanks to the Gazprom deal, the club also had the richest sponsorship in the Bundesliga: $127 million over five years. A lot of Schalke supporters instantly became Gazprom supporters—or at least, they had Gazprom's logo across their team shirts.

One German reporter was bold enough to ask Putin about the possible downside of this deal: "Should we Germans be afraid of Russians buying up everybody?"

Putin smiled his Putin-y smile.

"I think this should only make you happy," he replied.

The key person in brokering the deal was former German chancellor Gerhard Schröder. Since leaving politics the year before, Schröder had taken a prominent position with the company Nord Stream, which aimed to build a pipeline under the Baltic Sea from Russia to Germany. Schröder said the line would make for cheaper fuel costs; critics claimed it would make Germany more dependent on Russian gas. Gazprom's sponsorship of Schalke was intended to calm those fears. Having the Gazprom logo on Schalke shirts would familiarize ordinary Germans with the company. As a former Gazprom executive told Reuters, the deal would "create the image of a respectable Russian who takes care of your heating."

Along with nervous Germans, there were offended Russians. Gazprom's investment in a German soccer club was even more suspect than Abramovich's purchase of Chelsea. After all, Gazprom was owned by the state—Russian resources were being used to buy wins for a German team. Alexey Miller addressed the concerns.

"These investments are justified economically and, most importantly, politically, by entering the German market, by having Gazprom in the subconscious of the German people," said the company's CEO. To any Russian who might object, the message was clear: there was no greater victory for the country's national champion than planting its flag in the middle of Germany.

Gazprom promoted its brand in other countries. The company signed a deal to provide fuel to Chelsea's facilities. A sponsorship with Red Star Belgrade saved the Serbian club from bankruptcy. The most important brand placement was with Europe's biggest sports competition: the UEFA Champions League. The 2012 deal, paying $40 million per season, brought Gazprom into an elite group of UEFA sponsors that included FedEx, MasterCard, and Sony. The company's logo was also seen on millions of TV screens. That year, the Champions League Final drew three times as many viewers as the Super Bowl, across Europe and around the world. "This helps bring our brand to a completely different level," said Miller.

Now that it was cavorting with major global companies, Gazprom had to clean up its image. As recently as 2009 the company earned bad press for reducing gas flow to Europe because of the Kremlin's disputes with Ukraine. After signing the UEFA deal, Gazprom started talking about peace and harmony. Beginning in 2013 the company organized a social program for children called Football for Friendship. In the first year, over 600 kids from across Europe took part in the program's events. Football for Friendship eventually involved children from 200 countries and won international awards. Alexey Miller spoke of the program's success in cultivating mutual respect and shared universal values. "I am convinced that together we will make the world a better place," said the Gazprom boss. The company wasn't simply trying to gain customers with its soccer ventures. Russia's national champion wanted to prove that its pipelines flowed with the milk of human kindness.

Alexey Miller had big dreams for Zenit and Russian soccer. He looked to create a super league that could bring together Russian clubs with the strongest Ukrainian teams. This new association would challenge the top leagues in western Europe and be the centerpiece of a Champions League–style competition across the former Soviet Union. More importantly, a Eurasian federation would allow Russia to separate from UEFA. No UEFA meant no Financial Fair Play Rules, freeing Zenit to spend millions without European auditors inspecting the books.

A Russian-led super league didn't take off in soccer. In hockey, on the other hand, Gazprom and other national-champion companies joined together to create a league that stretched across the old USSR and beyond. As with Gazprom's soccer initiatives, the driving figure was a true fan. Alexander Medvedev (no relation to Dmitry) was director of the company's export operations. A Moscow native with Communist Party connections, he had risen through trade offices and international banking in the perestroika years. After the Soviet collapse, he led an investment group in Vienna before moving to Gazprom.

While the end of the Soviet Union was good for Medvedev's career path, he lamented the decline of Russian hockey. In May 2007 he angrily watched the national team fall short again in the World Championships, this time with a third-place finish in Moscow. After the tournament, he was summoned to the Kremlin. Putin also wanted hockey championships, not bronze medals.

Medvedev was joined by two greats of Soviet hockey: former goalie Vladislav Tretiak, who now led the Russian Hockey Federation, and Slava Fetisov, head of the Sports Committee. Putin posed the question to his guests: how could Russian hockey get back on top? Tretiak proposed a return to the old Soviet-style league, under the federation's control, to prepare players for the national team. Medvedev and Fetisov had a different plan: a new, North American–style league, with franchises rather than clubs. Franchises would be owned by major corporations, which would invest money in salaries and arenas. With more money and better facilities, Russian players would stay in Russia, rather than leaving to the NHL or Europe. This would allow more opportunities for the national team to train together. By funding the new hockey league, Russia's national champions would bring championships back to the nation.

Putin liked the idea. In fact, he later took credit for the whole scheme, just as he did with Abramovich's purchase of Chelsea. "I was the initiator; I came up with it," the president told a Moscow newspaper. "It seemed to me that after the confrontation—in the good sense of the word—between North American and Soviet hockey, a lot was lost in hockey. The sharpness disappeared. It seemed to me that if it was possible to recreate this struggle between European and North American hockey on a new basis, in the current condition, it would be very interesting. It would breathe new life into the sport."

Putin's Kontinental Hockey League launched in 2008, with Medvedev as the first president. Gazprom was a key sponsor, along with eight other Russian companies. The KHL imported many features of a North American league. There was a draft of amateur players and a mid-season all-star game. The league's 24 teams were organized into divisions, with the top teams in each division competing in playoffs at the season's end.

Before the inaugural season, the league built buzz by luring players from the NHL. Alexander Radulov, a promising young Russian, left Nashville for Ufa, in the Ural Mountains. Canadian goalie Ray Emery, who had led the Ottawa Senators to the Stanley Cup Finals, signed with Atlant Moscow for $2 million.

The splashiest signing was one of hockey's biggest stars, Jaromír Jágr. The high-scoring Czech forward, a former MVP and two-time Stanley Cup champion, joined Avangard Omsk for $5 million over three years. Fans packed the airport in the Siberian city when Jágr arrived. His move to the KHL was compared to David Beckham's jump to Major League Soccer the year before. "It's hard to imagine better advertising for our league," announced *Sovietsky Sport*.

With Jágr on the ice, a Gazprom executive as boss, and the Russian president claiming to be its founder, the Kontinental Hockey League had some momentum coming over the boards. But it also faced stiff challenges. Top of the list, of course, was preparing the national squad. To ensure this North American-style league was strengthening the Russian team, Putin's government-imposed limits on the number of foreign players each team could sign. "We need victories!" declared Sergei Naryshkin, the president's chief of staff and chair of the KHL board.

There were also bigger aims than hockey wins. The name "Kontinental" was deliberate. From the start, Medvedev and Fetisov envisioned the league KHL reuniting the old Soviet empire as a new sports empire. Putin had even bigger aims: "I would like to see the KHL become a European league," he told an interviewer, "to expand its borders at the expense of the Czech Republic, Slovakia, and Switzerland, and become a full-fledged European hockey league."

The KHL did expand into Europe, with franchises in Zagreb, Bratislava, and Prague. The additions were short lived, however. European teams couldn't keep up with the expense of playing in the Russian league. The exception was Helsinki Jokerit. One of the most storied clubs in Finnish hockey, Jokerit was owned by the colorful businessman Harry Harkimo, host of Finland's version of *The Apprentice.* Like another well-known host of *The Apprentice,* Harkimo wanted to run for political office, but he was in debt after building a new home for his hockey team, the 14,000-seat Hartwall Arena. So, in 2013 Harkimo cashed out. He sold both the arena and a 49% stake in the team to some of Putin's wealthiest friends, Gennady Timchenko and the brothers Arkady and Boris Rotenberg. Timchenko and Boris Rotenberg both held Finnish passports, and Harkimo stayed on as team CEO, giving the appearance of Finnish control. But the club was now in the hands of the oligarchs. To seal the turn, Jokerit jumped from the Finnish league to the KHL.

At first, the Russians' purchase of Jokerit stoked fan excitement. Like Abramovich at Chelsea and Alexey Miller with Zenit, the new owners put up a hefty dose of cash to sign players. Hartwall Arena was full during the team's first season in the KHL, which finished with a loss to CSKA Moscow in the conference semifinals.

But world events loomed larger than hockey. The Rotenberg brothers were put on the international sanctions list following Russia's incursion into eastern Ukraine in 2014. Timchenko and Harkimo shuffled the ownership shares, roping former Jokerit and NHL star Jari Kurri into the mix—all in the hope of hiding the Russian co-owner in the shadows. Helsinki hockey writers saw through the ruse and became more critical of the club's ties to Putin.

The turning point came at the start of the 2020 season. That summer, Putin ally Alexander Lukashenko claimed victory in the Belarusian presidential elections, giving him a sixth term in office. Lukashenko then ordered a violent crackdown on protestors in Minsk who opposed the rigged results. As police in black body armor fired rubber bullets into crowds and hauled people to jail,

Jokerit prepared to open the season in the Belarusian capital. Kurri said the match would go ahead.

Jokerit fans and the Helsinki press raised a storm. Fans threatened to boycott their own team's home games if Jokerit played in Minsk. Kurri and his team were caught between their Finnish supporters and league officials tied to the Kremlin. On the day of the game, the team's plane was ready to make the flight from Helsinki to Minsk. Jokerit didn't show up. Putin had wanted his league to give Russia a foothold in the European Union. The standoff in Helsinki showed that European fans would be noisy about human rights as well as hockey.

Four thousand miles away, at the far end of the Kontinental Hockey League, things were in better order. In 2014 President Putin made a visit to Vladivostok, the port city of 600,000 people on Russia's Pacific coast. The regional governor he had appointed two years earlier, 46-year-old Vladimir Miklushevsky, was making a name for himself as an energetic and popular administrator.

Miklushevsky gave the president a glowing report of recent developments in Vladivostok and the Russian Far East. There was economic growth, infrastructure projects, expanded opportunities for early-childhood education. A new maternity clinic had opened; salaries were increasing; fishing was strong. And there was another important development, one worthy of adding in a report to the president. The handsome young governor leaned over the conference table.

"You know that we created the Admiral hockey team last year," Miklushevsky said.

The governor touted the Admirals' success in their first season. More importantly, the team was drawing fans. "We have the most crowded arena in the KHL—99 percent capacity," Miklushevsky reported. "You can't buy a ticket. We are even thinking of putting in additional stands.

"Of course, the team is not an end in itself," the governor clarified. "The team is an example for many boys, girls even, because even girls in our country also play hockey."

"All of this is correct," Putin said. "I definitely support it. Hockey is one of the most popular sports in our country."

Miklushevsky's report showed the KHL's importance in Putin's Russia. It was indeed the president's league—a means of extending influence into neighboring countries as well as solidifying the regime's control across Russia. When Putin came to office, he deplored the fragmentation of Russia in the 1990s. An essential part of his program was unity. Politically, Russia had to be unified under strong, centralized leadership. Economically, the state-owned companies had to attend to Russia's national interests. Culturally, the people of Russia had to be bound together by a shared national idea. In telling Miklushevsky that hockey was one of the country's most popular sports, Putin wasn't simply talking about entertainment or recreation. The KHL established a common bond across the length of Russia. Unlike the top soccer or basketball leagues, made of teams based only in European Russia, the hockey league reached from Vladivostok in the East to Yaroslavl in the West.

The hockey league also connected present-day Russia to the Soviet past. The four divisions were named for legends of Soviet hockey: players Vsevolod Bobrov and Valeri Kharlamov, and coaches Anatoly Tarasov and Arkady Chernyshev. The championship trophy bore the name of one of the USSR's greatest heroes, cosmonaut Yuri Gagarin.

At the same time, the KHL looked like a North American league. In Vladivostok kids took photos with the Admirals' mascot, a cartoon walrus in a blue officer's uniform, complete with gold braids and epaulets. Cheerleaders shook poms-poms on the arena steps, dressed in short skirts and *telnyashki*, the blue-and-white striped T-shirts worn by Russian sailors. For pregame introductions, players skated through dry-ice fog and colored lights. Like most other cities in the KHL, Vladivostok built a multi-purpose entertainment complex for the team. The Admirals' new arena was named for Fetisov—not only because he was a hockey legend and not only because of his role in founding the league. Fetisov's name was in lights on the arena because of the new job he got from Putin, as Vladivostok's appointed delegate to the upper house of the Duma.

The KHL was flashy. It was not profitable. Like Putin's Russia, the league's fortunes rose and fell with oil and gas prices. In theory, the national champions were supposed to provide a solid financial foundation across the league; in practice, the league was divided among haves and have-nots. "The KHL is not a realistic business project," acknowledged the marketing manager of Metallurg Novokuznetsk. Although owned by the global steel manufacturer Evraz, whose principal shareholder was Roman Abramovich, Metallurg could not build a winner in the middle of Siberia. Deep in debt, the team moved to a lower league, one of ten franchises to drop out of the KHL for financial reasons.

Medvedev and Fetisov expected the KHL to challenge the National Hockey League. It never came close. In attendance and revenue, the KHL was far behind Europe's hockey leagues let alone the NHL. The Swiss and German leagues drew more fans, while each team in the Swedish league earned more from television rights than the entire KHL.

But that didn't matter. The KHL was not intended to be a commercial project, neither were Gazprom's sponsorships of European soccer. They were political projects. Like Moscow's Soviet leaders, Putin's government marshalled the country's resources to build the façade of an economically powerful state. With its ups and downs, the KHL was representative of Russia's path in the Putin years. There were the trappings of a global pro league: new arenas, colorful uniforms, dry-ice fog, and light shows. Yet foreign players in Russia still complained of poor facilities and unpaid salaries and crooked referees.

Russia's leagues still draw the world's athletes with generous contracts. Especially in women's sports like basketball and volleyball, Russian teams offer salaries far richer than athletes can earn in the US or Europe. This is what drew Phoenix Mercury star Brittney Griner to play for Yekaterinburg during the off-seasons from the WNBA. Yet when she was sentenced to nine years in a penal colony in 2022 for possessing less than a gram of prescribed hash oil, Griner learned that the riches Russia promises carry no protections. Europe's soccer clubs and associations made the same realization: Russia's loot is a treacherous trap.

CHAPTER 10

OLYMPIC DREAMS

ONE OF THE MOST REMARKABLE EVENTS in Vladimir Putin's first stint as president took place on July 4, 2007, at the Real Intercontinental Hotel in Guatemala City. Putin was in his second term as president, with approval ratings near 80%. Russia's economy had continued to rise, and the oligarchs had been tamed. The president traveled halfway around the world to gain confirmation of Russia's return to the ranks of great nations. He was attending the 119th session of the International Olympic Committee, putting his clout behind Sochi's pitch for the 2014 Winter Olympics. There was an expectation of something historic. Across Russia, viewers tuned in to the live broadcast of Sochi's presentation.

Politicians from Austria and South Korea were also at the meeting, representing bids from Salzburg and PyeongChang. But Putin took part in a way no one expected. When it was Sochi's turn, the president rose from his seat in the front row, between Irina Rodnina and Slava Fetisov. To everyone's surprise, he took the stage and spoke.

"Mr. President, members of the International Olympic Committee, distinguished guests, ladies and gentlemen: it is a great honor for me to address you today and to present the bid of Sochi to host the Olympic winter games in 2014."

Putin's speech highlighted the special landscape of Sochi, where visitors could enjoy a warm spring day on the Black Sea and then travel a short distance into snow-covered mountains. Russia was prepared to build first-class venues, he said, while paying attention to the environment and security. The venues would have lasting value by developing Russia's sports infrastructure. The $12-billion cost would be guaranteed by the government, Putin promised. He even mentioned the ancient Greeks, founders of the Olympic Games. According to local legend, Prometheus was chained to cliffs near Sochi. "It was Prometheus who gave people fire," Putin said, "fire [that] ultimately is the Olympic flame."

The speech was not great. What was remarkable was how the president spoke. This was a rare instance when Putin did not speak through an interpreter. He joked, he smiled, he invited the world in accented English. Russian athletes "have scored many victories and made many contributions to the Olympic movement," Putin said. "But we have not had the honor to celebrate the Winter Olympics."

He finished with a crescendo in French: "*The Olympic dream of millions of Russians awaits your decision.*"

A brilliant performance—one we cannot imagine today: Putin speaking in a language he doesn't command, going out of his way to impress an international audience.

It was 3:00 AM in Sochi when IOC members announced their decision. Crowded in the city center, over 20,000 people cheered and drank. A newspaper correspondent from Moscow overheard a conversation between two revelers.

"We beat everybody!" shouted one guy. "We ripped up the Americans!"

"The Koreans," his friend corrected.

"Them! And the Americans, too!"

"Maybe the Americans voted for us," the friend suggested.

"Now they will definitely realize we are a power," shouted reveler number one. "A superpower! We'll pound all of them."

In winning the bid, Russia had proved itself to the world. But now came the work. A resort city of more than 300,000 people, Sochi had little of the infrastructure needed for an Olympics, especially venues for winter sports. The host region needed hotels, athlete accommodations, ice arenas, bobsled runs. "In the mountains there were only goat trails," said Elena Anikina, chair of the Sochi bid committee. When the IOC evaluation committee visited, organizers hung banners around Sochi depicting what venues and facilities would look like after they were built. "It was practically a theater performance," Anikina acknowledged to a Russian reporter. "Now we can admit that."

IOC members were swayed by Russian promises to create something of Russian proportions. By contrast, the responsible bid from Salzburg, where infrastructure was already in place, didn't even make it past the first round. Rather than relying on the boring Austrians, the IOC was lured by the new Russia—and its charming president. "Putin's visit was decisive," said one Olympic committee member.

Putin was right to mention Greek mythology in his pitch. The 2014 Winter Olympics played out like a classical tragedy. Like the tales of the Greeks, hubris was the main character's driving motivation. The president said the IOC decision was an "an assessment of Russia, a recognition of its growing capabilities." But he was not satisfied with Russia simply being a trusted, welcoming nation. It also had to be a victorious nation, an unchallengeable power. Sochi was the summit of Putin's presidency. The world saw his Russia in all its grandeur and strength. But to attain those heights, he unleashed afflictions that still haunt Russia today.

Putin was the protagonist of this tragedy. Yet the drama of Sochi featured a large cast. To tell the story, let's call the principals to the stage and see how each played a part in this epic of ambition and corruption.

We begin with the straight man: Dmitry Chernyshenko, head of the Sochi organizing committee. When he still headed the Sports Committee, Slava Fetisov tapped the 39-year-old computer programmer and sports-media executive to lead the Olympic bid. Chernyshenko grew up in Sochi; he skied in the mountains above the city before there were resorts. Tall and good-looking, with a pleasant smile and calm manner, Chernyshenko worked on Russian media campaigns for 3M, Mars, and Proctor & Gamble. He spoke the language of Western execs and corporate PR—the ideal person to work with sponsors, media companies, and the IOC.

Chernyshenko did his job well. Looking at reports the Sochi committee sent to Olympic headquarters, one gets the impression of an efficient, well-managed operation, like an American or European non-profit. He visited London, Lausanne, and New York City. He spoke of economic development and future opportunities for sports and recreation. Chernyshenko gave the Sochi Games a gloss that dazzled the IOC and Western sponsors.

Most importantly, the Olympics would be an important step in Russia's continued process of democratization. According to Chernyshenko, the Olympics and Paralympics would introduce new ideas about volunteerism, care for the disabled, and recycling. Russians would become more attentive to global issues like diversity and sustainability. "The main thing is to leave a legacy," Chernyshenko said in a 2011 interview. This word—"legacy"—was a mantra for the IOC. Even before the Games began, Chernyshenko assured Olympic bosses that Sochi's positive legacy was evident.

Chernyshenko also reported that preparations were ahead of schedule and on budget. Architects and engineers from around the world contributed their expertise. Western firms recruited the workers needed to build hotels, highways, rails lines, and arenas.

"What will the total cost be for the Games?" asked a *New York Times* writer in a 2012 interview with Chernyshenko.

"It is important to understand that there are two, clearly outlined budgets to consider," he answered. On the one hand, Chernyshenko explained, there was the budget for staging the Olympics and Paralympics. This sum, $1.8 billion, is what he was responsible for. Then there was the budget for facilities and infrastructure. These expenses would total $5.9 billion, with half funded by the state and half by private investors.

"However, you should keep in mind," Chernyshenko added, "these budgets do not include the programs on renovation of the region that are not directly linked to the Games."

Let's take note of Chernyshenko's "however." This word provided a good amount of budgetary wiggle room—enough to fit tens of billions of dollars and the offshore accounts of Putin's good friends. To meet some of those friends and find out how they cashed in on the Olympics, we call to the stage the oligarchs we met in Finland: Arkady and Boris Rotenberg.

The Rotenbergs were not run-of-the-mill oligarchs with an interest in hockey; they were as close to Putin as anyone in Russia. The brothers had known Putin since they were kids at the martial arts club in Leningrad. Boris Rotenberg went to Helsinki in the 1990s, using his wife's connections to get into oil trading. His older brother was briefly in Finland as well but soon returned to St. Petersburg. Back in his home city, Arkady opened a professional judo club with start-up money from another Russian oil trader in Helsinki, Gennady Timchenko. Arkady's club did well. Judokas won multiple European titles and Olympic medals. The club also built a housing complex and yacht club. Judo was big business in St. Petersburg.

Arkady Rotenberg moved into bigger business, thanks to his ties with Putin. "Knowing high-level government officials has never been an impediment to business in our country," he admitted in an interview with *Kommersant*, "but it is hardly a guarantee of success." In fact, Putin got Rotenberg into a business that was assured of success: alcohol. In 2000 the new president signed a directive combining multiple distilleries into a state-owned company, Rosspirtprom. Putin then appointed his friend head of this new national champion of vodka.

Along with brother Boris, Arkady Rotenberg jumped from vodka to banking. The Rotenbergs then got into building pipelines. In 2008 their company bought a set of Gazprom subsidiaries for $348 million. The following year Gazprom awarded them no-bid contracts to build sections of the Nord Stream pipeline. Revenue jumped to $2 billion. "Everything is fair," Arkady assured. "There is nothing criminal here, believe me."

No-bid contracts were the norm for Sochi, with the Rotenbergs taking full advantage. The brothers' various companies, most registered in Cyprus, had contracts for 21 different projects. They built the Sochi airport, a gas pipeline, highways, a thermal power plant, port facilities, the media center, and the Formula One racetrack that would host the Russian Grand Prix. In total their companies were paid $7.7 billion, either directly from the government or through Gazprom contracts.

Rotenberg companies received more for Sochi projects than the entire cost of the 2010 Vancouver Olympics. And the payouts were far above what was budgeted. The pipeline was nearly four times more expensive than what was initially planned. The power station cost two and a half times more than it would have cost in Europe. Cost overruns certainly didn't hurt the brothers.

In 2009 they jumped more than 300 places on *Forbes* list of richest Russians.

If this tragedy had a prophet, it was Boris Nemtsov: physicist, journalist, dissident.

Nemtsov first became involved in politics after the Chernobyl nuclear disaster in 1986, when he was a 26-year-old researcher. He was an active critic of the Soviet regime, and then ran for office in the early 1990s, serving as governor of central Russia's Nizhny Novgorod region. Nemtsov was a born leader—handsome, smart, energetic, eloquent. Boris Yeltsin tapped him to be deputy prime minister, and he was rumored to be the president's chosen successor. As we know, that didn't happen.

Nemtsov led the opposition against the man who elbowed him out for Russia's top job. He criticized Putin for suppressing civil rights and democracy. Nemtsov also posted detailed reports on Putin's corrupt links with Gazprom and the webs of influence that enriched his friends. He even dared expose the palaces and yachts Putin enjoyed. "Putinism and corruption are the same thing," Nemtsov said. The president's $75,000 gold-plated toilet was proof.

Of all his investigations into Putin's graft, Nemtsov's 2013 report on Sochi made the biggest splash. Along with co-author Leonid Martynyuk, Nemtsov mapped the no-bid contracts and ownership schemes playing out behind the infrastructure projects. Backed up by a lengthy Excel file showing cost overruns, the report revealed the Sochi games to be the most expensive in Olympic history. A year before the torch was lit, the pricetag was already $50 billion, with an estimated $20–$30 billion lost in corruption.

"They are criminals," Nemtsov declared in an interview with Russian media after the report dropped. He pointed out one project in particular: the 30-mile highway connecting Sochi's Black Sea coast to the mountain ski venues. Planners decided to build a four-lane highway with a railway alongside, running through the rocky gorge of the Mzymta River. The contract went to Russian Railways; in essence, state funding for the project, budgeted at $3 billion, went to a state-owned company. But along the way, others got involved. Russian Railways subcontracted with various construction companies, some having little experience with actual construction. This was the case with SK Most, a company in Gennady Timchenko's portfolio of assets.

The route to the mountains required intensive engineering: over three dozen bridges and nine tunnels. Construction devastated vegetation in the gorge, making the river susceptible to flash floods. One winter flood washed cranes and equipment downstream. Two years later, another flood flushed construction waste from the tunnels. An 18-mile stretch of the river was bottled with toxic sludge.

Washed-out tunnels and bridges added to the cost. But Nemtsov charged that the biggest drain on the budget was the man running the operation, Russian Railways head Vladimir Yakunin. Another of the president's St. Petersburg buddies, Yakunin had a *dacha* in the lake development launched by Putin and Sergei Fursenko in the 1990s. Yakunin also bought a plot of land in an upscale village outside Moscow not long after Russian Railways got the Sochi contract. The house he built featured a 1,400-square-meter sauna, a garage big enough for 15 cars, and a 50-meter swimming pool. Yakunin's published income at the time was $1.5 million per year; the house was valued at $75 million. In fairness, Yakunin didn't own the property himself. It was registered to shell companies in Cyprus and Panama.

As Yakunin's palatial crib was going up outside of Moscow, the cost of the highway outside Sochi was also climbing. When the route finally opened, the final bill was more than $9 billion. As Nemtsov and Martynyuk noted in their report, Russians got a 30-mile highway to a ski resort at a cost more than three times what NASA spent to send a rover to Mars.

Nemtsov's report stung. Yakunin filed a lawsuit. Putin launched an anti-corruption probe. A few low-level officials were nabbed as scapegoats. The most damaging effect was that Russians lost confidence in the government's handling of the Games. A survey conducted one month after Nemtsov's report found that more than 65 percent of Russians believed public funds were not being used effectively. Nineteen percent of people believed funds were stolen. Pollsters acknowledged that attitudes might improve when the games opened. Yet, they added, this would all depend on the Russian team's performance.

February 7, 2014. The stadium went dark. Athletes from 88 countries were in their seats, along with 40,000 spectators. Over 45 million people across Russia were watching on television, together with hundreds of millions more around the world. The opening ceremony was about to begin: a pageant of music and dance, theater and visuals. There was an expectation of something vast, something worthy of Russia.

High above the stadium, Konstantin Ernst was ready for the show. The head of Russia's Channel One TV network had been planning for years. He even had veto power over the stadium design. The British architectural firm Populous had originally designed an open stadium, since a roof wasn't necessary in Sochi's subtropical climate. But a roof was necessary for Ernst's opening ceremony. The top went up, bumping the cost to $780 million. Four years later, the roof was removed for the World Cup.

With his long dark hair, large frame, and open shirt collar, Ernst resembled an imposing film producer—the look he was going for. Ever since he was young, the son of a prominent physicist, he had loved movies. During the perestroika years, when he was in his 20s, Ernst went to work for Soviet television. By 1996, he was CEO of Boris Berezovsky's ORT network.

Ernst kept his job after Putin stripped ORT from Berezovsky and turned it into the state-owned Channel One. The film buff-turned-broadcasting executive became the president's "unofficial minister of propaganda," in the words of *New Yorker* writer Julia Ioffe. Like Russia's other networks, Channel One cast Putin as the country's unquestionable leader, but without the clunky excesses of other broadcasters. Ernst followed the Putin line: the Russian people were heroic, and the strong Russian state was necessary. But he presented the message with the creative touch of a skilled filmmaker. Indeed, the network's original series and documentaries were praised for their quality. Entrusting the opening ceremony to Ernst was a masterstroke, much like London organizers turning to Oscar-winner Danny Boyle to helm their opening ceremony.

Keep in mind how important the opening ceremony is for the Olympics. What most people remember of London 2012, for example, is Mr. Bean performing the theme to *Chariots of Fire* and James Bond jumping from a helicopter with the Queen. Ernst's productions did not feature Bean or Bond. Something like that required self-deprecating humor—a value not commonly associated with the Russian people.

Ernst went for spectacle rather than spoof. Three horses of light galloped above the ground, from one end of the stadium to another—a reference to 19th-century writer Nikolay Gogol. A young girl wandered through a colorful landscape of onion domes and matryoshka dolls. A troop of naval cadets marched across the 18th-century map of St. Petersburg, the imperial capital founded by Peter the Great. Decades of Soviet rule were symbolized by red locomotives, machine gears, and rocket ships. The night was capped by Vladislav Tretiak and Irina Rodnina lighting the cauldron, accompanied by Tchaikovsky's *Nutcracker.*

Ioffe described Ernst's reaction: "As the show concluded and chants of 'Ro-ssi-ya!' echoed through the stadium, Ernst leaped from his chair in the command center. 'We've done it!' he yelled."

Ernst had delivered a brilliant display of great Russia. "They were a grandiose, bombastic celebration," political scientist Nina Kramareva told me. "For many Russians, it was just what they needed after so many years of internal troubles and being disrespected by the West."

The games were underway. Now Russia had to win.

Enter Dr. Grigory Rodchenkov, the chatty, curly-headed, bespectacled chemist who ran Russia's national anti-doping laboratory. "It's impossible to overstate what the Sochi Winter Olympics meant to Russians and to the regime of Vladimir Putin," Rodchenkov wrote in his memoirs. "The games were a glittering jewel in Putin's crown."

For this jewel to truly shine, Rodchenkov understood, Russian athletes needed to win. This was a tall order. Four years earlier at the Vancouver Winter Games, Russia managed only three gold medals. The operation Rodchenkov designed would change that. His cocktail of steroids would give Russian athletes the boost they needed to win, and his lab would ensure everyone tested clean.

The FSB provided a much-needed assist. A year before the games, the security agency's engineers figured out how to open the bottles athletes used to submit their urine samples. Each athlete submitted samples in two bottles: bottle A, which was tested immediately, and bottle B, which was saved for later testing, if needed. The bottles' Swiss manufacturer claimed the lids were impregnable. After months of tinkering, the FSB broke the lock. Thanks to these "magicians," as Rodchenkov called them, a doped athlete's sample could be opened, the dirty urine replaced with clean urine, and the caps resealed—all without detection.

As both a scientist and former distance runner, Rodchenkov had no aversion to doping. When you watch him devise a doping program for amateur cyclist Bryan Fogel in the documentary *Icarus,* you see the chemist's geeky enthusiasm for pharmaceuticals. Like Soviet researchers in the 1960s who first experimented with steroids, Rodchenkov saw drugs as a technology that could safely help athletes.

"Steroids reduce fatigue and trauma, and can help muscles recover more quickly," he wrote in his memoirs. "I am not aware of any studies concluding that these substances are harmful in moderate dosages."

Rodchenkov prepared a moderate doping strategy for the Sochi Games. His bosses in the Sports Ministry wanted to dope everybody on the Russian team, but he was specific about which athletes would benefit most from the drugs. He identified 36 older athletes who needed a fast-acting, low dose of steroids to help with recovery. These athletes would receive his cocktail of three types of steroids dissolved in vermouth. Athletes swirled the mixture in their mouths, getting the drugs' boost while avoiding the most detectable metabolites.

The other reason Rodchenkov resisted his bosses' push to dose more athletes because his lab couldn't launder that much tainted urine. At the end of each day's competition, hundreds of sample bottles were delivered to the lab in Sochi for testing. Rodchenkov ensured that the lab was outfitted with the most advanced equipment of any anti-doping facility in the world. But its most important feature was the hole drilled by his assistant, covered by a plastic wall plate and hidden behind a filing cabinet. Any Russian athlete who had taken Rodchenkov's cocktail had their samples removed from the rest of the delivery. Bottles A and B were passed through the hole to Evgeny Blokhin, stationed on the other side of the wall in a room without security cameras—and away from the prying eyes of the World Anti-Doping Agency.

Blokhin was an FSB agent. For this operation, he dressed like a plumber so he could move in and out of the lab without notice. Each night, he brought sample bottles with dirty urine to the nearby FSB station, where the "magicians" opened the supposedly unbreakable seals. The FSB station was stocked with four freezers of clean urine, stored in jam jars and soda bottles, with each athlete's name written on the label. The dirty urine was thrown out, clean urine poured in. The magicians resealed the bottles, and Blokhin the plumber brought them back to the lab building. The bottles went through the hole, Rodchenkov's team tested the samples, and the athletes were recorded as clean in the WADA database.

At first, the elaborate process had some bumps. On the second night of the games, Blokhin's crew had trouble with the caps, with some taking up to an hour to crack open. Rodchenkov and his assistants waited in the lab, sucking down cigarettes and coffee as they watched the clock. In his plumber disguise, Blokhin raced back and forth in the dark with each resealed bottle.

The scheme also didn't yield much at first: Russia won only two gold medals in the first week. Yet the second week brought better results. Rodchenkov pointed to Alexander Tretiakov in skeleton, Alexander Legkov in cross-country skiing, and Alexander Zubkov in bobsled as beneficiaries of his doping plan. All three were older athletes who shaved a few hundredths of a second off their times to win gold. "So, yes," the chemist boasted, "the cocktail made a significant difference to Russia's medal count."

Russia's final count was 13 gold medals, tying the record for most gold medals at the Winter Olympics, set by the Soviet Union at Innsbruck in 1976. Rodchenkov's lab also finished with a perfect score: eight athletes were nabbed for doping but not one Russian.

For the closing ceremony on February 23, Konstantin Ernst created another masterpiece. The show paid homage to

Tchaikovsky, Tolstoy, Rachmaninoff, and other greats of Russian culture. Dancers from the Bolshoi and Mariinsky ballet companies performed. One thousand children from across Russia sang the farewell. To bring the Games to a close, a 26-foot-tall animatronic polar bear blew out the cauldron with frosty breath—then shed a glistening tear. Putin applauded as his Olympics came to an end.

Is it better for a ruler to be loved or feared? Is it better to be leader of a welcoming land or a formidable power?

The Sochi Winter Games brought Russia plenty of love. A record 2.5 billion people watched the Olympics on TV and streaming video. Konstantin Ernst's opening and closing ceremonies were breathtaking celebrations of Russian culture. Reviews from foreign journalists and visitors were overwhelmingly positive. "The Games ran smoother than any of the nine Olympics I have covered," wrote Bill Plaschke in the *Los Angeles Times*. Sochi, declared Dmitry Chernyshenko, "showed the new face of Russia to the world."

Even Putin's critics in Russia acknowledged the Olympics' success. "Putin's fairy tale, which many did not believe in, has become a reality," wrote journalist Georgy Bovt after the closing ceremony. The Sochi Games "showed the world we are not Mordor."

Nevertheless, Putin chose the path of fear. Just hours before the closing ceremony, he gave the order to his Orcs to seize the Ukrainian region of Crimea. For the previous three months, Ukraine's capital was engulfed by mass demonstrations against President Viktor Yanukovych, a Putin ally. Under pressure from Moscow, Yanukovych had decided to pull the country away from the European Union into closer ties with Russia. Tensions in Kyiv reached the breaking point as the Winter Games were underway. Police killed 99 people and injured over 1,000, yet demonstrators held the square. Faced with unbreakable resistance, the government gave in. Police left Kyiv to the protestors, Yanukovych fled the capital, and parliament stripped his power.

The situation in Kyiv gave Putin the pretext to seize Crimea. The Games in Sochi gave him cover.

Why did he do this? Why waste all the positive energy Sochi generated to seize a neighbor's territory? According to Nina Kramareva, Sochi and Crimea were not contradictory to Russia's president.

"Putin wanted to put Russia's best foot forward," she told me. "He had no problem whatsoever that this foot was wearing a military boot."

On the evening I talked to Kramareva, the power in her Kyiv neighborhood had been knocked out by another Russian missile strike. From a friend's apartment, she told me about Sochi and Russian politics, about Putin's plans and the views of officials she interviewed. As she explained, the 2014 Winter Olympics were less about wooing the world and more about building national pride. The transformation of Sochi, the opening and closing ceremonies, the victorious medal count—all of this was intended to show Russians that Russia was wealthy, cultured, advanced, and, above all, strong.

When played for a domestic audience, the invasion of Crimea was not a break from the good vibes of the Games. Together, the Olympics and the military action were the culmination of Russia's post-Soviet resurrection. Russia was able to host the world, stage a top-class spectacle, win the most medals, *and* carry out a seamless military operation to take back its own land. Both the Sochi Games and the Crimea operation showed that Russia was unquestionably a great nation, a triumphant nation, a feared nation. The 1990s were over, once and for all. No one was telling Russia what to do.

CHAPTER 11

THE MASTER SPORTSWASHER

SITTING NEXT TO PUTIN at the Sochi closing ceremony, with an equally satisfied smile, was Thomas Bach, president of the International Olympic Committee. Sixty years old at the time, the gold medal–winning fencer for West Germany was elected just six months earlier. The first congratulatory call he received came from the Kremlin.

A few weeks after the IOC election, Bach and Putin met in Sochi, where they opened the new train station linking hotels on the coast with the mountain venues. Built by the Rotenbergs' construction company, the station had already flooded twice. But there was only glowing praise from the IOC president. The new structures were "magnificent," Bach proclaimed.

This first visit to Russia was not free of difficulties, however. Bach had to ask Putin a pointed question. Four months earlier, in June 2013, the Russian parliament passed a law banning distribution of "propaganda of non-traditional sexual relationships." Human rights organizations condemned the discriminatory law, and there were fears that LGBT athletes and spectators would experience hostility in Sochi. Bach raised these concerns to Putin, who had signed the law. Apparently, the president's reply settled concerns. Bach announced that the Sochi Winter Games would be free from all discrimination. "This is a principal pillar of the Olympic Movement and the IOC that will be upheld," Bach declared while standing alongside Putin.

As we've seen, Thomas Bach's predecessors were perfectly willing to adjust Olympic pillars for Moscow's liking. Avery Brundage was adamant about the pillar of amateurism, except for Soviet athletes. In 2014 the IOC no longer stood for amateur sport. Instead, its guiding principle was that sport expressed universal values—inclusion, diversity, acceptance. People around the world were inspired by sport; therefore, sport could have no barriers.

These values were rooted in the Western traditions of democracy and human rights. By contrast, Putin's Russia was moving in a decidedly anti-democratic, repressive direction. How would the IOC continue to sing the chorus of tolerance while the Kremlin was persecuting Russia's LGBT community—not to mention killing journalists and jailing pro-democracy demonstrators?

For Putin, it was never a problem. Russia's involvement in world sports allowed Moscow to wear a cloak of international legitimacy and even voice support of equality and openness. When critics outside Russia objected, when they pointed to wars and censorship and discrimination, the Kremlin charged them with mixing sport and politics. Having the backing of people like Thomas Bach only confirmed this defense. The sportocrats in Switzerland were nobly apolitical; they served the highest ideals of humanity. If they supported Moscow, how could Moscow be wrong?

As the Sochi Games came to an end, Bach had every reason to smile about his partnership with Vladimir Putin. The number of worldwide television broadcasters increased since the 2010 Vancouver Olympics. Digital coverage of the Games grew exponentially.

When it came to TV and digital media, the IOC's most important market was the United States—not because it had the most viewers, but because it brought in the most money. NBC paid $775 million to carry the Sochi Games. This stack of cash was essential for the Olympic movement as a whole. Roughly a quarter of the IOC's entire budget came from NBC.

The Olympics were likewise important for NBC. Both the Winter and Summer Olympics brought truckloads of advertising dollars. Ad sales for the Games were especially valuable because, unlike other sports, more women than men watched the Olympics. The larger female audience allowed for a wider range of sponsors, rather than only beer and car companies.

Initial ratings for NBC's coverage of the Sochi Games were promising: 31.7 million Americans watched Friday night's opening ceremony, and an average of 27.7 million viewers tuned in during the first weekend of competition. Over the whole two weeks of the Olympics, NBC averaged 17.2 million viewers per night. Among the major networks, CBS was far behind in second place, with an average of 9.6 million viewers per night.

The partnership between the IOC and NBC was a win-win. Even though he was new to the job, Thomas Bach understood there was no more important corporate partner for the success of the Olympics than the American media company. So when he sat down at a Sochi restaurant with Brian Roberts, the CEO of Comcast, NBC's parent company, Bach was ready to make a deal. There would be no bidding wars for US broadcasting rights, as there had been in the past. For the right price, the IOC would extend the current contract beyond the 2020 games in Tokyo.

The European sportocrat and the American executive agreed to terms. The Peacock network would broadcast the Olympics through 2032. For each round of the Summer and Winter Games, the IOC would receive a billion dollars, for a total of $7.5 billion.

Bach had this agreement in his pocket when he sat down next to Putin in the Sochi stadium. As he watched the end of the 2014 Games, the IOC's new boss could be satisfied that the Olympics were secure for years to come.

With the haul of American television money, Olympic sportocrats could afford to be generous. A year after the Sochi Olympics, the IOC announced it was returning its share of the Winter Games' $50-million operating surplus to the Russians.

Wait a minute! The most expensive games in Olympic history ended up turning a profit? How could that be?

The shell game worked much like Dmitry Chernyshenko had explained to the *New York Times*: The cost of actually staging the Sochi Games was roughly $2 billion. Costs for building venues and infrastructure were kept separate from this operational budget, even though the Games required the new construction. Indeed IOC demands made specific infrastructure necessary, such as highway lanes open only to Olympic officials. Yet organizers in Russia and sportocrats in Switzerland didn't count these expenses in their official calculations, allowing them to boast that Sochi's books were in the black.

"Financial indicators show that these were the most successful Games compared to previous editions," said Chernyshenko.

"All recent editions of the Games have either made an operational profit or broken even," added an IOC spokesman when announcing the Sochi surplus.

The IOC and Sochi organizers could talk all they want about surpluses. The number that stood out was $51 billion. The sum first unveiled in Boris Nemtsov's report was forever draped around Sochi's neck like an enormously expensive albatross. The bird also had a bad stench, stinky enough to scare away potential hosts for future Olympics.

Eight months before the Sochi games, the IOC opened bidding for the 2022 Winter Olympics. Six cities submitted bids. But over the next year, before IOC evaluators made their site visits, four cities dropped out of the running. Stockholm withdrew its bid in January 2014, with politicians citing the lack of support for using public funds. Kraków dropped out after a May referendum; 70 percent of voters rejected the use of public funds for the games. A month later, the west Ukrainian city of L'viv ended its bid, due to Russia's invasion of eastern Ukraine's Donbas region.

Three cities remained: Oslo, Beijing, and Almaty, Kazakhstan. The favorite was clearly Oslo. Winter sports were wildly popular in Norway, and the country's capital already had the infrastructure to stage the Games. Plus, the 2018 Winter Games were slated for PyeongChang, South Korea, so it was Europe's turn on the Olympic merry-go-round.

Yet Norwegians were spooked by Sochi. In their commentaries, critics pointed to the high costs of the 2014 Games as one more example of Olympic overruns. All Summer and Winter Games had run huge deficits, so excess costs of $51 billion were not an aberration. Sochi was a warning of where the Olympics were headed.

The final nail for the Oslo bid were revelations about the perks IOC officials demanded: preferred treatment at hotels, complete control of public ad space, and a reception hosted by the royal family, with the King and Queen picking up the tab. Critics in Norway fumed that Olympic sportocrats had started to behave like the authoritarian satraps they were accustomed to hanging out with. "The Olympics are still a beautiful event," wrote one Norwegian commentator, "but those who own them have become rotten to their core."

After Oslo dropped its bid, only two candidates remained for 2022: Almaty and Beijing. Faced with the choice of two authoritarian regimes, IOC members cast their votes for the regime they already knew. The Sochi Games proved that you didn't need to put the Winter Olympics in a wintry city; you just needed mountains and snow a reasonable distance away, which Beijing offered. Putin's government had built highways and railroads to link the host city to mountain venues. Xi Jinping's government would surely do the same.

Beijing was the IOC's choice, but the Olympic bosses were backed into a corner. In wealthy, democratic countries, voters and politicians were unwilling to pay the cost of the Olympics. It appeared the only places where the Games would find a home in the future were countries like Russia and China, where regimes could brush aside criticism and do whatever was necessary to put on a good show. For some sportocrats, this was just fine. "Dictatorships can hold such events with ease," said Gian Franco Kasper, head of the International Ski Union, to a Swiss interviewer. "They don't have to ask the people."

Negative response to Kasper's comments showed that doing business with dictators wasn't the best PR move for sports federations. The IOC couldn't write off the world's democracies and rely only on the likes of Putin and Xi. The Olympics were broken, in large part due to Putin's games. Bach and the Olympic bosses had to fix them.

In 2019 Olympic officials announced a slate of reforms for future host candidates. No longer would host cities be expected to build new venues and infrastructure to accommodate the Games, as had been done in Russia in 2014 and Brazil in 2016. Instead the IOC stated its preference for existing venues or temporary structures. And hosts were no longer required to be cities. A region or even an entire country could bid for the Games, allowing for pooled resources.

IOC officials tried to cover up Sochi's high price and sneered at candidates that backed out of the bidding for 2022. Ultimately, however, Putin's $51-billion Olympics led to changes in how the Games were planned, proposed, and selected. The result is that future Winter Olympics in the French Alps and Utah will use existing or temporary venues.

To his credit Thomas Bach understood the IOC needed to change. Sepp Blatter was another matter. At the time Olympic officials in Lausanne were wrestling with the effects of Sochi, FIFA leaders down the road in Zurich were mired in scandal.

The governing body of world soccer had been under scrutiny since December 2010, when Blatter, the organization's president, announced Russia would host the World Cup in 2018 and Qatar would be the tournament's site in 2022. FIFA's choice of Qatar was widely criticized. The tiny Persian Gulf state had no football tradition and little infrastructure. Plus, it was on the edge of the Arabian desert, where temperatures in the summer could reach 120 degrees.

Unwilling to back out of the mess it made, FIFA moved the tournament to November and December, throwing league schedules around the world into disarray. Blatter turned a blind eye to reports that migrant workers building venues in Qatar were being persistently mistreated, and he rejected charges that the Qataris had bought votes for their bid.

FIFA's choice of Russia was also suspect. Many saw England as the front-runner for 2018, with Spain and Portugal's joint bid right behind. But the English were knocked out in the first round of voting. Some would say this was FIFA payback for a *Sunday Times* report that the Russians were buying votes. Russia's win looked to confirm the accusation. "How did Russia end up winning the bid for the 2018 World Cup?" said Prime Minister David Cameron. "I will let you fill in the blanks on that one."

Across the Atlantic in the FBI's Lower Manhattan office, investigators were at work filling in the blanks. Before FIFA's World

Cup decisions were announced, agents in the Eurasian organized crime unit were looking into allegations of Russian vote-buying. The unit's chief, a longtime anti-mob investigator named David Gaeta, suspected the Russian mafia of having its hands in world soccer. Gaeta made a visit to London, where he met someone with well-placed contacts in Moscow, former British intelligence agent Christopher Steele. From his Russian sources, Steele was alert to the vote-buying scheme. The retired spy passed the tips to Gaeta.

Rumors of a Russian fix sparked an FBI investigation into FIFA. Gaeta entrusted the case to a young agent in the unit, Jared Randall, whose career as a high school soccer player established him as the office's resident expert on the sport. IRS agent Steve Berryman, a fellow soccer fan, added his experience in money laundering. But Randall and Berryman didn't go after the Russians; instead, their investigation steered toward Chuck Blazer, the sole American on FIFA's executive board. Randall and Berryman found that Blazer had embezzled upwards of $20 million from CONCACAF, the soccer federation governing North America and the Caribbean. When the agents paid him a visit in November 2011, Blazer flipped immediately.

With Blazer's cooperation, Gaeta's team was able to build their case. Fixed with a wire, Blazer met FIFA colleagues at the 2012 London Olympics. The recorded conversations provided the basis for the first set of 14 indictments against FIFA officials. On May 27, 2015, Swiss police and US agents arrested the seven indicted officials in Zurich and seized computers and documents at FIFA headquarters.

The raid was perfectly timed. The world's soccer bigwigs were in Zurich for the FIFA congress, where Blatter would be on the ballot for his fifth consecutive term. Police ruined the festivities, making their arrests at the delegates' hotel, the five-star Baur au Lac.

When reporters descended on the hotel, they were especially eager for Russian reaction. Rumors circulated among the press that the head of the country's delegation, FIFA executive committee member Vitaly Mutko, would be called in for questioning.

"World Cup in Russia is no problem," said the smiling Mutko as he moved through the gauntlet of microphones. "Is very good temp, is open new stadium, is no problem."

"What about the criminality?" asked a reporter.

"Is no criminality, no criminality in Russia," Mutko replied. "In Russia, bidding is open, is no problem."

"Have you been questioned?" asked another reporter.

Mutko shook his head. He didn't understand the question, but he gave an answer anyway—with a smile.

"In Russia, is small money."

That was the extent of Mutko's comments in English. He had more to say a few days later on Russian television. "In geopolitical terms, the target is certainly Russia," Mutko said of the FIFA raid. Russia supported FIFA and Blatter, so the US targeted FIFA and Blatter. Moreover, the Americans were denied the 2022 World Cup in favor of Qatar; now they wanted revenge.

"These are links in the same chain, failure after failure," Mutko said. "And they can't find the reason why they are rejected, why African and Asian countries don't vote for them."

Fifty-six years old at the time, his black, combed-back hair threaded with gray, Vitaly Mutko had risen steadily in Russian sports. He was president of Zenit before the Gazprom years, then head of Russia's top soccer league, then chief of the country's soccer federation, before being named in 2008 to a new post created just for him, Minister of Sport. When Mutko came in, Fetisov was out—his sports agency was absorbed into the new ministry. But Slava did not leave empty-handed. He got his new job representing distant Vladivostok, and he had offshore accounts in Cyprus plump with proceeds from the sports-betting business his office had run.

Word on the Moscow street was that Slava had the tendency to run off at the mouth. By contrast, Mutko had better credentials than those of the Olympic medalist and Stanley Cup–winner; he had worked in the St. Petersburg mayor's office in the '90s. Putin needed someone he could trust. By 2015 connections to world sports were crucial. The view from the Kremlin was that a hostile, US-led campaign had Russia backed into a corner. The Ukrainian protestors who forced out Viktor Yanukovych were neo-Nazis following orders from Washington and Brussels. Yanukovych's successor, Petro Poroshenko, was a tool of NATO and EU expansion. The intervention in Crimea was necessary to protect Russians. Likewise, Russia was forced to invade the Donbas region of eastern Ukraine in August 2014 to preserve its sovereignty.

According to Moscow, the Americans responded to these justified actions with illegal sanctions, coercing other countries to discriminate against Russian citizens. With economic, political, and military pressure, the US was trying to push its way into the former Soviet region. Washington believed that Moscow was wrong to insist on defending Russian interests in Russia's own part of the world.

"I hear this all the time," Putin said at a 2015 economic forum, "that Russia wants to be respected. Don't you? Who does not want to be respected? Who wants to be humiliated? It's a strange question. As if this is some exclusive right—'Russia demands respect.' Does anyone like to be neglected?"

Putin could pout all he wanted. The fact of the matter was that in the months after Sochi he asserted Russian power in the region—and his own power as president—in brutal fashion. Aside from the forced annexation of Crimea and the invasion of eastern

Ukraine, here is what else Russia did during that time in the name of earning respect:

- July 17, 2014: Malaysia Airlines Flight 17, en route from Amsterdam to Kuala Lumpur, was shot down over eastern Ukraine by a Russian-made BUK anti-aircraft missile. All 283 passengers and 15 crew members were killed.
- July 31, 2014: Journalist and human rights activist Timur Kuashev was abducted in the southern city of Nalchik. He was found dead the next day, with signs of poisoning. According to German, Dutch, and Russian investigative reports, the FSB's poison team was in Nalchik at the time of his death.
- February 27, 2015: While walking near the Kremlin with his girlfriend, Boris Nemtsov was shot four times in the back. Five Chechen men were convicted for taking 15 million rubles to kill Nemtsov, although investigators never found out who paid them. Security cameras at the site were all turned off at the time of the shooting.
- Spring 2015: Continuing the work he started with Nemtsov, opposition activist Alexey Navalny founded the Democratic Coalition to oppose Putin. Courts prevented the party from running candidates in elections.
- May 26, 2015: Another opposition leader, Vladimir Kara-Murza, was hospitalized for poisoning. Kara-Murza was in a coma for a week before reviving. Two years later, he survived another poisoning.
- Fall 2015: Russia carried out airstrikes in Syria in support of dictator Bashar al-Assad. Human rights organizations documented instances of Russian planes bombing schools and hospitals.

Moscow deflected any questions on these events. Ukrainians shot down the Malaysian airliner, claimed the Kremlin. Chechens killed Nemtsov. There was no proof of Russian strikes on Syrian hospitals. As for how those events might impact the World Cup in Russia, the question was not even valid. Anyone who asked was mixing sports and politics, Moscow charged.

World governing bodies backed this line of defense. "We are involved in football and we will not allow politics to get in the way," Sepp Blatter said while visiting Russia. "If a few politicians are not particularly happy that we are hosting the World Cup in Russia, then I always tell them: 'Well then, stay at home.'"

Putin returned the support. When Blatter visited Russia in July 2015 for the draw of World Cup qualifying groups, Putin praised soccer's embattled boss at a gala event in St. Petersburg. "I believe people like Mr. Blatter, the heads of major international sports federations, deserve special attention and gratitude," said the Russian president. "If anyone should be awarded Nobel Prizes, it is these people."

And when asked about the FIFA investigation, Putin had the same response as when asked about Russian missiles destroying Syrian hospitals: "I do not believe a single word."

Ultimately, however, not even Vladimir Putin could protect Blatter. In September 2015 Swiss police searched Blatter's office and seized his computer, turning up evidence that he and his cronies had paid each over $80 million in bonuses. FIFA's major sponsors called for a change. The following month, the federation's executive council suspended Blatter. The next year, FIFA banned Blatter from all soccer-related activities. But the ousted sportocrat still had a friend in the Kremlin. When the 2018 World Cup Final was played in Moscow, Blatter was in the dignitaries box.

With all the money changing hands among FIFA officials, was any coming from Moscow to Switzerland? The FBI had started down this trail back in 2010. After the Feds turned their attention to Chuck Blazer, more allegations surfaced of Russian cash for FIFA votes. A report by Russian investigative journalists turned up emails revealing Moscow sports officials' plans to bribe Blazer,

European soccer boss Michel Platini, and other FIFA leaders. Christopher Steele offered further evidence of payoffs. Before compiling his infamous dossier on Russian interference in the 2016 US election, Steele passed intel to the FBI that an oligarch paid a bribe to Blatter, with Putin's approval.

None of these reports led to legal charges. Steele himself acknowledged there was no proof of Russia buying votes for the World Cup. "Don't expect me or anyone else to produce a document with Putin's signature saying please X bribe Y with this account in this way," the retired spy told London's *Sunday Times*. "Putin is an ex-intelligence officer. Everything he does has to be deniable."

"FIFA has gone through sad times, moments of crisis," declared Gianni Infantino after his election in 2016 to succeed Sepp Blatter. "But those times are over. We need to implement the reform and implement good governance and transparency."

Infantino talked about big changes, yet much about FIFA's way of doing business remained the same, including the fondness for Russia. "Football is a team sport," the new president said during his first visit to Moscow. "We are a team that will organize the greatest event in the history of football. The best World Cup ever, in a fantastic country like Russia."

As the World Cup approached, it was getting harder to stomach FIFA's blather. Russia was acting less like a reliable player in international affairs and more like a rogue state. On March 4, 2018, two agents with Russian military intelligence, the GRU, attempted to kill a former Russian officer living in Britain. The Russian exile, Sergei Skripal, was found unconscious that afternoon on a park bench in Salisbury. His 33-year-old daughter Yuliya was next to him, slipping out of consciousness and foaming at the mouth.

The GRU agents had used a perfume bottle to spray the nerve agent Novichok on the handle of Skripal's front door. British police said the bottle contained enough poison to kill thousands of people. It ended up killing only one: a young Salisbury woman whose boyfriend found the discarded bottle and gave it to her as a gift. Skripal and his daughter survived. The house was so contaminated with poison it had to be completely rebuilt.

In response to the attack, the British government expelled 23 Russian diplomats. Other EU countries, Australia, and Canada likewise expelled Russian diplomats. Even President Donald Trump declared that Russia was responsible for the attack, and his administration expelled 60 Russian diplomats.

Shortly after the assassination attempt, the world also learned the truth about the Malaysia airline disaster. In May 2018 the multinational team investigating the destruction of MAL Flight 17 announced that the BUK rocket had come from a missile brigade of the Russian army. According to witnesses and satellite data, the brigade had moved the missile launcher across the border into Russian-held Ukrainian territory on the morning of the attack. After the plane was downed, the brigade moved the launcher back to Russia.

The Dutch and Australian governments declared Russia legally responsible for the plane's destruction and demanded compensation for families. Governments of other European countries, Canada, and the United States echoed this statement, calling on Moscow to acknowledge responsibility.

"There is nothing that would make us trust these findings," Putin replied. Russia had not been involved in the investigation, he said. And in all likelihood, the Ukrainians were responsible.

The president commented on the investigation at the St. Petersburg Economic Forum. With sanctions over military action in Ukraine, diplomatic protests over the poisoning, and now the MAL 17 report, Putin faced an array of challenges. Yet he looked into the audience at the economic forum and saw French president Emmanuel Macron and Japanese prime minister Shinzo Abe in attendance. Russia was still a world power, and Putin was still a world statesman.

"We are seeing in the world today a situation where everyone pretends to be playing football, while actually following the rules of judo," he said. The result was neither football nor judo, he added, continuing the sports analogy. "Just chaos. This is where we are headed."

The implication was clear: The Americans had created this world of chaos. Russia alone stood against the arrogance of American power.

A few weeks later, Macron joined Putin in Moscow's Luzhniki Stadium to watch the French national team in the World Cup Final. The president of Croatia, Kolinda Grabar-Kitarović, was there to cheer her team. Conor McGregor was also in Putin's guest box, as was Mick Jagger. Surrounded by world leaders and celebrities, with hundreds of millions around the globe tuned into the match, Vladimir Putin had no reason to concede to investigations or sanctions.

In 2007 Putin had traveled to distant Guatemala and spoke in halting English to gain the trust of the IOC. A decade later, the leaders of world sport were kowtowing to Putin. The most obsequious was Gianni Infantino. In his press conference before the Final, the FIFA president gushed about Russia's World Cup. His words could have come straight from the playbook: "The World Cup has changed Russia. It has become a real football country. Football is now part of Russia's DNA. It has also changed the perception of the world about Russia. Everyone has discovered a beautiful country, a welcoming country, full of people who are keen to show to the world that what maybe is sometimes said is not what happens here."

In 2014 tweets and blog posts introduced a new word into the universal lexicon: "sportswashing."

The term was first used by human rights organizations to spotlight how the authoritarian government of Azerbaijan used the European Games to sanitize its image. Amnesty International applied the term to Sheikh Mansour's purchase of the Manchester City soccer club and Qatar's hosting of the World Cup. According to these NGOs, sportswashing took place whenever an authoritarian government with a record of suppressing human rights spruced up its international reputation by engaging in world sport.

Without question, the master sportswasher was Vladimir Putin. In his decades as ruler of Russia, journalists were killed and political opponents jailed. Independent media outlets were shut down, international human rights organizations banned, and opposition parties harassed. Yet Moscow's connections with world governing bodies ensured that Russia maintained its reputation as a "reliable country."

Sportswashing also had domestic benefits. Putin built his legitimacy as a leader who restored the Russian state and revived Russia's international prestige. Hosting the Olympics and World Cup confirmed this image. Highways in central Russia's most populated regions were obstacle courses of craters and cracked pavement. But the 30-mile highway from Sochi to the Olympic ski resort proved that Russia was able to build world-class infrastructure.

Authoritarian regimes gain a boost at home and abroad from sportswashing. But what do the governing bodies get out of the deal? Surely, there are bribes paid to top officials. Yet there must be something else that international federations get from their cooperation with the Putins of the world.

For one, it's helpful to have a big, imposing country stand up to the Americans. The US pays the bills, but it can also be irritating. Vitaly Mutko was on to something when he said the Americans fail to understand why they don't get the votes within world federations. Moscow talked of sport's universal values—openness, inclusion, neutrality. At the same time, Russians engaged in the under-the-table deals that drove world sports. This was more to the sportocrats' liking than goody-goody Americans with their investigations and sanctions.

As the head of the international skiing federation admitted, sportocrats prefer to hold their events in authoritarian countries. "The fact is that it is easier for us to have events in dictatorships," said Gian Franco Kasper. "From a business standpoint, I say: I only want to go to dictatorships. I don't want to argue with environmentalists."

The fact of the matter is: fans don't want to argue with environmentalists either. They want to watch sports. Political scientist Alexandra Yatsyk was still living in Kazan in 2018, when World Cup matches were played there. She marveled at how well everything was organized for the visitors: security, transportation, fan zones.

"I saw the joyful mood of international fans," she told me. "They were able to move around easily. They were welcomed. Local people didn't have this same experience, but fans don't notice such things."

Fans didn't notice the lack of independent media or open elections. They weren't bothered by international sanctions, or occupying soldiers, or rampant corruption. All they noticed was that Putin's government pulled off the World Cup without a hitch. As Yatsyk observed, "They went to the matches; they drank beer; they had their entertainment."

CHAPTER 12

CRASHING TO EARTH

"And the Oscar goes to…*Icarus*."

Applause swept through the Dorothy Chandler Auditorium when Greta Gerwig and Laura Dern announced the award for Best Documentary. Director Bryan Fogel leaped to his feet. Bursting with excitement, he made his way to the stage with the film's producers. Fogel took the gold statuette in his hands, placed it by his feet, and unfolded his speech.

"We dedicate this award to Dr. Grigory Rodchenkov," he said, pausing for another burst of applause, "our fearless whistleblower who now lives in grave danger. We hope *Icarus* is a wake-up call—yes, about Russia, but more than that, about the importance of telling the truth, now more than ever."

Icarus was indeed a wake-up call—in the way great documentaries are. After its premiere at the Sundance Film Festival in January 2017, Netflix paid $5 million for the rights, giving Fogel's film a worldwide platform. As buzz about *Icarus* built through the year, Fogel was invited to speak to members of Congress and media outlets from *Meet the Press* to the BBC.

Fogel acknowledged that he never intended to tell the story of Russian doping. He wanted to make a film about the science of doping, to learn what advantage athletes actually gain from drugs and find out how someone like Lance Armstrong could go years without testing positive. His film was actually two films: first, a chronicle of his own doping regimen for an amateur cycling race, as designed by Rodchenkov; and then, after Rodchenkov was caught in an investigation during filming, a rapid-fire exposé of Russian doping at the 2014 Winter Olympics.

Fogel himself was stunned by the sudden turn. "I never imagined that, through event after event, that two years into the making of this film, I would find myself essentially sitting on a nuclear bomb of information," he said in an interview. The bomb's shock wave had far-reaching effects, Fogel understood. Rodchenkov's revelations cast a cloud over decades of Russian and Soviet participation in international sport.

"Do you just wipe out all of Olympic history and start over?" Fogel asked.

Without question, Rodchenkov's escape to the United States in November 2015 was a major event in the history of international sport. After decades of rumors, the world was confronted with proof of Moscow's cheating. Yet the discovery of Russian doping goes beyond Grigory Rodchenkov. There were many gears in Moscow's doping, and when they began to fail, a chain reaction followed. Fogel's nuclear analogy is appropriate. But this wasn't a bomb. It was the breakdown of a power plant. Like the disaster at Chernobyl, it would require more than a two-hour documentary to put the whole catastrophe on screen. We would need a miniseries.

Episode One would begin with an idealist. A young man with boyish good looks and an easy smile. A romantic who married a girl two months after their first date. A moralist who didn't drink or dance at his own wedding. A fool who thought he could change Russia.

In 2008 Vasily Stepanov answered a newspaper ad to work for the new Russian Anti-Doping Agency (RUSADA). Raised in

Chelyabinsk, Stepanov had parents with the means to send him to the United States for high school. He took college courses without earning a degree, then held jobs without finding a career. One benefit of his time in America was becoming fluent in English. RUSADA regularly sent the American-educated Russian to international events. For the most part, though, his job involved collecting urine samples at competitions in Russia.

Stepanov found his work disheartening, and not only because he was hauling bottles of piss. No one at events in Russia cooperated—not federation officials, not coaches, certainly not athletes. In telling his story to British sportswriter David Walsh, Stepanov recounted offers of bribes from some officials, outright resistance from others. He reported the obstacles to RUSADA director Vyacheslav Sinev.

"Relax, Vitaly. Relax," Sinev answered. "This is Russia. Things take time."

Stepanov believed his work would help keep sports clean and fair. He had played soccer in high school and ran marathons after his return to Russia. His amateur naïveté was pierced by a sprinter he met at a competition, Yuliya Rusanova. On their first date, he told her about RUSADA's campaign to stop doping. She told him to stop being an idiot.

"I am using doping; everyone is using doping," she said. "To be a top athlete, this is what it takes," she added bluntly. "End of lesson."

Stepanov reported the conversation to Sinev. His boss brushed off the runner's remarks, and laughingly advised Stepanov to keep his distance. Stepanov asked her to marry him on their fourth date.

A two-month courtship did not lead to a harmonious marriage. A big problem was that Rusanova was following the doping program set by her coach as she trained in the 800 meters, while her husband was earnestly trying to end doping.

Four months into the marriage—and after two unsuccessful trips to the registry office to get divorced—Stepanov was sent to the Vancouver Winter Olympics with the RUSADA team. Unhappily married and unhappily employed, the 28-year-old idealist was exhausted. He reached out to WADA officials to tell them what he knew. There was no orderly system for testing in Russia. The only athletes suspended were those with no chance of competing internationally. When top athletes tested positive, they paid RUSADA to have the result recorded as negative. According to Stepanov, the anti-doping lab in Moscow was part of the whole scheme.

WADA officials could offer no help to the young whistleblower. The organization was set up in such a way that only RUSADA could investigate doping in Russia. When he returned to Moscow, Stepanov sought out the Sports Ministry's head of anti-doping, Konstantin Vyrupaev, whom he knew from his early days at RUSADA. Vyrupaev passed along the instructions he had received from his boss, Sports Minister Vitaly Mutko: "We are in Russia and we live by our own rules. The Russian Ministry of Sport decides who should be sanctioned and who should be a hero and who will win medals."

Stepanov emailed notes of his meetings with Vyrupaev to Stuart Kemp, a WADA official he had met in Vancouver. The conversations revealed hard lessons about anti-doping in Russia and the country's view of world sport:

1. WADA is not really battling doping; it's all politics.
2. All countries and especially Europe are afraid of Russia and try not to let us win any medals anyway possible.
3. Russia will always work by double standards, as prohibited [lists are] mostly politics and there is no really bad health consequences for athletes.

The correspondence with Kemp went on for four months, amounting to some 200 emails. This inside view of RUSADA lasted until Stepanov lost his job. His boss, Vyacheslav Sinev, was replaced by Nikita Kamaev, and Stepanov was one of a dozen RUSADA employees let go with the change at the top. Yet even after his ouster from Russia's anti-doping agency, Stepanov could still pass along information about Russian doping. He had another well-placed source—his wife.

Episode Two would begin with a young girl in Kursk, dreaming of the Olympics. Years later, Yuliya Rusanova recalled watching the Sydney Games on television: "When I was watching Russian athletes compete, I was getting very emotional. I looked at them as gods, as the people out of this world. I was crying when they were losing and felt happiness when they were winning."

Rusanova started competing at age 17. She was fast. But as she moved up the competitive ladder, she learned there was more to winning races. Girls from Moscow were fast too; plus, they had better shoes. They also had better coaches, who gave them pills to run even faster. Her own coach in Kursk resisted when she asked for pills. She wasn't at the level where doping would help, he claimed. Yet after she was hospitalized with tuberculosis, her coach asked the doctor if performance-enhancing drugs would help her recover more quickly. The doctor said yes. So at age 19, with the physician's approval and on her coach's suggestion, Rusanova started doping.

In the following months, Rusanova took oral anabolic steroids and injections of testosterone and EPO. She cut 12 seconds off her time in the 800m and won the National Championship in her age group. Rusanova had her eye on the European Championships, even the Olympics. That would require a time below two minutes, a goal within reach. Yet the closer she came, the more she realized she needed better drugs, not drugs administered by her coach in Kursk—who was also sleeping with her.

To get the boost she needed, Rusanova set up a meeting in Moscow with Dr. Sergei Portugalov. A longtime researcher in pharmacology, Portugalov had drafted the plans for Soviet doping at the Los Angeles Olympics. When Yuliya met him, he was a professor and deputy director at the sports science institute in Moscow. He was also the source for drugs among Russia's top athletes. Before their first visit, Yuliya waited in the hall while Dr. Portugalov finished meeting with a couple of swimming coaches.

Portugalov listened to the young sprinter's doping history, then he prescribed a new steroid for her: Oxastenon, a combination of oral turinabol and oxandrolone. He gave careful instructions on when and how to take the pills, and provided his cell number in case she had problems. Then he set his fee. Like other top athletes, Rusanova would pay Portugalov a percentage of her winnings: 5% from any international meet, and if she reached the European or World Championships, $700 for bronze, $1,000 for silver, and $1,600 for gold.

The next year, 2011, Rusanova won the 800m at the National Indoor Championship with the fastest indoor time in the world that year: 1:58:14. She finished third at the European Indoor Championship in Paris, behind Russian teammate Mariya Savinova. Rusanova finished second behind Savinova again at the National Outdoor Championship, with a time of 1:56:99. The London Olympics were a year away, and Yuliya was already hitting times good enough for the 800m Finals. Another second faster and she would be on the podium.

Then, just before the World Championship in South Korea, she got bad news from her coach: a urine sample had tested positive for EPO. Her coach assured Yuliya the problem could be taken care of. He had a friend who was a friend of the anti-doping lab's director. For 30,000 rubles (about $1,000), the coach's friend would have his friend, Dr. Grigory Rodchenkov, turn the positive to a negative. Rusanova paid the money. It was the necessary cost of winning, just like the fees to Portugalov.

Unfortunately, the drug test was the first in a string of setbacks that year. Rusanova finished last in the Finals in Korea. A few months later, she suffered an injury that kept her out of qualification races for the Olympics. She watched Mariya Savinova win gold at London.

When she was ready to train again, Rusanova decided it was time for a change. Savinova's personal coach, Vladimir Kazarin, agreed to take her on, but only if Rusanova kept her husband, the former RUSADA snoop, away from his camp. Kazarin also proposed a new program of steroids—along with human growth hormone. Training at Kazarin's camp, with Vitaly left behind in Moscow, Rusanova looked ahead to the Rio Games. She was ready to be done with her husband—finally done. The divorce papers simply needed to be signed. Then came word from Moscow of another test result.

In 2009 the world governing body of track and field, the IAAF, began testing athletes' blood passports. Rather than detecting substances present in the body at a specific moment, the passport analyzed blood tests over an athlete's career to measure changes in markers. Variations in certain markers over time indicated whether the athlete had engaged in blood doping or steroid use, even if the drugs had never been detected.

In February 2013 Rusanova was informed that her blood passport showed abnormalities. The national track coach, Alexey Melnikov, advised her to admit guilt and take a two-year suspension from the IAAF. If she fought the charges, he advised, the suspension would likely be four years.

"I did everything you told me," Rusanova said.

Melnikov was apologetic, but he brushed off any blame. The Russians simply didn't understand how blood passports would change things. "We didn't really see the danger until spring 2012," he insisted.

"The world that I imagined to myself collapsed in front of my eyes," Rusanova recalled. She was shocked but also bitter. "I'm being sanctioned and the people that set up such doping system in Russia will not be punished at all."

Rusanova simply had to sign a document and take the two-year suspension. She simply had to sign her divorce papers and end her rocky marriage. Instead, she decided to stick with her do-gooder husband and take the path he had urged all along. She decided to come clean.

The third episode opens in Istanbul, at a hotel near the airport. Yuliya and Vitaly have arranged a clandestine meeting with Jack Robertson, WADA's chief investigator. They brought along a 10-page letter to WADA, detailing Yuliya's whole doping journey. Yuliya had the journal in which she recorded the drugs and doses she took over the years, along with testing control slips for all her submitted samples. She had a bottle of steroids Kazarin gave her. And on her phone was a recording of the meeting with Melnikov.

A former special agent with the US Drug Enforcement Agency, Robertson had led the investigation that finally snared Lance Armstrong. As for Russia, however, WADA kept his hands tied. The obstacles were all the more frustrating because he had more than one Russian whistleblower. In late 2012 the agency heard from discus thrower Darya Pishchalnikova, the silver medal winner at the London Olympics. Nevertheless, WADA refused to act. Instead they forwarded Pishchalnikova's complaints to Moscow. RUSADA took action right away: Pishchalnikova was banned ten years for doping.

Robertson later told *ProPublica* that WADA resistance to investigating Russia came from the agency's president, Sir Craig Reedie. A longtime sports administrator in Britain and IOC vice president, Reedie stalled at any new indication of Russian doping. "He had to be literally pressured into every investigation," Robertson said.

Not getting anywhere inside the lines, Robertson reached out to Hajo Seppelt, a veteran reporter with the German television network ARD. Seppelt had investigated some of the biggest stories in sports doping: the doping of children in the former East Germany, doping in cycling, doping in cross-country skiing, doping in China, doping among Kenyan marathoners. Roberston put Seppelt in contact with Vitaly and Yuliya in March 2014. The reporter raced to Moscow to meet them.

Vitaly was surprised someone was finally paying attention. It had been four years since he first spoke to WADA officials in Vancouver. Now all of a sudden there was a German reporter in their apartment, looking like a German reporter—tousled hair, rectangular glasses, serious face. Seppelt wanted to make a documentary for ARD. He had other sources willing to speak off camera. But the documentary would have more weight if someone spoke on camera. He asked Yuliya and Vitaly if they'd be willing.

The Stepanovs agreed on one condition. They had to be out of the country when the documentary aired. Once the program ran, Yuliya's running career would be over and they would be in danger in Russia. They were now parents of a baby boy (Yuliya also took Vitaly's name after their son's birth). They needed to be safe, and they needed to work.

Seppelt worked to open the Stepanovs' path to Germany while pursuing leads for the documentary. Meanwhile, Yuliya gathered more evidence. With her phone's video camera, she recorded conversations with Kazarin, Melnikov, and Portugalov. She also recorded a conversation with Mariya Savinova, the Olympic champion in the 800m. This one hurt. As she came to know her rival, Yuliya found Savinova to be a kind person. She felt unable to betray a friend's confidence by passing along the video she recorded in Savinova's apartment. Yet she also knew the words of an Olympic gold medalist mattered more than anyone's.

"Well really, what should we do?" Savinova said in the clip used in the film. "How should it go differently? That is our system and in Russia that only works only with drugs.... My coach fortunately works with Melnikov, and he helps to cover up the tests. They allow him to change the dates for the controls. Oxandrolone is very quickly out of my body out again. It takes less than 20 days. We have tested that—my husband has very good contacts to the doping control laboratory."

Handing the video to Seppelt, Yuliya knew her relationship with Savinova was over. Her relationship with Russia was over as well. Ten days later before Seppelt's documentary aired in Germany, the Stepanovs flew to Prague, then boarded a train to Berlin. "I think that Russia will not forgive something like this," Yuliya said at the end of the documentary.

The day the program ran, she and Vitaly took the SIM cards out of their phones so they couldn't be located.

As Episode Four begins, Dr. Grigory Rodchenkov is sitting in front of a camera in his Moscow lab. He is relaxed in his short-sleeve shirt. Hajo Seppelt sits on a lab stool opposite him. Rodchenkov agreed to an on-camera interview with Seppelt, believing it was for a documentary about the Sochi Games. But now Seppelt was asking about allegations that Rodchenkov set up doping programs for athletes.

"You should be very careful to believe cheaters," Rodchenkov replied.

Seppelt pressed further. "Have you ever accepted money to cover up doping?" he asked in English.

"Did I ever take money?" Rodchenkov repeated. "From people who wanted to cover up doping?

"I never took money from people who try to cover up doping. The first question is: No.... You can see many rumors. But it's again.... All people are referring to me. Okay, we know Grigory and he wants to solve problem. It is not the case."

The day after the documentary aired in Germany, Rodchenkov met with Sports Minister Mutko and the director of RUSADA, Nikita Kamaev. They all believed the charges would quickly go away. "I prefer to operate with facts, concrete facts," Kamaev told the Russian press, "not blurry photos taken from under a skirt on a cell phone."

But the charges didn't go away. A week after Seppelt's program aired, Rodchenkov received a letter from WADA informing him that an independent commission would investigate the new revelations. The letter instructed him to retain the lab's stock of A and B samples. Commission members would arrive in a few days to collect them for testing.

The Sports Ministry stalled the WADA team's visa applications, giving Rodchenkov an extra day to cover his tracks. He and his team went to work. The letter stated Rodchenkov should keep all the samples; it then referred specifically to samples taken in the previous three months, which the lab had already been required to keep under WADA rules. Rodchenkov latched onto this apparent loophole. He would get rid of all samples older than three months and turn over only the recent samples.

The lab staff hauled over 8,000 BEREG-Kit bottles to a garbage truck, which dumped them in a landfill 20 miles outside Moscow. Rodchenkov counted 37 dirty samples in the remaining bottles. Their contents would have to be swapped out. A call went to the FSB magicians, who came to the lab and opened the sealed bottles. The original urine was poured out, clean urine poured in, and the magicians sealed up the bottles. Meanwhile, one of Rodchenkov's assistants scrubbed the computer files, changing the documentation to remove reference to positive tests.

The WADA team arrived the morning after everything was finished. Even after the mop-up operation, Rodchenkov wasn't entirely confident. The remaining samples were on their way to Lausanne for testing. Plus, the IOC still had samples from the 2008 Beijing Olympics. If those samples were retested, Rodchenkov estimated there would be 20 positives among Russian weightlifters and track athletes.

Rodchenkov was worried, but he also had no respect for the people stirring up trouble.

Episode Five opens with Rodchenkov in a low-lit room in Lausanne's elegant Palace Hotel. Sitting across from him in a lush armchair is Dick Pound, a 72-year-old Canadian lawyer and long-time IOC member. Sitting next to Pound is Dr. Olivier Rabin, WADA's science director: young, fit, and French, with degrees from University College London and the Sorbonne and research experience at America's National Institutes of Health.

For three hours, Rabin asked questions. For three hours, Rodchenkov stonewalled. "I told him several times that I didn't know what he [was] talking about," Rodchenkov later wrote. As he swatted away Rabin's questions, Rodchenkov looked over at Pound. The head of WADA's special investigation appeared to be asleep.

Rodchenkov knew he could dupe these morons. Moreover, he had word from his boss that the head of WADA, Sir Craig, wanted the scandal to go away. Reedie had sent an email to Nataliya Zhelanova, Vitaly Mutko's doping control advisor, essentially apologizing for the investigation. Sir Craig valued his friendship with the Sports Minister. "There is no intention in WADA to do anything to affect that relationship," he wrote.

Rodchenkov had little regard for the 323-page report that Pound's investigation compiled. Released on November 9, 2015, the report confirmed the charges made in the ARD documentary: there was a systemic culture of doping in Russian track and field, with coaches providing drugs to athletes and then colluding with the anti-doping lab to ensure negative test results.

Evidence pointed overwhelmingly to Rodchenkov as the central figure in covering up positive drug tests. The chemist dismissed Pound and his investigators as "dorks who understand nothing." He called a lawyer in Lausanne and made plans to appeal at the Court of Arbitration for Sport. "We will overturn this nonsense," he said when Bryan Fogel called later that day.

But the report forced Reedie's hand. A letter came to Rodchenkov the day after the Pound Report was released: WADA was stripping the Moscow lab's certification. From now on, samples from Russian athletes had to be tested outside Russia. Later that day, Rodchenkov was summoned to Mutko's office. The Minister told him to submit his resignation.

"As long as they weren't getting caught, they kept their mouths shut," Rodchenkov said of Yuliya Stepanova and other athletes who testified. Now it was his turn to flip. A week after resigning, he went to Moscow's Sheremetyevo Airport with a ticket Fogel had sent him. He had only a carry-on, as if he were going to LA for a short trip. Inside were the laptop he had used in Sochi and the hard drive from his office computer in Moscow.

Rodchenkov was unsure of what to reveal when he first arrived in Los Angeles. He feared for his safety, but he also knew he had to tell the story of Sochi, to show the audacity of the whole scheme. The urine-swapping lab had been, in his words, a "perfect operation." Somebody had to take credit for it, and that somebody would be him. As he later wrote in his memoir, "I was the main actor in the Sochi scandal."

The sixth episode opens with Rodchenkov at a conference table, surrounded by Fogel's cameras.

After he arrived in Los Angeles, Rodchenkov learned that Vyacheslav Sinev, the first director of RUSADA, had died in Moscow. Two weeks later, Sinev's successor, Nikita Kamaev, was also dead, purportedly of a heart attack. Like Rodchenkov, Kamaev had been fired after release of the Pound Report. Also like Rodchenkov, he was planning to come clean, to reveal what he knew in a book. Kamaev and Sinev were the only other men who knew the extent of Russia's doping cover-up. Now, only Rodchenkov was left. He knew the truth needed to come out, and he wanted to make sure he was the one telling it.

"Does Russia have a systemic, state-wide doping program in place to cheat the Olympics?" Fogel asked.

"Yes," answered Rodchenkov.

"Were you the mastermind of the state-wide system that cheated the Olympics?"

"Of course. Yes."

Rodchenkov laid out the whole story: the lab in Sochi, the swapping of urine samples, even how many Russian medal winners had been doping at the 2008 and 2012 Summer Olympics. He expressed no contrition. He was not like Vitaly Stepanov, a naïve young man who believed sport should be clean. He was also not like Yuliya Stepanova, an athlete who turned on a corrupt system when she realized how it used people like her and then threw them away.

In his book Rodchenkov had nothing but contempt for the Stepanovs. Yuliya was a "has-been" runner with "an axe to grind." In fact, both the lab director and the young runner had been part of the same corrupt machine. Its fundamental design went back to the earliest days of Soviet sport. In the following decades, it was adapted and expanded. Rodchenkov was a cog in this machine—yes, an important one, but a cog nonetheless. Once smaller cogs like Yuliya Stepanova stopped doing their job, once they started being noisy, the whole system grinded to a halt.

The failure of the Russian sports machine began for the most Russian of reasons: the science couldn't keep up with the West. For decades, Moscow's chemists had devised fixes to doping tests. Rodchenkov equipped his lab with millions of dollars' worth of Western tech, so Russian athletes could elude detection. But his lab had no answer to blood-passport analysis. Yuliya Stepanova and others weren't washed-up cheaters trying to settle scores. They had trusted coaches and chemists who claimed their machine was better than anything in the West.

Ultimately, it wasn't. What Rodchenkov never admitted in his memoir or *Icarus* or anywhere else is that he got out-scienced.

Episode Seven opens with the the *New York Times* headline: RUSSIAN INSIDER SAYS STATE-RUN DOPING FUELED OLYMPIC GOLD.

Reaction in Russia to the May 2016 article was swift and furious. Rodchenkov was denounced as a defector and a cheat. "A criminal will say anything," said Kremlin spokesman Dmitry Peskov.

Vladimir Putin made his own statement on the doping scandal a few weeks later. Rodchenkov was a person "with a scandalous reputation," the president declared. But there were larger forces at play. The doping charges were yet another example, Putin stated, of how "one state dictates its will to the entire international sports community."

Putin played upon the greatest fear of the governing bodies, that international sport would again be torn apart by boycotts. "We are now witnessing a dangerous relapse of political interference in sport," he stated. "Yes, the forms of interference have changed, but the essence is the same: to make sport a tool of geopolitical pressure, by using it to form a negative image of countries and peoples. The Olympic movement, which plays such a tremendous unifying role for humanity, may once again be on the verge of a split."

Russia's president spoke the language of the sportocrats. Sport had the power to unite people, but the Americans, with their calls for a total ban on Russian athletes, were unfair and discriminatory.

This was the statesmanlike version of Putin's response. In interviews with Russian media, he spoke more directly, calling Rodchenkov an "idiot," someone who was mentally unstable, and a stooge of American intelligence agents. Some in Russia said even worse. "Rodchenkov simply needs to be shot for lying," said Leonid Tyagachev, former head of the Russian Olympic Committee, "like Stalin would have done."

Rodchenkov and the Stepanovs were traitors; their revelations were lies. Nevertheless, heads had to roll. Rodchenkov's direct supervisor in the Sports Ministry, Yuri Nagornykh, resigned. Alexey Melnikov and Vladimir Kazarin, the coaches Yuliya Stepanova had recorded, were made scapegoats. After they were given lifetime bans by the IAAF, Russian media pinned the blame on them for the entire scandal.

Valentin Balakhnichev likewise pointed to the coaches after he was ousted as head of the Russian track and field federation. Balakhnichev also voiced an argument widely expressed on Russian sports sites, that the whole scandal was conjured by WADA for the organization's own benefit. "They turned a Russian fly into an international elephant," he claimed, "to gain new powers, a staff of informants, and an exorbitant budget."

This view of the doping scandal, that it was part of a global anti-Russian conspiracy, connected with a common belief in Russian politics and society at the time. International institutions, under the influence of the Americans, were biased against Russia. There was power to be gained—and profits to be reaped—by discrediting Russia, weakening Russia, humiliating Russia. Punishments handed down after the doping allegations were like economic sanctions imposed after the military actions in Ukraine: malicious, unfair, and intended to force Russia back into a humbled, subordinate position. The West—particularly the United States—could not abide that Russia was again a world power. When it came to sports, the Americans, Canadians, and Europeans had to make up stories of doping to keep Russians out of the arena. This was the only way they could win.

Leonid Tyagachev expressed the view of many Russians in his radio interview about the doping scandal, the interview in which he called for Rodchenkov to be shot. Russia had shown its greatness to the world through international sports. But Russia didn't need international sports to maintain that greatness. The nation could stand on its own.

"We are such a strong country," Tyagachev said. "In sports, we have shown the world our great importance, our great victories, our development. All this shows we are the right people, on the right path. If we are unjustifiably insulted, we do not need the Olympic Games. We do not need this treatment. We will not kneel."

CHAPTER 13

PUTIN'S POODLES

"BEYOND A REASONABLE DOUBT." Richard McLaren stressed this point in his news conference in Toronto on July 18, 2016. A veteran sports lawyer and professor at Western University in Ontario, McLaren led the new investigation WADA launched after publication of Rodchenkov's allegations in the *New York Times*. McLaren insisted that his team followed the principles of criminal law: They only presented evidence that was established "beyond a reasonable doubt." If evidence they gathered did not meet this standard, it was not included in the report.

In less than two months, McLaren's investigators examined thousands of pages of documents on Rodchenkov's computer drives. They interviewed the former director of the Moscow lab as well as anonymous witnesses. Lab analysts re-tested Russian athletes' urine samples from Sochi and London. Cross-checked against Rodchenkov's records, the tests confirmed his accounts of manipulated samples. Analysts also looked at the 37 urine samples Rodchenkov's staff swapped out in advance of WADA's visit to the Moscow lab in 2014. In three bottles, the urine inside didn't match the DNA of the athlete whose name was on the label. Inside one bottle was urine from two different people.

According to McLaren, evidence showed that the anti-doping labs in Moscow and Sochi operated within a state-directed system to protect doped Russian athletes. Throughout the 95-page report, the phrase was repeated over and over: "beyond a reasonable doubt."

The view was different in Moscow: the McLaren Report proved nothing. There were no facts. The so-called "investigators" did nothing more than rehash Rodchenkov's insinuations. Just like the economic sanctions imposed on Russia, the report was a conspiracy to "settle scores," said Irina Rodnina, now a Duma member.

The Moscow buzz was accurate: there was indeed a conspiracy behind the doping revelations. But it was not directed *against* Russia. Rather, there was a conspiracy within WADA and the IOC to protect Russia.

After the McLaren Report was released, the world's athletes demanded justice. Canadian cross-country skier Beckie Scott and German fencer Claudia Bokel, chairs of the WADA and IOC athlete committees, heard from hundreds of international athletes demanding strong punishment of Russia. Yet when the IOC executive council met on July 24, athlete concerns were brushed aside. Thomas Bach announced the IOC would not ban the entire Russia team from the upcoming Summer Olympics, due to begin in Rio on August 5. Instead, the federations governing the 28 sports in the Games would decide the eligibility of each Russian athlete. If a canoeist or swimmer could prove they were clean, then the governing bodies of those sports would allow them to compete.

Bach explained the logic of this decision to the full IOC membership at their meeting in Rio. A complete ban would have been the "nuclear option," he said, resulting in "death and devastation." This was opposed to Olympic principles. "The Olympic movement stands for life and the construction of a better future," Bach said.

A few days later, at the Rio Games' opening press conference, a young Russian reporter cut through Bach's high-minded rhetoric. Standing up hesitantly in the press room, she asked the IOC president a question from the heart.

"It looked like you personally were helping us. Is it true?"

Still today, there is no clear answer to this question. Why did Thomas Bach allow Russian athletes to compete? Was he pressured by Moscow? Or bought, as some athletes charged? Perhaps the most accurate take on the situation was the headline that ran on the front page of the German tabloid *Bild*, below a photo of Putin whispering in Bach's ear: PUTIN'S POODLE.

There were plenty of Russians who saw the IOC decision as anything but helpful. After Bach passed the buck, the various sports federations acted quickly to suspend Russian athletes from the Rio Games. The entire weightlifting team was banned. Of 30 members of the rowing team, only four were cleared. Most notably, the IAAF banned Russia's entire track and field team. There were appeals for one Russian runner, Yuliya Stepanova, to be given special permission to participate as a neutral. The IOC refused.

In total 118 Russian athletes were banned from the 2016 Summer Games. One of the most famous was pole vaulter Yelena Isinbayeva. At age 34, the world record-holder was planning her fifth and final Olympic appearance. Isinbayeva was known around the world as the greatest female pole vaulter of all time. She was also one of the most marketable athletes in track and field, with the black hair, blue eyes, and sharp cheekbones of a Slavic supermodel. Adidas featured her in a global campaign before the Beijing Olympics. The following year she jumped to Chinese sportswear company Li-Ning for $7.5 million.

Isinbayeva was also known for speaking her mind. At the 2013 World Championships in Moscow, she defended the infamous gay-propaganda law. Targeting Swedish athletes who wore rainbow-colored nail polish, she vented about foreigners disrespecting Russian "tradition." She later claimed her remarks were misunderstood due to her poor English.

Isinbayeva's words were even sharper when she spoke in Russian, particularly in the wake of the doping scandal. Yuliya Stepanova "should be disqualified for life," she told R-Sport. Isinbayeva unleashed on Instagram after the IAAF confirmed its ban of Russian track and field athletes: "Let all those pseudo-pure foreign athletes breathe a sigh of relief and win their pseudo-gold medals in our absence. Strength has always been feared."

With 271 athletes cleared for competition, Russia still had one of the largest contingents at the Rio Games. As was his custom, Putin hosted a reception at the Kremlin for the departing Olympians. This send-off had a somber tone. The Games would be diminished because of the Russians' absence, he intoned. Competition will have lower quality and medals will have lesser value—all because of "political manipulation."

The president then called on Isinbayeva to speak to her fellow athletes. The track star stepped to the podium in the ornate Alexander Hall, before paintings of St. Alexander Nevsky, the medieval prince who defended the motherland against invaders from the West. She began to speak, then broke down in tears.

"We were suspended without evidence," she said after wiping her eyes, "brazenly, rudely, without any chance to justify ourselves."

She turned to the president.

"Vladimir Vladimirovich, I ask you, protect us from this lawlessness. We really need your support, your advice, because today athletes are left defenseless. We truly believe in you—and we love you. We must punish everyone who has had a part in this."

Putin looked on sympathetically, glancing to the floor as Isinbayeva appealed for his protection. He had a difficult path. On the one hand, he denounced governing bodies for their unjust treatment of Russian athletes. On the other hand, he had to make a show of following their stipulations so Russia could be fully restored to international sport. He was especially careful when speaking about the IOC, mindful that Bach had indeed helped the Russians. Putin criticized WADA, the sports federations, and the International Paralympic Committee, which banned the entire Russian team from the 2016 Paralympics. But he did not say a harsh word about Bach and the IOC.

Putin's doublespeak was on full display a few weeks later when he welcomed the Rio medal winners back to the Kremlin. Even with its reduced team, Russia did impressively well, earning fourth place on the medal table with 19 gold and 56 total medals. The president saluted the athletes for their courage. Russians truly represented the Olympic ideals of justice, equality, and mutual respect. By contrast, the president noted, others in the world insolently trampled these ideals.

He then backed off. "Yes, of course, we are aware of our own mistakes," he admitted. "We are working to improve our country's anti-doping system."

And then he attacked again. "The international anti-doping organizations need to improve their work to ensure they are free from political pressure," Putin said. "After all, what are they—a military organization or something?"

Moscow sports officials followed the strategy set by their leader. On the conciliatory side, there was a show of cleaning up RUSADA and the sports agencies. "We made a lot of mistakes," said Vitaly

Smirnov, former head of the Russian Olympic Committee, who was appointed to reform the country's anti-doping system. "It was an institutional conspiracy," admitted acting RUSADA director Anna Antseliovich to the *New York Times*.

At the same time, Moscow went on the offensive. In September 2016 the hacker group Fancy Bear posted documents stolen from WADA computers showing Western athletes had permission to take banned medications. Russian media reports on the hacks singled out gymnast Simone Biles and tennis stars Serena and Venus Williams, who had been prescribed drugs on the WADA banned list.

The hacks were a perfect tactic. The stolen documents were proof of the double standard Russians faced in world sport: everyone dopes, but only Russia is punished. Yet there was also deniability. "How can one possibly prove that the hackers were from Russia?" asked Vitaly Mutko.

Turns out it was pretty easy to prove when they left behind one of their laptops while trying to hack a military conference in the Netherlands. The laptop verified what American and European investigators long suspected: the hackers were not only Russian; they were officers in the Russian Military Intelligence Directorate, the GRU.

Investigators found that the GRU's hacking unit started targeting WADA computers on July 18, 2016, the day the McLaren Report was released. Most of the hacking was done from Moscow. Using spear phishing messages and spoofed websites, unit members nabbed login names and passwords. On occasion, a few traveled overseas on diplomatic passports to hack WiFi networks. In Rio they tapped routers at hotels where WADA and IOC officials were staying during the Olympics. They did the same a month later during an anti-doping conference in Lausanne.

The GRU unit expanded attacks to the US Anti-Doping Agency, the IAAF, the Court of Arbitration for Sport, FIFA, and dozens of other sports organizations. The Fancy Bear website posted the spoils of these raids: medical records, test results, and emails about doping violations, relating to nearly 250 athletes from 30 countries. This was all on top of their work to undermine November's US presidential election. 2016 was a busy time to be a Russian hacker.

Moscow attacked the governing bodies, and Moscow placated the governing bodies.

"The Russian anti-doping system has failed," Putin stated in March 2017, "and this is our fault."

Sir Craig Reedie welcomed Putin's statement. The World Anti-Doping Agency set up a roadmap for re-certifying RUSADA and the Moscow anti-doping lab. The Russians made progress, with new staff, new policies, and international consultants to supervise reforms. One clear signal that Moscow meant business came in May 2017 when Putin's favorite pole vaulter was removed as chair of RUSADA's board. Yelena Isinbayeva had condemned the doping investigation at every turn. She "did not reflect a culture change," said WADA deputy director general Rob Koehler, head of the committee overseeing Russia's re-certification.

WADA's roadmap had two main conditions for reinstatement of the Moscow lab and RUSADA. For one, the lab had to turn over its complete computer files. This would provide full transparency, showing which test results had been altered during Rodchenkov's time as director.

Second, Moscow had to publicly accept the McLaren Report's findings. The Canadian professor's work for WADA had been Earth-shaking. After release of his first report right before the Rio Games, McLaren and his team continued their trek through the mountains of evidence. Their second report, released in December 2016, was even more damning. The investigation concluded that over 1,000 Russian athletes were involved in the cover-up of positive doping tests, going back to the 2012 London Olympics. The report pointed to Vitaly Mutko as being ultimately responsible. Putin's former Sports Minister, now Deputy Prime Minister, had known what Rodchenkov was doing in the Moscow lab and in some instances gave specific instructions.

This key finding kept the Russians from signing off on the McLaren Report. Moscow could admit to widespread doping in Russian sports. Officials could even acknowledge there had been an "institutional conspiracy." But while a scheme carried out by people working in state jobs was acceptable, the charge of a government-run doping program, led by the former Sports Minister, was not.

Fortunately, the IOC helped them out again. WADA had already conducted two investigations, the Pound Commission in 2015 and the McLaren Commission in 2016, based on interviews, documents, recorded conversations, and forensic tests. For Thomas Bach, however, these inquiries weren't good enough. The IOC launched its own investigation into Russian doping, led by someone with more Olympian heft than Canadian lawyers: the former president of Switzerland, Samuel Schmid.

The Schmid Commission didn't break any new ground. Its members reviewed the same evidence McLaren's team had pored through, then they poked holes in McLaren's findings. Of particular concern was the accusation of a state-directed doping program. Schmid posed the allegation directly to the man who had been in charge. "State-doping support system has never existed in the Russian Federation," Vitaly Mutko assured him. Individuals within state offices "might have been connected to each other," Mutko said, but there was no state-directed program.

Mutko's denials got the spotlight in Schmid's final report. Released on December 2, 2017, the judgement weighed in at

30 pages, compared to over 1,300 pages produced by the WADA investigations. The Schmid Commission agreed with previous findings that there was "a widespread culture of doping in Russia." And yes, individuals in state positions were involved. But no, the IOC commission did not find proof that "the highest State authority" knew about the doping. To be sure, Mutko denied any knowledge. The evidence, therefore, did not allow the Schmid Commission "to establish with certitude who initiated or who headed this scheme."

Here was the loophole the IOC needed. The Sports Ministry and Russian Olympic Committee were cleared of initiating the doping scheme. These institutions were not guily, but they were still legally responsible; therefore, some punishment was necessary. Three days after the Schmid Report was released, the IOC Executive Board announced its sentence: the Russian Olympic Committee was suspended from the upcoming Winter Olympics in Korea, and Sports Ministry officials were prohibited from attending.

Russian sports officials were banned, but Russian athletes were not. If they were verified as clean, athletes from Russia could compete in Korea—but not, the IOC decided, as representatives of Russia. Instead, their uniforms would read "Olympic Athlete from Russia." When an "OAR" competitor won a medal, the Olympic flag rather than the Russian tricolor would be raised. If the medal was gold, the athlete would take the podium to the Olympic anthem.

Bach could congratulate himself on the Solomonic solution based on the Schmid Commission's investigation. RUSSIA BANNED FROM WINTER OLYMPICS, read headlines around the world, giving the appearance of tough action by the IOC. Yet clean Russian athletes were still allowed to compete.

In fact, the Schmid Commission report provided cover for a decision the IOC had already made. Before Bach announced the plan for Russian athletes competing in Korea, the IOC was in talks with Nike to design uniforms for the OAR team. Just as with the Rio Summer Games, the IOC never considered banning the entire Russian team from the 2018 Winter Olympics.

Beckie Scott discovered this as she relayed the concerns of athletes around the world. Serving as chair of WADA's athlete committee, Scott heard from individual athletes and athlete committees. There was consistent demand for a complete ban on Russia. Evidence presented in the McLaren Report "should have been enough to disqualify and not enable a country to participate at the Olympic Games," she said in an interview with the BBC in August 2017.

Immediately after her interview, Scott was scolded by the heads of the IOC's Athlete Committee, American hockey player Angela Ruggiero and French canoeist Tony Estanguet. The world's athletes would be "accurately informed about the facts, the actual situation," they wrote, but only after Samuel Schmid's report was released. Just as the McLaren Report was more than Moscow could accept, it was too strong for the IOC.

Within WADA, deputy director Rob Koehler also got pushback when he pressed for stronger penalties against Russia. The IOC wanted Russian athletes in the Games, one of his WADA bosses told him. And since the IOC paid a big share of WADA's budget, the agency had to quiet down about punishing Russia. "It was stated directly to me that 'Russia is the most powerful sporting nation,'" Koehler said in an interview with HBO's *Real Sports*. "'The IOC is a 50 percent partner. And we don't want to piss them off, so back off.'"

I asked Koehler about the resistance he and Beckie Scott faced. Why was the IOC so determined to keep Russia in the

Games? After all, the doping revelations were a black mark on the Olympics. And surely, Thomas Bach did not want to go down in history as "Putin's Poodle."

"Russia puts a ton of money into the Olympics and into international sport," Koehler told me. "Money comes into the IOC, and money flows out from the IOC to all the federations and national committees. If you behave, you'll get money. Misbehave, and you won't. It's a well-oiled system to make sure people toe the party line. It's not the most ethical business. And there's a lot of pressure to uphold the status quo."

In the West, the IOC's punishment for the 2018 Winter Olympics was widely seen as too lenient. Viewed from Russia, however, the sanctions were another politically motivated insult. Yelena Isinbayeva vented her anger on Instagram: "What remains of Olympic principles, of the spirit of the Olympic, of the idea of the Olympic Games? Without Russia, it's a lame Olympics!"

Duma members howled that Russian athletes could not forsake their motherland by wearing some neutral uniform. There was speculation Putin would call for a boycott. The president, however, insisted this would be unfair to the athletes. Russia would still be proud of its Olympians, no matter what colors they wore.

Indeed, Russians turned out in force at the Winter Games in Korea. At the Olympic plaza in Gangneung, site of the hockey venues, I saw Russian flags and hockey jerseys. Many Russians wore T-shirts and beanie hats with the white, blue, and red stripes of the national flag, bearing the slogan "Russia in My Heart."

Russia wasn't the only country in fans' hearts. The Soviet Union held a warm spot as well. I saw red-and-white jerseys with the recognizable Cyrillic letters "CCCP." While walking past a row of Russian fans in the hockey arena, I glanced at a young man in a

Stalin T-shirt. I stopped in my tracks and did a double-take. "Wait a minute!" I said to myself. "Stalin—at the Olympics?"

For most Russians, hockey is the most anticipated event of the Winter Olympics. This was especially the case in 2018. Russians had not claimed gold since 1992, when the post-Soviet Unified Team won. In Korea they were the overwhelming favorites. For the first time since 1998, the National Hockey League did not release its players for the Olympics, which meant teams like Canada, the US, and Sweden would be without their best players. Russian NHL stars like Alexander Ovechkin were also absent. But former NHL players like Ilya Kovalchuk and Pavel Datsyuk were now playing in the Kontinental Hockey League, making them available for the Olympics.

The Russian team was stacked. And this was indeed the Russian team, not Olympic Athletes from Russia. The fans did not hide their true allegiance, nor did the players. "Yes, they took away our flag and anthem," Kovalchuk told *Sport-Express* before the Games, "but they did not take away our honor and conscience. We know that we are Russians, that we represent the best country in the world."

Overall, Russia's athletes won only two gold medals at the 2018 Winter Olympics. But one of those golds was in the sport that mattered most. On February 25, over 33 million Russians watched their hockey team win a thrilling overtime game over Germany for the gold. Inside the arena, cheering Russians in jerseys emblazoned with the double-headed eagle waved their nation's flag. As the Olympic banner was raised during the medal ceremony, fans joined the players in singing their country's anthem. Their voices were so loud, they drown out the Olympic anthem playing over the arena speakers. "We knew we'd do it if we won," Kovalchuk said of the team's decision to sing the anthem.

After the hockey game, Russian pride poured over social media. Twitter users posted GIFs of Russian and Soviet flags, photos of

Putin and Stalin. With the final win coming over Germany, there were references to the Soviet victory in 1945, even Alexander Nevsky's defeat of the Teutonic Knights in 1242.

But the real opponent was America. In the hockey tournament's group stage, the Russians had trounced Team USA, proving how weak the Americans were. After the gold-medal victory, homophobic and racist memes cast the United States as a decadent, mongrel country. According to tweets from Russian fans, the representative American was a Black athlete doped on steroids. The country's symbol was the rainbow flag. Russians were real men, and they proved it on the hockey rink.

There was no hint of neutrality when Putin welcomed the Olympians home from Korea.

"The games were historic for our great country," said NHL legend Pavel Datsyuk at the Kremlin. "We defended the honor of our country thanks to our Russian character."

As usual, Putin mixed conciliation and confrontation in his remarks. "We need to turn over a new leaf. We must learn from this lesson," the president said. "But I hope the international bodies will understand as well that sports should be kept away from topics that have nothing to do with it."

Putin's comments set the tone for the year ahead. RUSADA continued its reforms, following the compliance roadmap set by the World Anti-Doping Agency. The Russians made progress on all points, except for the two big ones: acknowledging the McLaren Report and providing WADA with the data from the Moscow lab.

On the first matter, the new Minister of Sport, Pavel Kolobkov, and the head of the Russian Olympic Committee, Alexander Zhukov, acknowledged that a "group of individuals" manipulated test results. But they did not concede to the charge of a state-directed doping program. Instead they acknowledged the

IOC's Schmid Report. As for the lab data, Minister Kolobkov said that as soon as WADA let the Russians back in, then an independent expert would be allowed into the Moscow lab to copy the computer files.

WADA leaders were inclined to take what they could get. Beckie Scott again stood on behalf of athletes, bringing forward demands from representative committees of different countries and sports federations. There was an "unprecedented global uprising," she said at the WADA Executive Council meeting in September 2018. The world's athletes did not agree with reinstatement of RUSADA.

Council members laughed out loud at Scott's appeal. One WADA official, who also wore hats in the IOC, asked why the anti-doping agency even needed an athlete committee. Didn't the IOC athlete committee provide enough representation? It appeared to him that the WADA athlete committee did little more than stir negative feelings toward sports officials.

In the showdown between the people who competed in sports and the people who ran sports, there was no contest. The executive council voted to reinstate RUSADA. Beckie Scott resigned from the committee overseeing Russian compliance and later from the WADA athlete committee. The sportocrats wanted Russia in the game, no matter what athletes said.

Not surprisingly the Russians did not prove as cooperative as promised. In December 2018 WADA sent a team of tech specialists to Moscow to get the lab data. They left empty handed—a disagreement on "access conditions" was the official explanation. WADA threatened to undo the vote to reinstate. The Russians invited them back. A month later, the WADA team made the trip again. This time, they left Moscow with 23 terabytes of files. Back at their computers in Lausanne and Barcelona, the IT crew went to work.

To understand what WADA's tech specialists found, it helps to recall the warning all of us have received from IT departments at work since the dawn of computers: deleted files are never really deleted. Even after we hit "empty trash," those angry emails and pirated videos are still lurking in the depths of our computers. The Moscow lab didn't get that lesson.

As they pored through the data, WADA's tech experts found evidence of deleted files, back-dated entries, altered command logs, and missing backups. On the December day when the WADA team was blocked from entering the Moscow lab, Russian IT guys were inside deleting over 450 database-backup files. They were even busier hitting the delete key before the return visit in January. WADA's tech experts identified over 20,000 data files and PDFs removed from the lab's servers. Digital footprints told the forensic team which files were deleted, when they were deleted, and who did the deleting.

WADA specialists also found planted information. The Moscow lab's IT director backdated file deletions to 2015, when Rodchenkov was still in charge. Russian tech guys also inserted texts into the lab's internal messaging system as supposed proof that Rodchenkov demanded bribes from doped athletes.

When WADA reported the discoveries back to the Moscow lab, the Russians insisted the files were accurate. "What about the backdating?" asked WADA tech specialists. "There was no backdating," replied the Russians.

Moscow might lie, but ones and zeroes don't. The Russians were caught covering up their cover-up of the biggest crime in sports history. In November 2019 WADA un-reinstated RUSADA and the Moscow lab. The anti-doping body went even further, imposing the toughest sanctions yet: For the next four years, anyone affiliated with the Russian Olympic Committee or the Russian government, from the president down, was barred from the Olympics and other international events. The Russian flag would not fly at events. Russian athletes could still compete, but only after proving they were clean. If approved these athletes would wear nothing that said "Russia" or showed the national colors. The sham neutrality of the Korea Winter Olympics would not be repeated. Finally WADA was throwing the book at the incorrigible Russians.

But other sportocrats came up with the save. Moscow appealed the WADA sanctions to the Court of Arbitration for Sport. In December 2020 the Court issued its ruling. Yes, the data cover-up was the culmination of a massive fraud, carried out in the "most cynical and sophisticated manner." Yes, the computer evidence clearly showed "Russian authorities remain as willing as ever to interfere with, and corrupt, the anti-doping system." WADA was therefore correct to call for robust punishment.

But, the Court added, there needed to be attention to "proportionality." Any punishment had to follow rules of natural justice and human rights. The three-man panel (Australian, French, and Italian) dialed back WADA's original slate of sanctions. The length of the sentence was cut from four years to two. And rather than having Russian athletes dress in completely neutral uniforms, the Court allowed for uniforms in the colors of the national flag. The word "Russia" could be on their uniforms, but only with the words "Neutral Athletes."

For a third time, Russia was getting a break. The IOC refused to ban the country's athletes from Rio, and then created the Olympic Athletes from Russia fiction for the Winter Games. Now, the Court of Arbitration for Sport was cutting down WADA's punishment—even while conceding that Russia had been caught red-handed. Again.

The view in Moscow, however, was that any punishment was an unjust punishment. "Russia is a great country and a great power, including in sports," said Duma member Dmitry Svishchev, who headed the national curling federation. "I don't think anyone has the right to punish us. This does not apply to our country."

In fact, this revised punishment was no punishment at all. Russia had a larger contingent at the Tokyo Olympics in 2021 than at Rio. Athletes wore white, blue, and red uniforms with the logo of the Russian Olympic Committee. When a Russian athlete won gold, a Tchaikovsky piece played rather than the Olympic anthem.

The emptiness of the sanctions was evident six months later at the Beijing Winter Games. WADA's initial punishment stipulated that no representative of the Russian government was allowed to attend the Olympics or any international sporting event. The CAS panel walked back this penalty, allowing for a Russian official to attend "if invited by the Head of State or Prime Minister." Guess who got an invitation to join China's head of state, Xi Jinping, at the Opening Ceremonies in Beijing.

Vladimir Putin was one of the few world leaders at the Beijing Winter Games. The US, Canada, Australia, and several European countries staged a diplomatic boycott in protest over the Chinese government's human rights record. Putin, however, was a reliable guest. After his meeting with Xi, where the two leaders made plans for an anti-NATO partnership, the Russian president blasted the West for mixing politics and sport: "This is fundamentally wrong and contradicts the very spirit and principles of the Olympic Charter."

Thomas Bach approved this message. "We can only get all humanity together," he said at the IOC meeting in Beijing, "if the Games stand beyond all differences and political disputes."

As the IOC president recited platitudes about the unifying mission of the Olympics, all the efforts to bring Russia to account for cheating were undermined by a 15-year-old girl in sequins.

Kamila Valieva was the favorite to win gold in women's figure skating at Beijing. Teammates Alexandra Trusova and Anna Shcherbakova were expected to join her on the podium. All three skaters were coached by Eteri Tutberidze, who had trained world champions for a decade. Like Soviet gymnastics coaches of the 1960s, Tutberidze devised a new strategy for winning medals: teach tiny girls with no curves how to perform terrifying jumps. More than any other skater, Valieva showed the success of this strategy. In her first season of senior-level competition, she set one record after another for high scores. In the team event at Beijing, she became the first female skater to ever land a quadruple jump in international competition.

Thanks to Valieva's performance, the Russians handily won gold in team skating. The medal ceremony was scheduled for the night after the final skate, but the International Skating Union stepped in before the medals were awarded. Rumors buzzed that Valieva had failed a drug test. Because she was a minor, however, the IOC could not post her test results, nor explain the situation.

The official silence stoked speculation in the media, both in the West and Russia. As it turned out, the cause of the snafu was Russia's non-compliance with WADA. Valieva had submitted a urine sample to RUSADA control officers at a competition in Chelyabinsk in late December. But the sample could not be tested in Moscow's decertified lab. Instead, it was sent to Sweden. The holidays created a testing logjam, then COVID hit the staff, so the Stockholm lab didn't finish testing Valieva's sample until just before the Games. Her sample tested positive for trimetazidine, a drug usually prescribed to patients with heart problems. For an athlete, the drug could improve heart efficiency and endurance.

RUSADA suspended Valieva, then un-suspended her, based on her story that the drug was her grandfather's. Valieva said her grandpa would grind pills in the kitchen to dissolve them in water, so that's how she probably ingested it. WADA and the International Skating Union were skeptical. They called on the Court of Arbitration for Sport to decide Valieva's fate. In a hurry-up hearing conducted by video link, the Court decided Valieva could compete in the women's event, given her young age and the delay in the lab's finding.

By the time Valieva took the ice, the scandal had been building for a week. According to commentators in the West, the teenage skater was another doped-up Russian athlete allowed to compete. In Russia she was a child of the motherland degraded by the West. "Kamila, do not hide your face," said Kremlin spokesman Dmitry Peskov. "You are a Russian. Walk proudly. Most importantly, defeat everyone!"

After the short program, it appeared Valieva would indeed defeat everyone. She went into the free skate with a two-point lead. As she stepped onto the ice, the final skater of the night, the week's tempest weighed on her. She skated again to Ravel's *Boléro,* the same routine that had won the team competition. This time, she stumbled backward on her second jump, then fell on the next combination. Later in the routine, she missed another landing and fell to the ice. She lifted her arms to finish the routine, then threw down a hand in frustration and bent over in tears.

Cameras were there as she stepped off the ice. "Why did you let it go?" Tutberidze asked. "Explain it to me. Why? Why did you stop fighting?"

The next moments are still difficult to watch. Valieva in tears; her teammate, Trusova, fuming at the judges' scoring, mascara streaming down her face; and their fellow Russian, Anna Shcherbakova, sitting alone, stunned, the neglected gold medal winner.

It was a low point for the Olympics. Even Thomas Bach remarked on Tutberidze's "tremendous coldness" toward the young skater. In his daily news conference, Bach spoke of the pressure Valieva must have felt. "Rather than giving her comfort, rather than trying to help her," Bach said, "you could feel this chilling atmosphere, this distance."

What was this sudden gasp of conscience from the IOC president? Was he criticizing Russia—in calling out how one of their young athletes was mistreated?

In his comments, Bach missed something important: performing at the highest level of international sport demanded technical precision and steely composure—skills built through ceaseless training and, yes, rigid coaching. Over the decades, the Moscow playbook had transformed sports, elevating the feats expected of athletes and, therefore, the demands imposed upon athletes. The Olympic goals of faster, higher, stronger came at a cost. The Soviets figured this out in the 1950s. The rest of the world followed their lead. After all, what was the difference between Eteri Tutberidze treating Valieva with "tremendous coldness" and Béla Károlyi imploring Kerri Strug to vault on her injured ankle at the 1996 Olympics?

It fell to a Russian to call out Bach's hypocrisy. Tatiana Tarasova was the daughter of Anatoly Tarasov, the legendary hockey coach who devised the Soviet team's relentless training regime. Tarasova herself was also a coaching legend: she trained more gold medal–winning figure skaters than anyone in Olympic history. Like Russian coaches in other sports, including her father, she was in demand around the world. Her skaters included not only Russians but also Americans like Michelle Kwan and Johnny Weir. She knew what was required to become an Olympic champion, and she had no patience with the IOC president clutching his pearls.

"Look at yourself!" she said of Thomas Bach's whining about harsh, distant coaches. "Who started all this?"

CHAPTER 14

KICKING RUSSIA OUT OF THE GAME

THOMAS BACH STEPPED to the center of the Beijing Bird's Nest to close the Winter Games. The stadium was bathed in dark-blue light. Ninety-one young men in white were arrayed behind the IOC president, each holding the flag of a participating nation—all except for Russia, which was still technically banned from the Games. Russian athletes were represented not by their national flag but by a white banner with the Olympic rings and supposedly neutral swirls of red, blue, and white.

Bach addressed the assembled Olympians, but his speech was directed to the world.

"Each and every one of you strived to achieve your personal best. We were deeply touched how you were wishing and cheering for your competitors to achieve their best as well."

Except for that moment after the women's figure skating Final when Alexandra Trusova fumed at the judges awarding gold to her teammate, Anna Shcherbakova. "Everyone has a gold medal. Everyone but me," she sobbed. "I hate skating. I hate this sport. I will never skate again."

Bach also said, "You not only respected each other. You supported each other. You embraced each other, even if your countries are divided by conflict."

Here he was referring to Russian skier Ilya Burov, who gave a congratulatory hug to gold medalist Oleksandr Abramenko of Ukraine. Indeed, a sportsmanlike gesture. But the euphemism "divided by conflict" was a bit disingenuous. During the course of the games, over 100,000 Russian troops were massed on the Ukrainian border.

"You overcame these divisions," Bach said, "demonstrating that in this Olympic community, we are all equal. We are all equal—regardless of what we look like, where we come from, or what we believe in."

Apparently, some were more equal than others. Before the women's skating Final, several former Olympians asked on social media why Kamila Valieva was allowed to compete after her positive test. "We were just told illegal drugs and abuse are OK," tweeted Canadian gold medalist Meagan Duhamel.

Bach's address continued: "The unifying power of the Olympic games is stronger than the forces that want to divide us. You give peace a chance. May the political leaders of the world be inspired by your example of solidarity and peace."

Vladimir Putin must have taken Bach's advice to heart. Back in Moscow, the Russian president was putting the finishing touches on a speech for the nation—and the world. Putin's fundamental message was peace: Russia wants peace, Russia seeks peace, Russia has the duty to bring peace to lands on its borders.

Broadcast on February 24, just a few days after the Olympic flame had been extinguished, Putin's speech announced the beginning of Russia's "special military operation." That morning, the Russian army launched the largest invasion in Europe since World War II. The target was Ukraine, but the ultimate enemy was the

United States. In Putin's words, "the dominant state" had broken treaties and brushed aside other countries' legitimate concerns. Russia had no choice but to defend itself.

"For our country, it is a matter of life and death," the president declared from the Kremlin, "a matter of our historical future as a nation."

Russia was primed for the fight long before Putin gave his speech. Going back to the Salt Lake City Olympics, Russians had heard the same rhetoric about world sports: Russia was a great nation, but it was constantly disrespected by the US and the international organizations controlled by the Americans. This perspective of world sports contributed to an us-versus-everyone mentality that dominated Russian politics and media before the invasion of Ukraine.

Throughout those years, Moscow's complaints about the unfair, American-dominated world order received an indulgent hearing from sports governing bodies. Sportocrats in Switzerland depended on dollars from American corporate sponsors and media contracts, but they also wanted to limit the "dominant state's" influence. Russia appeared to be a reliable partner in offsetting American power, just as the Soviet Union had been decades earlier. The debris of the Putin era—murdered politicians, downed jetliners, armed annexations—could all be swept under the carpet of political neutrality.

Russia's invasion of Ukraine brought that arrangement to an end. Unprovoked, deliberate, and cynically timed to the Winter Olympics, Putin's war was a defiant middle finger. After having gotten away with so much for so long, Moscow had every reason to believe the governing bodies of international sport would concede to this latest provocation. To everyone's surprise, the sports world finally decided it had enough.

At first the sportocrats dithered as Putin's tanks rumbled into Ukraine. Governing bodies posted mealymouthed statements that they were watching carefully. "We will continue to monitor the situation closely," said Formula One racing, which had a Grand Prix race in Sochi on the calendar for September. The International Ski Federation announced on the invasion's first day that World Cup events scheduled for the upcoming weekend in Russia would go on as planned.

The biggest sporting event on the immediate calendar was the Winter Paralympics, scheduled to begin on March 4. Initially, the IPC agreed to allow Russian athletes to compete as neutrals. Russia's team of 71 athletes arrived in Beijing. But the IPC faced a swell of opposition, with other countries threatening to pull out of the games if Russian athletes competed. Two days after arriving, the Russians were sent home.

Surprisingly, the IOC also reacted vigorously. Twice before, Putin had defied the Olympic Truce, the UN resolution calling on participating nations to refrain from warfare during the Olympics and Paralympics. In 2014 Putin had broken the truce by seizing Crimea; in 2008, Russian troops invaded Georgia while he was in Beijing for the opening of the Summer Games. This time, the IOC finally spoke up, condemning the Russian government's violation of the truce. The executive board went even further, calling on sports federations to remove or postpone scheduled events in Russia.

Federations were also pushed into action by their own athletes. Even though the Russian Grand Prix was months away, F1 drivers objected to racing in Sochi. "When a country is at war, it is not right to race there," said Max Verstappen. Skiers Ryan Regez of Switzerland and Sandra Näslund of Sweden, both gold medalists in Beijing, announced they were not competing in Russia. The following day, the FIS announced the season's remaining events in Russia were cancelled.

Principled athletes were especially decisive in soccer. Russia was slated to host a qualification game in March for the 2022 World Cup. Days before the invasion began, national federations in the same qualification group as Russia—Poland, Sweden, and the Czech Republic—asked FIFA what would happen in the event of war. FIFA didn't even answer. When the war began, FIFA president Gianni Infantino went before the press to say the federation was monitoring the situation.

"The first match is one month from now," Infantino said, referring to the upcoming qualification game between Russia and Poland. "We hope this whole situation will be solved before then."

At the time Infantino was doing his hoping, over 100,000 Russian troops had already crossed the Ukrainian border. Columns of tanks and armored vehicles, marked with the letter Z, were knifing through northern and eastern Ukraine. Russian missiles were pounding Kyiv and other cities. In euphemistically saying "the whole situation will be solved" in a month's time, Infantino expressed the view of many observers at the time: the Russian army would quickly overrun Ukraine, and then we can get back to business as normal.

While world soccer's boss was unwilling to stand up to Moscow, the sport's players were. The day after the invasion started, Robert Lewandowski phoned his teammates on the Polish national team to ask their views on the qualification match. The Bayern Munich forward had been national squad captain for nearly a decade, and his teammates were playing in leagues across Europe. Lewandowski put the question to each of them: Could the Polish team play Russia?

This was a serious question. Professional soccer players do not refuse to play international qualifiers. They faced reprisals from their national federation, or from FIFA. Their chances of playing in the World Cup would be dashed. Yet Lewandowski didn't have to convince anyone.

"We didn't think about the consequences or whether we might be punished," Juventus goalkeeper Wojciech Szczęsny told the *New York Times*. "We only cared about the outcome. We were prepared to forfeit the game. We were not going to play."

Szczęsny had a personal connection to the war—his wife, a popular Polish singer, had been born in Ukraine. Defender Tomasz Kędziora, whose club team was Dynamo Kyiv, was married to a Ukrainian. As soon as the war began, the soccer federation worked to get Kędziora and his family to Poland.

Even for Poles without family links across the border, the invasion of Ukraine had a profound impact. In the first weeks of the war, over 1.5 million refugees fled into Poland. Lewandowski's wife, Anna, mobilized employees at her business to provide care for Ukrainian children. Of course, Poles had their own history with Russian invaders. Between 1939 and 1941, tens of thousands of Polish intellectuals, teachers, and military officers were executed or deported to Siberia during the Soviet occupation of eastern Poland. The Red Army came back at the end of the war. This time, the Soviet occupation led to 44 years of communist rule, with Moscow threatening to crack down whenever Poles tested their independence.

So, when Lewandowski told the Polish federation that the national team was not playing, there was no objection. "We didn't have any doubts," said team manager Jakub Kwiatkowski. "It is hard to imagine that we would stand on a pitch and play a team that represents the invaders," he told Britain's talkSPORT.

The sportocrats pushed back. FIFA suggested the match be played at a neutral site, with the Russian team wearing neutral jerseys. The soccer bosses added a threat: play or else. The Polish answer was no. Not at a neutral site. Not with neutral uniforms.

The Poles were not playing the Russians. "If FIFA wants to kick us out, let them kick us out," said Kwiatkowski.

"It is the right decision!" tweeted Robert Lewandowski. "I can't imagine playing a match with the Russian National Team in a situation when armed aggression in Ukraine continues. Russian footballers and fans are not responsible for this, but we can't pretend that nothing is happening."

The national team's decision had the backing of the nation's leader.

"You don't play with bandits," tweeted Polish president Andrzej Duda.

"The world has created bonds of friendship with Russia that will last forever." Gianni Infantino's remark after the 2018 World Cup did not age well. In the days after Putin ordered his troops into Ukraine, Infantino was slammed.

Rob Harris of the Associated Press launched a direct strike at the FIFA press conference on the day of the invasion: "Will you be retaining your Order of Friendship medal that you received from Vladimir Putin after the 2018 World Cup? And in light of all the developments that have happened now do you have regrets about the 2018 World Cup or your glowing endorsements of Putin and his conduct?"

The question shook Infantino. He dodged with the usual pablum: "We are constantly reflecting on the role of sport. In particular, the role of sport to bring people together in a peaceful environment." It was obvious how empty the rhetoric had become.

"A grotesque, morally invertebrate fool," judged the *Guardian*.

"Let history damn Infantino," echoed the *Telegraph*.

British sportswriter David Walsh lumped Infantino together with Thomas Bach. The sportocrats "now look like idiots, unable to credibly denounce their friend," he wrote in London's *Sunday Times*. "They took his money and now pay for it with their reputations."

Infantino's hesitation was all the more stark as other soccer leaders quickly moved to cut ties with Russia. UEFA announced the day after the invasion that it was pulling that spring's Champions League Final from St. Petersburg. The federation also ended its lucrative sponsorship with Gazprom. Schalke 04 tore up its deal with the energy giant as well.

Roman Abramovich tried to get ahead of the anti-Russian wave. Two days after the invasion, the Chelsea owner announced he was handing club administration to the board of trustees. The following day, Chelsea released an official statement, calling the situation in Ukraine "horrific and devastating."

British authorities, however, did not let Abramovich cleanse himself so easily. The UK government froze Abramovich's assets and imposed a travel ban. The Premier League's board followed by disqualifying the oligarch as Chelsea director. Abramovich received government permission to sell the club, with his pledge to donate the proceeds to war victims. In May 2022 Chelsea was sold for £4.25 billion to a consortium led by Todd Boehly, co-owner of the Dodgers and Lakers. As of 2025 the money is still sitting in Barclay's bank, while the government and Abramovich's lawyers haggle over how the money should be distributed.

With the soccer world turning against Moscow, pressure on Infantino grew. On February 28 even the IOC flipped their allegiance. Noting that it acted "with a heavy heart," the IOC called on all sports federations to "not invite or allow the participation of Russian and Belarusian athletes and officials in international competitions." FIFA finally went along with the rest of the sports world. Russia got the red card from all international matches.

As their organizations banned Russians, Infantino and Bach took tight control of their statements. Bach issued a statement on the IOC website on March 12; Infantino spoke three weeks later at the FIFA World Congress in Doha. Their words were similar, as if they had shared notes. Both condemned the violence in Ukraine, "with heavy hearts." Both avoided any mention of past dalliances with Putin.

Another point of agreement was that their organizations were in no way responsible for the conflict. Bach and Infantino insisted their global institutions of influence and power actually had no influence and power. Governing bodies of world sport cannot keep peace, they declared. The Olympics and world soccer could help rebuild peace and mutual understanding—once the conflict was over.

Decisions of war and peace were entirely in the hands of politicians, maintained the leaders of FIFA and the IOC. In his speech to the FIFA congress, Infantino pointed out that Kyiv hosted the Euro Championship in 2012 while Moscow hosted the World Cup Final in 2018. Yet even though the capitals of Russia and Ukraine hosted soccer's biggest tournaments, the sport "did not solve the problems of the world. It did not even solve the problems of the region." Soccer tried. Soccer didn't succeed. Soccer can't be faulted.

All Infantino needed was a bowl of water to wash his hands.

As leaders of world soccer and the Olympics separated themselves from Putin, they likewise separated the innocent Russian athlete from the guilty Russian government. "This war has not been started by the Russian people, Russian athletes, or Russian sports organizations," Bach stated. In calling for exclusion of Russian athletes from international events, the IOC did not claim they were representatives of a country carrying out a war of aggression. Instead, Olympic leaders cited the practical concerns of safety and integrity of competition.

Athletes from other countries, however, were not so willing to distinguish Russian athletes from the Russian state. "I refuse to play against players who choose to represent the values and principles of Russia!" declared Polish goalkeeper Wojciech Szczęsny on Instagram. "I refuse to stand on the pitch, wearing the colors of my country and listen to the national anthem of Russia! I refuse to take part in a sporting event that legitimizes the actions of the Russian government."

Another argument for exclusion was that many Russian athletes were active members of the armed forces. The Soviet-era sports clubs affiliated with the military and security services, CSKA and Dynamo, still enrolled thousands of athletes. Most of the medals the Russian team brought back from the Beijing Winter Games were won by athletes with officer rank, who lived on military salaries. Russian armed forces regularly used these officer-Olympians in recruiting campaigns, and several military athletes gave explicit support for the invasion of Ukraine.

But what about Russian athletes who did not wear a military uniform, or speak in favor of the war, or enter the arena to their country's anthem? What about individual athletes who competed for prize money, or who played for a team in a pro league outside of Russia? Would these athletes also be excluded?

As soon as the war began, top-ranked tennis players Daniil Medvedev and Andrey Rublev distanced themselves from Moscow's aggression. After a semifinal match in Dubai, Rublev wrote on a TV camera with a black marker: "No war please."

Despite such criticism of the war, the All-England Tennis Club decided to ban Russian and Belarusian players from the 2022 Wimbledon Championships. There were discussions of a diplomatic solution, perhaps pairing a Russian and Ukrainian player as a mixed-doubles team or excluding Russians or Belarusians from the trophy ceremonies if they won. But Wimbledon organizers did not want Moscow to have any opportunity of hijacking the world's most prestigious tournament. "They didn't want it to be used as propaganda," Rublev explained to Russian journalist Vitya Kravchenko.

Kravchenko interviewed Rublev and fellow Russian player Daria Kasatkina in summer 2022, shortly after the Wimbledon ban. Walking through Barcelona, where they trained, the two young pros spoke candidly to Kravchenko about the impact of Russia's politics on their professional and personal lives. Rublev acknowledged he was considering giving up Russian citizenship to continue his career. Kasatkina likewise spoke of the war's effects on her own career prospects and those of younger Russian tennis players. "Sixteen- and 17-year-olds have some chance," she said. "They might have time to leave the country."

More significant for Kasatkina was that she would be in danger in Russia as a gay woman. The Kremlin had made her an exile, with its policies on sexual identity and its war in Ukraine. Yet Russia was still home. The 25-year-old tennis pro traveled the world and lived on the Mediterranean, but her heart was still in the country where she had been raised. Kravchenko asked if she accepted the possibility of never returning.

"Yes, I've thought about it," she said. Then she broke down in tears.

For one Russian athlete competing abroad, there was no need to fear a life in exile. Alexander Ovechkin would not have to change his citizenship. He was loved in Russia and in America—at least among Washington Capitals fans.

For two decades, Ovi was one of the NHL's biggest stars: a 12-time All-Star, three-time league MVP, and two-time cover model for EA Sports *NHL* video game. In 2018 he led the Capitals to their first Stanley Cup, earning playoff MVP honors and a place of reverence in the DC sports pantheon.

Ovechkin was also MVP of Vladimir Putin's stable of athletes. When Russia won the 2014 Hockey World Championship in Minsk, Ovechkin handed the trophy to Putin in the locker room. The president took a drink from the cup and gave Ovechkin a kiss. "Nobody could have missed the symbolism here," former *Sport Ekspres* journalist Slava Malamud told the CBC. "The marriage of sports and power."

Later that same year, Ovechkin lent his fame to the PR campaign supporting the invasion of eastern Ukraine. He posted a photo of himself on Instagram holding a sign that read, in English: #SaveChildrenFromFascism. Ovechkin added the line in Russian: "Our Grandfathers and Grandmothers witnessed the horrors of Fascism! We will not allow this in our time!" The post recited Putin's justification for the 2014 incursion into Donbass, the same justification for the 2022 invasion: Ukrainians are Nazis, and only Russian military action can stop them.

In 2017 Ovechkin took a more prominent role supporting the president's reelection campaign. As the face of Putin Team, a social media campaign launched by a PR firm working for the Kremlin, the NHL all-star was joined by other famous Russians backing the president's bid for a fourth term. Putin Team's roster included singers and actors as well as internationally known athletes like Yelena Isinbayeva and hockey players Pavel Bure, Ilya Kovalchuk, and Evgeny Malkin. The PR firm intended the campaign to reach an international audience, to show the world that Russians who were popular abroad also supported their president. Because of his fame in America, Ovechkin got the spotlight as the team's star.

Ovechkin's support for Putin was well known among hockey writers in North America, so there were questions as to how—or even if—he would address the invasion of Ukraine. On the day after Russian troops crossed the border, Ovi sat down for questions after practice. With his Ovechkin-brand Nike hat pulled low, the team captain's lively personality was turned down. His famous gap-toothed smile did not make an appearance. He searched for words when a reporter asked his thoughts about the situation in Ukraine.

"Umm, obviously it's a hard situation. Umm, you know, umm, I have lots of friends in Russia and Ukraine and it's hard to see the war, like, I hope soon it's going to be over and, umm, there's going to be peace in the whole world."

The next question was more direct: "Do you support the Russian invasion of Ukraine?"

"Umm, like, I'm Russian, right?" he answered. "It's not something I can control. You know, it's not in my hands. I hope it's going to end soon and there's going to be peace in both countries. You know, I don't control this one."

Ovechkin showed no hesitation to the next question: Did he still support Putin?

"Well, he's my president," he said right away. "But how I said, I'm not in politics. I'm an athlete. And umm, how I said, I hope everything is going to be done soon, you know. It's, umm, a hard situation right now for both sides."

Another reporter asked what Ovechkin thought of footage of the destruction in Ukraine.

"Umm, it's hard. It's a hard situation. Umm, you know, I have family back in Russia and, you know, it's scary moments. But, umm, you know, we can't do anything. We just hope it's going to end soon and, umm, everything's going to be all right."

Ovechkin stammered on for another minute. No one asked any follow-ups, such as: "You say you're not in politics, but what about Putin Team?" or "When you say Putin is your president, does that mean you support his decision to invade Ukraine?" No one would get another chance. After this meeting with the press, the Capitals and NHL ensured that the world's most famous Russian hockey player never again faced questions about his president's war.

Ovechkin's performance provided his defenders with talking points: He was only an athlete. The war was outside his control. He just wanted peace. His quick response to the question about suffering in Ukraine was especially clever: "I have family back in Russia." Ovi fans grabbed hold of that line to conjure scenarios of FSB agents holding his family hostage to ensure his support for Putin. This excuse is used still today to explain why Ovechkin has not removed the photo of Putin on his Instagram profile. Presumably, if Ovechkin changes the profile pic on his IG page, his family will be sent to Siberia.

Ovechkin's press conference drew a sharp response from another all-time hockey great. "Not only an alibist, a chicken shit, but also a liar!" tweeted retired Czech goalie Dominik Hašek, two-time Stanley Cup winner, Olympic goal medalist, and Hall of Famer. Hašek not only condemned Ovechkin's mealy press conference, he also called on the NHL to suspend the contracts of all Russian players. "Every athlete represents not only himself and his club," he tweeted, "but also his country and its values and actions."

Hašek's tweets set off a social-media storm. Some NHL fans were outraged Ovechkin didn't denounce the war Putin had launched. Others slammed Hašek for suggesting Russians be expelled from the NHL. Athletes have nothing to do with war, went the common argument. After all, American athletes weren't held responsible for U.S wars in the Middle East. If Russian athletes were banned, it would be like the internment of Japanese-Americans during World War II, wailed social-media philosophers. "Dom, I love you," one fan tweeted to Hašek, "but you're supposed to be between the pipes, not hittin' the pipe."

Hašek was not one to be quieted by Twitter critics. Like Poland's soccer players, he had no illusions about Russia. When he was three years old, Soviet forces invaded his country to extinguish Czechoslovakia's Prague Spring reform movement. Hašek was also aware of the real-life threats in an authoritarian state: when he was offered a million-dollar contract in the NHL in 1988, he refused to defect. The move would have ended his father's career as a teacher. A year later, when students went into Prague streets to protest the communist regime, Hašek and three teammates went AWOL from their army club to join the demonstrations.

As an athlete with strong political views, Hašek was disappointed by the NHL's response to the invasion. Yes, the league cut partnerships with Russian companies and stopped posting content to Russian-language media sties. But there was never discussion of removing the 56 Russian players from rosters.

"Our players play for their NHL teams, no matter where they're from," said commissioner Gary Bettman. "At this particular point in time, the Russian players are in an impossible situation."

Hockey fans in the US and Canada joined Bettman in expressing sympathy for Russian players. There was outrage when Canadian junior leagues announced a ban on drafting players from Russia. Wasn't this what Russian officials wanted, critics asked, to keep their talented young players locked inside their own country? Teenage prospects were losing the opportunity to develop their skills, because of some political event they had no connection to.

"Who is actually being punished by this decision?" asked a Vancouver hockey writer. "It isn't Putin or the oligarchs behind him. It's only the players—16- and 17-year-old kids who want to come to Canada and follow their hockey dreams."

In the moral calculus of sport, this was the worst crime of all—denying an individual athlete's dreams. The invasion of Ukraine was terrible. It was awful that Russian bombs were turning apartments to rubble and Russian soldiers were raping Ukrainian women. But how could that justify denying a Russian athlete their chance at an NHL contract, or Olympic gold, or a Grand Slam title? This same question was asked by hockey fans in North America and leaders of governing bodies in Europe. "We are here to support the athletes of the entire world to make their Olympic dreams come true," declared the IOC in its statement on Russian athletes participating in the Paris Games.

For most of us, this view of sports as a fulfillment of individual ambition is in the DNA of our games. The seeds of this belief sprouted on the schoolyards of 19th-century England and America. Sports developed here as an integral part of education, a way to train young people in moral character. Still today, this focus on sport as an exercise in personal growth and personal advancement remains at the root of our games, from children's select teams to pro leagues. Sports are not simply fun, or a way of keeping physically fit—sports make us better people.

To be sure, Russian athletes speak in terms of individual development, individual achievement, individual goals. But as we've seen, sports in Russia grew in a different political and cultural environment. This has not changed. If anything, the distinctly Russian view of sports has been reinforced in the Putin years.

There is no better example of this than the responses to Ovechkin's 895th NHL goal. When the Capitals forward broke Wayne Gretzky's scoring record on April 6, 2025, fans and media in North America celebrated the event as a historic sports moment. Ovechkin received the highest tributes an athlete can earn in America: He was a great guy, respected by teammates and rivals. As he neared the record, he showed class and humility. He had claimed a place among the GOATs in a long, consistent career.

In Russia, by contrast, Ovechkin's goal was a historic national moment, even a moment of "planetary scale," in the words of one commentator. Proof of the record's importance for the motherland came from Ovechkin himself. In the on-ice ceremony after his goal, Ovi thanked the cheering crowd: "And the last thing, all of you fans, for whole the world, Russian, we did it, boys. We did it. It's a history." Back home, these off-the-cuff lines, spoken in broken English to spectators at New York's UBS Arena, were altered to: "Russians, we did it!" The phrase was quickly immortalized. On TV, sports and news sites, social media, and even a video screen high above the Moscow skyline, the words "Русские, мы сделали это!"—"Russians, we did it!"—were indelibly attached to Ovechkin's goal.

Grammar snobs pointed out that this new slogan of national greatness was a bad translation of what Ovechkin actually said. Other grumblers objected altogether to Ovechkin being put on a pedestal, not because he was a hockey player, but because he was a hockey player who scored goals in America. On websites reporting the historic goal, their anger cast a noticeable shade over comments sections, with plenty of upturned thumbs showing support.

"Yes, he's Russian of course, but he's lived his whole life in the USA and played for a team from the USA," declared a user of VK Video, Russia's version of YouTube. "For me they've always been enemies and always will be. To kiss America's ass is a humiliation for Russians."

"We're sick of Ovechkin," posted another user of the video site. "He rakes in the dough and lives in a country that hates us. And what has he done for our guys fighting in Ukraine? But he'll get into the Duma soon enough. There's nothing but shit there."

"He's the definition of a foreign agent," wrote a reader of *Sport Ekspres*. "For how much he's making in America, he's probably the one in charge."

For haters and fans alike, Alexander Ovechkin wasn't simply a hockey player. He was a representation of Russia—a symbol into which Russian fans poured their pride, resentment, and anger.

He is not alone. Despite the posts of American fans and pronouncements of Swiss sportocrats, Russian athletes are not just athletes pursuing individual dreams of sports success. Their nation looks to them with its wounded, still-undeveloped sense of identity and purpose. As Duma member Dmitry Svishchev said of Russians in the NHL, "Every morning I wake up and see that our players have either scored or had an assist, that our goalies have again stopped so many shots. We have a lot to be proud of in these challenging times."

In spring 2022 when Svishchev made his remarks, Russia was an international outcast. The military push to Kyiv had been stopped, even as TV commentators in Moscow boasted that Russian soldiers would march to Berlin. Sanctions had crippled the economy; travel bans closed the borders. Despite all this, Russians could keep their heads up. They had hockey players in the NHL.

"You can see that our guys are in demand," Svishchev said. "You can't get rid of them. They're the backbone of the NHL. These guys are truly the pride of all our Russian people."

This was the aim of the Moscow playbook all along, the goal of all its strategies. If Russian competitors excelled in world sports, they would provide a distraction from present troubles, proof that Russia was a great nation despite its broken-down infrastructure, its rampant corruption, its uneven development. Russians are the backbone of the world's richest hockey league—one Russian is even that league's greatest scorer. Russians hold top rankings in world tennis. They win Olympic gold. They set world records. You can't kick Russian athletes out. They are the best. And they prove Russia is the best.

CONCLUSION

THE CROWD INSIDE the stadium roared in anticipation. This was a Russian arena—Moscow's Luzhniki Stadium—and a Russian crowd, more than 90,000 strong. Warmed by the afternoon sun, people shed their winter coats as they cheered. The stands swelled with waves of white, blue, and red flags.

Russia's largest stadium was filled not for a sporting event but a national celebration. The official occasion was the eighth anniversary of the "reunification" of Crimea. In fact, it was a rally in support of the invasion of Ukraine. Along with Russian flags, people waved banners emblazoned with the symbol of the "special military operation," the letter Z. The Latin character substituted for the Cyrillic "З" on signboards around the stadium:

Zа мир без нацизма (For a world without Nazism)

Zа Россию (For Russia)

Zа Президента (For the President)

The president himself was making his first public appearance since the invasion began three weeks earlier. Dressed stylishly in a puffy winter coat and beige turtleneck, Putin moved energetically around the midfield stage as he spoke into a hand-held mic. "We know what needs to be done next," he said to cheers, "how it needs to be done, and at what cost. We will fulfill all these plans, without question."

Of course, Putin couldn't have a rally without sports stars. Before the president roused the crowd with his speech, 10 athletes took the stage in their Team Russia gear, the letter Z prominent on their chests. The young women and men stood solemnly as the flag was raised and anthem played. The symbolism was clear: The world had barred these athletes from standing beneath their flag at the Olympics. Now they were able to show pride in Russia before their nation and their president.

Standing beneath the flag were medalists at recent Summer and Winter Olympics, including the games that concluded in Beijing just before the invasion. Joining them was Ivan Kulyak. The handsome blonde gymnast was known for his act of patriotism at a recent competition in Qatar. After winning bronze in the parallel bars, Kulyak stepped onto the podium—next to the Ukrainian gold medalist—with a makeshift Z taped to the front of his singlet. The International Gymnastics Federation promptly stripped his medal and banned him for a year. In Russia, Kulyak's defiance was celebrated. This brave defense of the motherland earned him a place on the Luzhniki stage, along with Russia's Olympians—a gold medal from the Rio Olympics around his neck.

There was one problem, though. Kulyak had not won gold at Rio. He had not even competed at Rio, or any other Olympics. Yet here he was, on stage with real Olympians, before tens of thousands of people and the president waiting in the wings, wearing a medal that wasn't his. It was not enough for Kulyak to be hailed for his support of Putin's war. He had to be a champion. Even if he was pretending to be a champion.

We can draw a line back through eight decades, from Kulyak's fake medal to Nikolai Romanov's twisted math after the Helsinki Olympics, from Moscow's anti-doping lab giving WADA investigators doctored computer files to Romanov lying point-blank to Avery Brundage, from Putin asking his sports officials "When will we win?" to Stalin demanding guarantees of victory. Through 80 years of Soviet and Russian participation in world sports, Moscow has had one goal: our athletes must be champions. Whether they actually win doesn't really matter.

Throughout those 80 years, Moscow has deflected accusations of cheating with the simple defense: everyone cheats. Go all the way back to Dynamo's British tour in 1945. Arsenal stocked their team with players from other clubs, just like Dynamo. It was American athletes, not Soviet, who first introduced steroids to international competition. Remember Nikolai Romanov's response to Brundage, when the IOC chief asked about Soviet training:

"We want to win. You don't criticize us for that, do you?"

Romanov's meaning was clear: In every country, athletes, coaches, and sports officials want to win. In every country, athletes, coaches, and sports officials find ways to get an advantage. How is Moscow's desire for wins any different?

While writing this book, I heard this question several times—at university lectures in Berkeley and New York, in interviews with journalists from Canada and Australia, in graduate seminars in Prague and Helsinki. What makes the Russian drive for sports victories unique? If Russians need to show their country's greatness by winning international events, what distinguishes them from Americans, who also like to watch their athletes win gold—and who also tend to think their country is the greatest on Earth?

To be sure, Americans are known for waving flags of white, blue, and red for their athletes, whether at the Olympics or Women's World Cup or other international events. And certainly, Americans get a patriotic surge at watching their athletes win. Yet while victories in world sport boost Americans' national pride, they are not fundamental to Americans' sense of identity. As a Czech colleague once explained to me: "Americans don't need to prove they're great. They *know* they're great."

Blunt, but true. During the 2024 Paris Olympics, viewers across the United States were thrilled by Simone Biles winning three gold medals. But there wasn't nationwide moaning when Biles slipped off the balance beam, costing her the chance to break the record for most total gold medals in gymnastics. Biles was the GOAT. For Americans, there was no dispute, even if she didn't set the medals record.

"But what about Larisa Latynina?" a Russian would ask. "She has nine gold medals—more than Biles's seven. This proves she is the greatest."

An American would likely answer with their own question: "Larisa who?"

The Russian would be offended by this ignorance of their great champion. But the reply illustrates how Americans understand their country's place in the world. American pride is rooted in the awareness of being a land wholly set apart—in geography, history, politics, everything. It is a new nation. There is no need for Americans to compare themselves to other countries. The greatness of the USA is a self-evident truth. Just like the greatness of Simone Biles.

By contrast, Russian pride is rooted in the awareness of being a distant land on the edge of Europe, a nation of rich traditions that have developed in a unique but not entirely separate way. Russia's distinct culture and its place on Europe's margins have cultivated a critical, morally superior view of its far-away neighbors. But there is also a sense of inferiority. Russians *believe* their country is the greatest, but they fear it's not. Their boasts need to be validated by others. Gold medals provide that validation.

Other than sports victories, Russia does not have many tangible proofs of its greatness. The US did not need to win the 2023 World Baseball Classic to certify its global standing. After all, it's the country that invented baseball—as well as airplanes, iPhones, chocolate muffins, and plenty of other things enjoyed around the world. By contrast, there is no innovative product, no practical thing that Russia offers the world. Even within the country, the government can't maintain infrastructure, health care, education, and other basics. Russia must import over 70% of its pharmaceuticals and medical equipment. The country exports gas, yet millions of Russians freeze through the winter due to decrepit central-heating systems in cities. As Nina Kramareva told me, "Russia has nothing concrete to offer its own people. It has to give them gold medals."

For Moscow, sports have historically been an instrument of state policy. In the words of former *Sport Ekspres* writer Slava Malamud, "Russian sports were artificially created in a lab for political purposes." By contrast, sports are deeply woven into the fabric of American life. Across the United States, in communities large and small, everyday social connections are linked to sporting events: Friday-night high school football and Saturday-morning kids' soccer, intramural basketball teams and church softball leagues, triathlons and turkey trots, Super Bowl parties and March Madness brackets.

Sports are not simply something Americans do: they shape Americans' thinking. Since the 1800s, athletics have had a constant presence in US schools and colleges. The ideals of sport—fair play, sportsmanship, teamwork—are fundamental to American education. Yes, American kids want to win. But from a young age, they are taught essential lessons from sports: be a good winner, be a good loser, and above all, don't cheat.

Of course, there are cheaters in American sports. When caught, however, they are typically scorned. Lance Armstrong has been a pariah ever since he lied to Oprah about doping. But imagine if his story went in a different direction, one in which he was elected to Congress after being stripped of his Tour de France titles, while the whistleblower who revealed his drug use, Floyd Landis, was forced into hiding in another country. This is what happened in Russia. Based on evidence in Grigory Rodchenkov's files, bobsledder Alexey Voyevoda was stripped of his two gold medals from the Sochi Olympics and received a lifetime ban. Yet Voyevoda ended up with a seat in the Duma, as a member of Putin's party. Meanwhile, Rodchenkov is in the US witness-protection program.

In pointing out this contrast between Russia and the United States, I'm not suggesting that sportsmanship and playing by the rules are exclusively American ideals. They are not. Canadian skier Beckie Scott told me how international athletes contacted her after the 2016 doping revelations, with appeals for Russia to be banned. "We heard from a lot of athletes around the globe," she said, "tons of people who were concerned about doping in their sports. They saw this as an opportunity to make a strong statement for clean sport, by excluding Russia from the Olympic Games."

As Scott explained to me, Moscow undermined the integrity of world sport not only with its doping program but also by compromising the world governing bodies. She already recognized Russia's influence in 2002, when Olga Danilova and Larisa Lazutina were caught doping. Scott had finished third behind Danilova and Lazutina in a race at Salt Lake City, so she expected to receive gold after their disqualification. Instead, she was disgusted to learn that the IOC encouraged the Russian skiers to lodge appeal after appeal. Olympic officials did not want to upset Moscow in 2002, just as they didn't want to upset Moscow in 2016, or 2018, or 2022.

"It would be one thing if they would just put it out there," Scott said of governing bodies, "that what they're really concerned about is the business of sport. Instead, they hide behind this idealism, that the principles of sport are something we should all aspire to—friendship, unity, fairness, equality. Athletes are cogs in an entertainment machine, and clean, fair sport is just a PR campaign. Anyone who dares to speak out is, almost without exception, targeted and ostracized. I know this because I lived it."

As Beckie Scott discovered, the world's athletes wanted Russia out, but the sportocrats made sure they stayed in.

By protecting Russia after the doping program was exposed, the leaders of world sport reversed the prediction IOC members made back in 1951, when they first admitted the USSR to the Games. Participation in the Olympics did not inspire Russians to adopt the ideals of fair play and sportsmanship. Instead, the leaders of world sport gave up those ideals to appease Moscow.

There will come a time when Russian missiles are no longer killing Ukrainian civilians. There will even be a time when Vladimir Putin no longer rules from the Kremlin. When that day comes, it would be unwise to quickly readmit Russia to full participation in international events. From Brundage to Bach, the men running world sports have been turned into compliant poodles by Moscow's rulers. For the sake of the governing bodies' credibility, the leash has to be cut.

Above all, it is in the interest of fair competition to keep Russia on the sideline. The Moscow playbook has been a guide for gaming the rules. In some instances, its strategies have had a beneficial effect, such as the Soviet emphasis on women athletes. But for the most part, Moscow has cheated to win—and then lied when the cheating is discovered. Without question Russian athletes have given the world extraordinary performances. But Russia, as a participant in world sporting events, cannot be trusted to follow the rules.

We can ask this question as well: Why would Russia even want to return to world sports? Moscow's politicians, journalists, and officials were complaining about the unfair treatment Russian athletes received from international governing bodies already in 2002, after the Salt Lake City Games. Doping penalties and bans over Ukraine have simply confirmed what Moscow sees as a persistent anti-Russian bias. Slava Fetisov, Irina Rodnina, and Larisa Latynina have all condemned the world's federations in harsh terms. They insist that any restriction on Russia's athletes is an unacceptable insult to the motherland.

To make matters worse in Moscow's eyes, international sports have become a cesspool of un-Russian immorality. Proof of this was the opening ceremony of the 2024 Paris Olympics, with its parade of drag queens and, in the words of a Russian Foreign Ministry official, "the drug-addicted rapper Snoop Dogg." As a popular news site declared, the Paris Games were the "Olympics from Hell." It was a good thing Russia didn't attend.

For many of us outside Russia, the Paris Olympics weren't all that hellish. Television ratings for the 2024 Summer Games soared over recent Olympics. Spectators bought more than 9.5 million tickets, setting an all-time Olympic attendance record. We might ask how much of this success came from removing the clouds of scandal. Ever since Moscow's doping program was brought to light, the Winter and Summer Olympics have been stained by Russian participation. By excluding Russia, the Paris Games lifted the inconvenient questions of how to include this uncooperative participant. At the very least, the Paris Olympics showed that the world can hold a spectacular athletic festival without Russia.

The Olympics are games, and games are meant to be fun—Paris reminded us of that. The joy of our games is lost, however, when one player needs to win at all costs. It's even worse when that player breaks the rules and then lies after getting caught. Yet this is how Russia has competed for decades. This is also how Russia has conducted its war in Ukraine. The country that denies its doping and cover-ups is the same country that denies targeting civilians in war, despite hard evidence to the contrary. Sport is important to Moscow because it is the one venue where Russia can prove its greatness to the world. But it is also the one venue where the world can hold Russia to account. After 80 years of deception, it's time to do that. Until Moscow acknowledges its cheating, and agrees to play by the rules, it has to be kept out of the game.

ACKNOWLEDGMENTS

THIS BOOK HAS DEEP ROOTS, reaching back over thirty years to when I was in college studying Russian language, literature, and history. Over the decades, I have gained insights into the Soviet Union and Russia from my professors and fellow students, from academic mentors and colleagues, from scholars and journalists, from military officers and diplomats. I owe thanks to them all. Above all, I'm grateful for my own students. Their curiosity and enthusiasm always made Russian history a joy to teach, even if the subject matter could be depressingly dark.

A special nod to former student Ken Zurcher—who, like many of my students, has far surpassed me in knowledge of this region—and to my colleague Alan Holiman. They provided help in translating tricky phrases in vernacular Russian. And thanks to Professor Maria Carlson, my former boss at the University of Kansas. Many observations in these pages bear the influence of her unmatched expertise in Russian culture.

The bulk of the book was written in the Czech Republic. The University of Hradec Králové's Institute of History provided me generous support as a visiting professor. Thanks to Jiří Hutečka for making this stay possible—and for your hospitality and friendship. I finished writing in the cafés and libraries of Prague, where I now serve as visiting professor at Charles University's Institute for International Studies. Thanks to Jan Hornát and Ota Konrád for steering my appointment. And thanks to Petra for celebrating with me when the book was finished.

Much of the source material came from library collections at the University of Minnesota and Kansas University. KU's Center for Russian, East European & Eurasian Studies supported my work there with a research fellowship. I also spent days at the International Olympic Committee's archive in Lausanne, Switzerland, and the records of Radio Free Europe at Budapest's Blinken OSA Archivum. Thanks to numerous archivists and librarians for help in accessing sources.

Only a few of the people I interviewed are mentioned by name in the text, yet everyone I spoke with shaped my understanding of Russian sport and politics. Thanks to Sylvain Dufraisse, Rob Koehler, Nina Kramareva, Sergei Medvedev, Simona Petracovschi, Beckie Scott, Stefan Szymanski, and Alexandra Yatsyk. These pages also echo with conversations I had for my previous book on world hockey, namely my interviews with Dominik Hašek, Alena Polenská, and the late Luděk Bukač.

Thanks to everyone at Triumph for putting this book into the world, especially to Josh Williams for recognizing its audience, and to Jesse Jordan for guiding the manuscript to the finish line. My agent, John Rudolph, believed in this project from the start and has been a constant source of support and wisdom.

I'm grateful for friends and family in Minnesota who gave encouragement throughout this project. To my Mom, Collette and Tom, Brenda and Georgia, the St. Peter beer gang, Geoff and Steph, Barb and Maura: I appreciate all the times you asked, "How's the book going?" Special thanks go to my father, who was my first coach and my first history teacher. None of this would have happened without you, Dad.

Above all, I owe truckloads of thanks to my children. They have shown kindness, patience, and understanding to their world-traveling, book-writing dad. With love and gratitude, I dedicate this book to them.